The Ethics of Giacomo Leopardi

Also Available from Bloomsbury

The Philosophy of Mario Perniola, Enea Bianchi
French and Italian Stoicisms, ed. by Janae Sholtz and Kurt Lampe
Kielmeyer and the Organic World, ed. Lydia Azadpour and Daniel Whistler
Nietzsche and the Earth, Henk Manschot

The Ethics of Giacomo Leopardi

A Philosophy for the Environmental Crisis

Alice Gibson

BLOOMSBURY ACADEMIC
LONDON • NEW YORK • OXFORD • NEW DELHI • SYDNEY

BLOOMSBURY ACADEMIC

Bloomsbury Publishing Plc, 50 Bedford Square, London, WC1B 3DP, UK
Bloomsbury Publishing Inc, 1385 Broadway, New York, NY 10018, USA
Bloomsbury Publishing Ireland, 29 Earlsfort Terrace, Dublin 2, D02 AY28, Ireland

BLOOMSBURY, BLOOMSBURY ACADEMIC and the Diana logo
are trademarks of Bloomsbury Publishing Plc

First published in Great Britain 2024
This paperback edition published 2025

Copyright © Alice Gibson, 2024

Alice Gibson has asserted her right under the Copyright, Designs and
Patents Act, 1988, to be identified as Author of this work.

For legal purposes the Acknowledgements on p. vi constitute
an extension of this copyright page.

Series design by Charlotte Daniels
Cover image: Wall after earthquake (© FredFroese / Getty Images)

All rights reserved. No part of this publication may be: i) reproduced or transmitted in any form, electronic or mechanical, including photocopying, recording or by means of any information storage or retrieval system without prior permission in writing from the publishers; or ii) used or reproduced in any way for the training, development or operation of artificial intelligence (AI) technologies, including generative AI technologies. The rights holders expressly reserve this publication from the text and data mining exception as per Article 4(3) of the Digital Single Market Directive (EU) 2019/790.

Bloomsbury Publishing Inc does not have any control over, or responsibility for, any third-party websites referred to or in this book. All internet addresses given in this book were correct at the time of going to press. The author and publisher regret any inconvenience caused if addresses have changed or sites have ceased to exist, but can accept no responsibility for any such changes.

A catalogue record for this book is available from the British Library.

A catalog record for this book is available from the Library of Congress.

ISBN: HB: 978-1-3502-9864-4
PB: 978-1-3502-9863-7
ePDF: 978-1-3502-9865-1
eBook: 978-1-3502-9866-8

Typeset by Integra Software Services Pvt. Ltd.

For product safety related questions contact productsafety@bloomsbury.com.

To find out more about our authors and books visit www.bloomsbury.com
and sign up for our newsletters.

Contents

Acknowledgements   vi

Introduction   1

1   Vices, trifles and illusions   21
     Problematising works   21
     Barbarous times in the *Zibaldone*   34
     The general spirit of the age in the *Operette*   55
     Exonerating humanity   68

2   Dreams and vision   99
     A philosophy that aims to cure in the Canti   99
     The property of works of genius: Should laughter or pity prevail?   118
     The limits of Leopardi's thought   144
     Resignifying Leopardi today   167

Conclusion: Planetary solidarity   189

Afterword   194
Notes   196
Bibliography   225
Index   235

Acknowledgements

Firstly, thank you to Howard Caygill, who introduced me to Leopardi's thought during my doctoral studies at Kingston University, and to those at the Centre for Research in Modern European Philosophy, whose feedback facilitated my work in its formative stages. I have presented different aspects of this research in a variety of forums, most recently at 'Derrida Today', for which I am grateful to Elina Staikou for the opportunity, and at the 'Contaminations' conference organised by Leopardi Studies at Oxford. Special thanks are due to those from Arizona State University, particularly Celina Osuna, as well as to friends from the Leopardi Writing Workshop held in Recanati in 2019, including special thanks to Christine O'Brien, for ongoing efforts nurturing a group I cherish.

I wish to express my deep gratitude for my encouraging and supportive friends: Mala Siamptani, Harriet Sinclair, Jenny Parker, Victoria Crossley, Woody Whyte, Heidi Edwards and many more, who have lent me moral support throughout the course of this project, oftentimes being patient with me in my absence. Thanks also to my family, particularly my parents, Verina and Rod.

To friends and staff at the University of Brighton, and Louisa Buck and Chris O'Neill, thank you for cultivating my belief in myself as a researcher. Finally, thank you to Eileen John for the mentorship, and to all those at Bloomsbury who have helped make this book a reality, and to all those who have lent their time, energy and expertise to help strengthen my work.

Introduction

Our relationship with nature is broken. Every day we are offered mounting evidence that the ways of understanding that dictate how we engage with the Earth facilitate its destruction. As Elizabeth Kolbert has shown so proficiently in her Pulitzer prize-winning *The Sixth Extinction: An Unnatural History* (2014), today, we find ourselves at the very heart of a catastrophe, in which the cataclysm for the sixth mass extinction event, responsible for the sudden and dramatic contraction of life on Earth, is us. As Vandana Shiva highlights in *Making Peace with the Earth* (2013), in which she shows the devastating environmental impact of the myths of corporate globalisation, we are driving up to three hundred species to extinction every day.[1] In his response to the 2022 report of the Intergovernmental Science-Policy Platform on Biodiversity and Ecosystem Services (IPBES), which is akin to the IPCC climate change reports, Patrick Vallance argued that ambitious political commitments must be made to redress our overexploitation of the planet, if we are to survive.[2]

Today, humanity faces a series of intertwined crises on a planetary scale, the three central issues of which have been identified as climate change, nature and biodiversity loss, and pollution. Industrial farming, which supports the unrestrained extractive and exploitative cultures of those whose lifestyles have the biggest impact have destabilized the climate system of our self-regulated planet, has caused the loss of 75 per cent of agricultural biodiversity.[3] Current dominant food systems fail to adequately account for the needs of nature, leading to the destruction of habitats and disruption of natural processes. Combining factors such as these exacerbate unhealthy ecosystems in which zoonotic infectious diseases – those shared between humans and vertebrate animals – can thrive.[4] This ecological debasement of the world we share is closely bound up with how we choose to live, particularly in rich countries with proportionately higher carbon footprints, and in the behaviours that we permit from the richest in society, from companies, and from our governments and politicians.

In this study, I highlight the relevance today of the work of the Italian poet and philosopher Giacomo Leopardi (1798–1837), the eldest son of a provincial aristocratic family in Recanati, a small town in the Marche Region that belonged to the conservative Papal States. I call upon Leopardi's philosophical thought to problematize the concept of nature we have inherited from the Enlightenment and to consider how his work, despite having some important limitations, issues critical guidance in terms of how to think on the planetary scale in light of the contemporary challenges facing us. Throughout, I consider Leopardi's early recognition of the effects of modern ways of life that fail to prioritize creativity, bodily senses, passion, enthusiasm, the imagination, communal or familial love, citizenship and courage, and which examines, oftentimes with humour, the dearth which derives from this. Assessing Leopardi's understanding that we have too readily abandoned our opportunities to flourish and dream, I firstly trace his account of the lack of regard we show for ourselves and our nonhuman kin in contemporary life, which paves the way for the destructive relationship with nature we are increasingly suffering the effects of. After my examination of these problematising works, I consider how Leopardi reconstructs his own ethics out of the resources he finds in the ancients, and combines with his contemporaries' insights, a philosophy for the environmental crisis. As I hope to show, this philosophy centres itself on curing the ailments Leopardi previously identified, by bringing solidarity, resolve and consolation to the heart of his writing.

Assessing the foundations of modernity

According to the English poet Matthew Arnold (1822–88), a disciple of Wordsworth and Goethe, Leopardi's work was characterized by his 'mental lucidity', the foundation of which was Leopardi's ability to comprehend ideas that were still in their inception.[5] Patrick Creagh, whose 1983 English translation of the *Operette* I refer to throughout, gives a comprehensive introduction to Leopardi's life, which he described as composed of an outer one 'practically without incident and an inner one of extraordinary intensity', writing:

> By the age of twelve Leopardi knew more than his tutors, and thereafter was self-taught. He virtually lived in his father's vast but random library, engaged in 'seven years of mad and desperate study', taught himself Greek, Hebrew, German, Spanish and English (to add to his Latin and French), translated and commented on the classics, wrote essays on philology and literature, produced (at the age of fifteen) a long, stodgy but incredibly learned *History of Astronomy*, and emerged at twenty as one of the most erudite men in Europe, and a hunchback who was never again to know a day's true health.[6]

While Leopardi suffered extensively with his health, his response to those who only assessed his pessimism through with recourse to such preliminary means was often cutting. Such accounts of his work continue to appear even today, as can be seen by the description given in the article 'The Disease of the Italian Poet Giacomo Leopardi (1798–1837): A Case of Juvenile Ankylosing Spondylitis in the 19th Century?' (2017), in which the authors wrote:

> The acknowledgment of a physical cause of Leopardi's disease contributes to reevaluate his 'cosmic pessimism' as an original expression of his thought, so leading a general revaluation of the figure of one of the most important European thinkers of the 19th century.[7]

The theme of Leopardi's 'cosmic pessimism', of which I will give a full account, purveys this study, underpinning the communal ethics he settles on, as I uncover through an examination of the inspiration he drew from ancient Stoic philosophers, such as Marcus Aurelius, Lucius Annaeus Seneca and Epictetus.

A tree cut off at the root

Of all the prescient insights we can find in Leopardi's impressive oeuvre, there is one excerpt in particular that strikes me as bearing significant potential to be of transformative value today, as we face the challenges of the ongoing environmental crisis. In the August of 1820, adding to the extensive collection of notes that made up his notebook, the *Zibaldone*, Leopardi reflected:

> It is no more possible for man to live cut off from nature, which we are constantly drawing farther away from, than it is for a tree cut off at the root to bear flowers and fruit. Dreams and vision. Something to talk about again in a hundred years. We do not yet have an example from the past of the progression of excessive civilisation and an unrestrained violation of nature. But if we do not turn back, our descendants will leave this example to their descendants, if they have any.
>
> [217]

This passage captures Leopardi's remarkable capacity to see the potential costs of a way of life based on excess and a lack of restraint, the consequences of which, he believed, we would ultimately find ourselves confronted with. Taking issue with those habits of living which he took to be detrimental to true vitality, Leopardi's insights represent an early warning of a theme that would later be taken up by the Nobel Prize winner and Bengali social reformer Rabindranath Tagore. In his 1922 essay 'The Robbery of the Soil', Tagore's description of our relationship with nature includes a similar warning:

> The temptation of an inordinately high level of living, which was once confined only to a small section of the community, becomes widespread. The blindness is sure to prove fatal to the civilisation which puts no restraint upon the emulation of self-indulgence.[8]

Throughout this study, I consider the implications of Leopardi's warning against extracting resources faster than the planet has the capacity to replenish. I also note the numerous examples we find in his work of his recognition of the detrimental nature of the indulgence Tagore would later write of, noting in particular those bad habits 'among the leisured classes', which were harmful to the body. One example of this from the *Zibaldone*, which was also recorded in 1820, was his observation that writing was particularly damaging:

> On entering the world, a young man wants to become someone. This desire is certain and common to all. But today a young man of private means has no way of achieving this other than the one I mentioned, or through writing, which is just as harmful to the body. So glory today is dependent on activities that are bad for one's health, whereas once the opposite was true.
>
> [131]

When I come to consider the limits of Leopardi's thought, despite his concern of resource depletion, I will draw heavily on the work of the Indian environmental activist Shiva, who cited Tagore at the outset of her work. I demonstrate how Shiva's work unpacks the violent consequences of the war with nature for which Leopardi comes to advocate and suggest a reworking of his philosophy to forego this aspect and instead supplement his ethics of solidarity with the contemporary vision of environmental justice we find in the work of Shiva. To begin, I situate Leopardi's opposition to nature in relation to the philosophical optimism of the eighteenth century, which he critiqued. Following this, I utilize the arguments of a range of contemporary theorists, whose work I call upon to highlight how we can find new ways to reformulate our relationship with nature, in a manner that can help call a material halt to outdated frameworks of thought that justify the unceasing exploitation of the Earth's resources.

Two hundred years later than Leopardi had imagined, a vast array of initiatives now attest to the widespread recognition of our need to reassess our relationship with the natural world. These include but are not limited to the Paris Agreement, Conference of the Parties (COP) summits, the Green New Deal, the Bridgetown Initiative. Youth activists like Vanessa Nakate and Greta Thunberg have reinvigorated arguments that the climate scientist James Hansen passionately set out in *Storms of My Grandchildren*, (2009), where he rallied against the generational and racialized injustice of continuing to accept 'business as usual' in relation to the environmental crisis.[9] Across the globe, people, other organisms, biomes and ecosystems are increasingly confronted with the adverse effects of human action and inaction, experiencing a greater frequency and intensity of natural hazards, such as earthquakes, landslides, floods and sinkholes, to a degree that concerns those working in disaster risk management.[10] Ways of life that have always been attuned to the needs of nature have been violently silenced and ignored for centuries, and in the past few decades, we have seen countless warnings of environmental collapse issued from scientists, activists and journalists go unheeded. Today, a key part of our challenge is to confront the lack of political will required to meet the scale of our collective challenges.

In his work, Nathaniel Rich has traced the movement of lobbyists acting in corporate interests from wholesale denial to division as a tactic to preserve their profits. As he has written in *Losing Earth: A Recent History* (2019):

> It is not yet widely understood, though it will be, that the politician who claims that climate change is uncertain betrays humanity in the same fashion as the politician who fabricates weapons of mass destruction in order to whip up support for a profiteering war. It is not yet widely understood, though it will be, that when a government relaxes regulations on coal-fired plants or erases scientific data from a federal website, it is guilty of more than merely bowing to corporate interests; it commits crimes against humanity. The rejection of reason – the molten core of denialism – opens the door to the rejection of morality, for morality relies on a shared faith in reason. Actions to hasten carbon dioxide emissions are the ineluctable corollary of climate denialism. Once it becomes possible to disregard the welfare of future generations, or those now vulnerable to flooding or drought or wildfire – once it becomes possible to abandon the

constraints of human empathy – any monstrosity committed in the name of self-interest is permissible.¹¹

When Leopardi proposed in 1820 that an unrestrained violation of nature would be 'Something to talk about again in a hundred years', it is exceptionally unlikely that he could have foreseen the extent to which corporate entities would attempt to derail such a conversation. Today, as Rich argues, has becoming increasingly clear that corporate interests have been aware of the risks associated with their business models for decades. Moreover, their abdication of responsibility, which in the first instance depended on a recourse to claims that climate change was uncertain, according to Rich, amounts to a crime against humanity.

Adding to growing bodies of work that analyse the unequal effects of corporate growth at the expense of environmental justice, in her book *Oneness vs. the 1%: Shattering Illusions, Seeding Freedom* (2020), Shiva discussed the 'The Money Machine of the 1%'. Introducing the concept, which threatens to destroy the planet and the societies from which it draws its support, she writes:

> The money machine, facilitated by the mechanical mind, allows the 1% to extract wealth from nature and society, defining their 'extractivism' as scientific, economic and human 'progress'. The denial of self-organisation, intelligence, creativity, freedom, potential, autopoietic evolution and non-separability in nature and society is the basis of the domination, exploitation and colonisation, enslavement and extraction, of nature and diverse cultures, of women and indigenous people, of farmers and workers through brute power and violence. The result is an ecological crisis; a human crisis of hunger and poverty, of deepening inequality, of marginalisation and alienation, of uprooting, dispossession, and the creation of refugees. Linear, extractive systems based on violence are at the root of economic inequality, and the polarisation of society into the 1% and the 99%; they are the basis of new forms of enslavement, and an unprecedented exercise of disposability and extermination.¹²

The logic of this machine, she explains, is to: 'bulldoze, destroy, aggregate and accumulate, externalise and excavate'.¹³ As testimonies and evidence of the results of such practices are increasingly brought to the fore, a desperate need for resistance is revealed. This can come in the form of a secure sense of solidarity and strength of will, one which I argue we can unearth from a thorough engagement with Leopardi's work that goes beyond his critique of modernity, that can then put to use in the service of a collective vision for environmental justice.

An ethics of survival and optimistic will

In *Questions of Cultural Identity* (1996), the cultural theorist Stuart Hall described his view of 'reconstruction work', underscoring the political potential of relocating and reactivating the past. Giving in account of this approach, Hall elucidated:

> Narratives of historical reconstruction may reject such myths of social transformation: communal memory may seek its meanings through a sense of causality shared with psychoanalysis, that negotiates the recurrence of the image of the past while keeping open the question of the future. The importance of such retroaction lies in its ability to reinscribe the past, reactivate it, relocate it, *resignify it*. More significant, it commits our understanding of the past, and our reinterpretation of the future, to an ethics of 'survival' that allows us to *work through the present*.[14]

Prompted by this call for an 'ethics of "survival"', I aim throughout my analysis of Leopardi, to illustrate how his work can be seen as an example of what Hall describes as 'reconstruction work', by virtue of his ambition to synthesize ancient insights and practices with contemporaneous concerns. Providing the reasoning for adopting such an approach in the monumental *Zibaldone*, Leopardi set out his ambition to recover from ancient civilisation that which has been lost, when he writes:

> We need still to *recover* much from ancient civilisation, by which I mean the Greeks and the Romans. Consider the many ancient institutions which have very recently been *revived*: schools and the use

of gymnastics, bathing and similar practices, [...] The tendency over these recent years, more than ever before, toward social improvement, has brought about, and continues to do, the *renewal* of many ancient practices, both physical, and political and moral, which had been abandoned and forgotten during barbarous times, from which we have *not yet entirely emerged*. The current *progress* of civilisation is still a *revival*; it consists, for the most part, in *recovering what has been lost*.

[4289]

With such claims in mind, in my analysis, I show how Leopardi renews the critiques of anthropocentricism he finds in ancient critics like Lucian of Samosata, in addition to highlighting how he revived the practices of Stoic philosophers. I elucidate Leopardi's recollection of the ideas of thinkers like Aurelius, who lived from A.D. 161–80, and directs us to 'look upon earthly things below as if from some place above them' to promote our consideration of human reality, in a manner that encompasses its social, geographical and emotional aspects. In addition, I also examine the centrality of the theme of consolation in Leopardi's thought, a theme that traverses Seneca's *Natural Questions*, and which I relate to today's endeavours to respond to the environmental crisis.[15]

In my account of Leopardi's work, I argue that appreciation of his influence on the development of Western philosophy currently fails to do due service to the significance of his ideas. I show how his Leopardi's influence can be seen in the work of Schopenhauer, for example, who contributed to familiarity with Leopardi's ideas in Germany, counting him among the great pessimists, when he wrote: 'Do you know that the three greatest pessimists were in Italy in *one and the same* year? ... Byron, Leopardi and I. But none of us got to know any of the others.'[16] As I will also examine, long before Nietzsche declared God to be dead in *The Gay Science*, Leopardi, who Antonio Negri described as a 'precursor to Nietzsche', considered the ethical implications of the decline of Christianity at great length. According to Nietzsche, who owned a copy of Leopardi's *Operette morali* and who Negri has shown was familiar with Leopardi from at least 1869, described the poet as 'the modern ideal of a philologist', and a 'poet-scholar' like Goethe.[17]

Leopardi's philosophy, as I will show, also featured in the work of Walter Benjamin, who cited repeatedly throughout *The Arcades Project* from Leopardi's 1824 operetta 'Fashion and Death'. Seeking to show how the impact that Leopardi's thought has had on contemporary theorists has been significantly underappreciated, I respond by using the work of the Italian theorist Sebastiano Timpanaro, whose contribution to the development of Western Marxism is defined by his classical analysis of Leopardi's account of human mortality, as a case study. Illuminating in turn many of Leopardi's hidden influences, I provide an account of Timpanaro's reading of the poet's philosophy, including his examination of Leopardi's 1836 poem 'La ginestra', which is known in English as the 'Flower of the Desert', 'Flower of the Wilderness' and 'Broom'. This examination leads me to propose my own account of the strengths of Leopardi's late poem, which focuses on the significance of the themes of revival, renewal and consolation, bringing home the value of developing an ethics of solidarity, which I argue can aid our survival as a species and help us in our endeavours to halt and turn back our destruction of the Earth's ecosystems.

The current lack of familiarity with Leopardi's work represents an opportunity to appreciate how the insights of the prescient philosopher can speak directly to many of the issues we find ourselves needing to grapple with today. In my contribution to attempts to remedy this dearth in scholarship, I demonstrate how Leopardi's ideas attended to the deeply rooted nature of racism in the project of modernity, building on the work of Hall and Paul Gilroy to reveal the ongoing significance of Leopardi's critique of civilisation's reliance on the trade of sugar, coffee and other commodities. I also highlight the relationship between Antonio Gramsci's account of the importance of the conviction '*that the source of his own moral forces is in himself*' and the value Leopardi ascribed to 'works of genius' a term he took from Germaine de Staël's novel *Corrine* (1807), where she gave an account of the nobility found in the conscious strength portrayed in the works of ancient sculptors.

Informed by the ideas of Gramsci, one of a number of Italian political philosophers who have faced imprisonment in Italy, I examine the often problematic presentation of the relationship between humans and nature to be found in Leopardi's work, which encouraged Gramsci to rejection comparisons of his thought to that of the poet.[18] Arguing that despite its significance, this limit does not discount other theoretical benefits of Leopardi's thought, I consider Leopardi's ethics and aesthetics in relation to Gramsci's depiction of the power of cultivating the conviction that our 'own moral forces' are within ourselves, which he explained when he wrote:

> [A] man ought to be so deeply convinced that the source of his own moral forces is in himself ... that he never despairs and never falls into those vulgar, banal moods, pessimism and optimism. My own state of mind synthesizes these two feelings and transcends them: my mind is pessimistic, but my will is optimistic. Since I never build up illusions, I am seldom disappointed. I've always been armed with unlimited patience – not a passive, inert kind, but a patience allied with perseverance.[19]

In my presentation of Leopardi's ethical thought, I show how the exemplary figures in his late philosophical poem prompt our recognition of our own power, serving as the encouragement we need to govern our own optimistic will with patience, perseverance and fortitude.

Highlighting the dormant power of Leopardi's late ethics, particularly in relation to the ongoing environmental crisis, I wish to show that there is more to Leopardi than the staunch critique of post-Enlightenment thought he is commonly known for. By drawing attention to the moments in his thought when his consolatory philosophy is most prominent, I demonstrate how this arises in response to his more well-known critique. Bringing to the fore the various ways Leopardi has influenced philosophers who English readers may be more likely to be familiar with, including Arthur Schopenhauer, Friedrich Nietzsche, Walter Benjamin, Susan Sontag, Paul Gilroy and Eugene Thacker, I suggest that we might return to Leopardi today as part of the work of reconstruction that Hall advocated for. In doing so, I suggest that we can take up the opportunity to use key aspects of Leopardi's work as the foundation from which to build an expansive environmental ethics, showing how his ethics values vitality, solidarity amongst and beyond humans, and the potential of the imagination, which he focuses on in addition to ridiculing human folly and false pride, which continue to be prominent in contemporary political life.

Against defeatism

In *Staying with the Trouble: Making Kin in the Chthulucene* (2016), Donna Haraway effectively captured an important problem one repeatedly encounters when discussing possible responses to the environmental crisis, where she wrote:

> Both the Anthropocene and the Capitalocene lend themselves too readily to cynicism, defeatism, and self-certain and self-fulfilling predictions, like the 'game over, too late' discourse I hear all around me these days, in both expert and popular discourses, in which both technotheocratic geoengineering fixes and wallowing in despair seem to coinfect any possible common imagination.[20]

Pushing back against such defeatist thought, I argue such lines of thinking bear too heavy a risk of being demotivating, self-fulfilling and inaccurate. I intend to take for granted our deep immersion in an ongoing environmental crisis, not in order to encourage despair, pacifism or shame, but to show that reading Leopardi closely today can help us to metabolize the harsh truths our present confronts us with, in a way that serves, rather than undermines, us. As Haraway has noted, a common refrain one encounters when acknowledging the environmental crisis is the argument that all there is left to do is for us to relinquish our power and resign ourselves to the fact that there is no sense in having any active trust in each other and playing for a resurgent world.[21] I believe that, in attending to the current crisis, it is crucial to protect ourselves from the appeal of such conclusions.

More specifically, I suggest that we stand to benefit from a careful critical engagement with Leopardi's thought concerning the danger of turning away from harsh realities, in which he gives us guidance on how to manage painful emotions more effectively. From considering his work in this light, I demonstrate how his thought can help us learn to confront, console and overcome our fears, particularly in the face of claims that it is 'too late', or that we 'are too far gone', which too readily overlook the preventative potential of more generative lines of thought. Such an approach to reading Leopardi today, I argue, can help us recognize the power we too readily relinquish, and open up spaces of opportunity in which we can use our power with resolution, in united attempts to remedy our relationship with the rest of nature. Overall, my aim is to highlight Leopardi's role in activating an enthusiasm, which arises from his insistence on a truthful accounting of the present.

Affirmative thought and pessimism

This book builds on the work of the Italian political philosopher Antonio Negri, in particular the 2015 translation of his study of Leopardi, *Flower of the Desert: Giacomo Leopardi's Poetic Ontology* (*Lenta ginestra: Saggio sull'ontologia di Giacomo Leopardo*). This work examines Leopardi's late, and I will argue, philosophical poem 'La ginestra', which is also known as 'Flower of the Desert' or 'Wild Broom' in English language scholarship on Leopardi's work. The central figure of Leopardi's poem is a plant from the Genisteae tribe that is abundant in the vicinity of Mount Vesuvius. Bearing sweet pea shaped yellow flowers, it is comparable with the exception of the lack of spikes on its stems, to the evergreen gorse widespread across the UK, and thrives on disturbed soil in Western, Northern and Central Europe, and is commonly known as 'broom', in reference to the suitability of its long, slender and tough branches for making brooms. The original title of Negri's study, 'Lenta ginestra', refers to the gentleness embodied by the plant in the last stanza of Leopardi's poem, examined in detail within this study.[22]

Negri's work was written during a time of deep personal crisis. In Rome in April 1979, the philosopher was arrested and subsequently incarcerated in Padua on the basis of spurious, politically motivated charges. He found himself falsely accused of being an accessory to the abduction and assassination of the Italian prime minister at the time, Aldo Moro, who was killed on 9 May 1978, in a seminal event in Italian political history. By virtue of his role as one of the leading thinkers of 'Autonomia Operaia', the Italian Workers' Autonomy movement, Negri was accused by the Italian state of being the theoretical weight behind Italian terrorism since 1971.[23] Subsequently cut off from his comrades and witnessing the systematic decimation of the political movements in which he had participated, Negri came to the sobering realization that his work, and even his life itself, would need a new foundation.[24] Seeking this groundwork, he turned to three disparate figures who had been important to him since his youth: Baruch Spinoza, Leopardi and Job from the Old Testament.[25] While his study of Spinoza and Job has been widely recognized, his work on Leopardi, first published in 1987, remains largely overlooked today, despite the value of its ability to demonstrate the global significance of Leopardi's philosophical thought. Outlining the approach he adopted in *Flower of the Desert*, Negri wrote:

> As Auerbach taught us for literature, and Deleuze for philosophy, only an interrogation brought to bear on the present opens up a schema of interpretation capable of traversing the reality of *poiesis* – be it poetic or philosophical – without dissipating its historical quality but rather recapturing it, in the will to make the truth, constructive power [*puissance*].[26]

His insistence on the importance of bringing an interrogation of Leopardi to bear on the present informs my approach, in which I seek to recapture the constructive power of Leopardi's ethics in order to apply it to contemporary life. Examining the poet's fierce, often harsh, and constant polemic against the fundamental principles of calamity and human misery, Negri noted in his work: 'It is indeed instrumental reason, in its capitalist definition, which Leopardi opposes, just as Adorno and Horkheimer do at more than a century's distance.'

Reflecting on this seemingly shared attribute across these thinkers, he continued, remarking:

> Can these positions be related to one another? In no way, if one considers their presuppositions, the culture and language to which they belong. But it could become possible if we conceive instrumental reason as a historical constant of capitalism and its development, whatever its degree of maturity and conceptual formalization. So then, faced with the same phenomenon, it is possible that the distinct judgments, stated with more than a century of distance between them, retain their value and justify conceptually the analogy they present.[27]

Negri's analysis of the constructive power of Leopardi's work and his prescient insights with regard to the overdevelopment of reason inform my work. In this study I examine Leopardi with an appreciation in mind of Patrick Creagh's insight that: 'all his ideas were a long time in wood before being bottled'.[28] According to Creagh, who translated Leopardi's *Operette Morali* (Moral Essays), critics who proclaim to find sudden conversions in his work often fail to register how one of its most prominent features was the way Leopardi continuously sought to combine numerous, philosophical, emotional and autobiographical insights, which he allowed to mature separately. Considering the generative potential of Leopardi's ethics for contemporary application, I examine the precise ways in which some of the themes Leopardi introduced in his early work altered with the development of his philosophical thinking. In doing so, I trace some of the external influences that helped to shape Leopardi's ideas, considering their significance as I explore the immense network of opportunities his reflections bring to light, examining his work's rich potential to serve as a stark reminder of how far back in human history our anthropocentric impulses reach.

In the first part of this work, I consider how Leopardi's thought was shaped by the effects on eighteenth century philosophy of the disastrous Lisbon Earthquake of 1755, which struck on All Saints Day morning, killing an estimated 60,000 people in Lisbon alone.[29] Despite various attempts to align Leopardi's pessimism with that of Schopenhauer, I aim to show that Leopardi's philosophy was marked by a demonstrable concern with taking living well as the highest value. Taking inspiration from critics' assessments of the affirmative aspects of Nietzsche's ethics, which I suggest shares comparable features with Leopardi's philosophy, I go on to suggest that the importance of the theme of consolation for Leopardi's work has been largely neglected. Building on Negri's study, which examines the significance of Leopardi attempt to reconstruct an ethical perspective through his philosophical poetry, I seek to build on Negri's study, *Flower of the Desert*, in which he examines the significance of Leopardi's attempt to reconstruct an ethical perspective through his philosophical poetry. As he wrote in a footnote in *Subversive Spinoza*, where he summarised his analysis:

> I attempted a five-part periodization of Leopardi's work. In the first period Leopardi confronts the dialectical culture of the beginning of the nineteenth century; in the second he shifts his focus toward a radical sensualist theory, with points of extreme pessimism; in the third and fourth periods Leopardi attempts, with various different motivations, to develop an approach to history and strives to reconstruct an ethical perspective; in the fifth period, he theorizes human community and the urgency of liberation. This historical pattern of the development of Leopardi's thought and poetry agrees with the broad lines traced back by the best Italian interpreters of Leopardi, above all Cesare Luporini and Walter Binni.[30]

The Italian critic Walter Binni, to whom Negri refers here, and whose work examining Leopardi's thought has yet to be translated, examined, in the final chapter of his study *La protesta di Leopardi* (1973), the ethical-poetic conclusion of the Leopardian experience set out in his poem 'La ginestra'. In my own account of this poem, I show how Leopardi's work forms part of what he sought to devise as a cure to the maladies of modernity, which he had identified earlier in his writing life, operating as a sort of resolution to the wealth of ideas he had previously grappled with.

Growing recognition of Leopardi's insights

Finding promise in the increasing recognition afforded to the significance of the relationship between Leopardi's work and an environmental crisis that has arisen out of a war with nature, I strive to analyse the complexity of this relationship. Such recognition may be seen in light of the seven-year project, which culminated in 2013, of translating the *Zibaldone* into English. Although a presentation on Leopardi's work was delivered by Geoffrey Bickersteth for the Annual Italian Lecture at the *Proceedings of the British Academy*, as long ago as 1927, broadly speaking, Leopardi still has yet to gain the widespread attention he deserves outside of Italy.[31] The University of Birmingham is now home to the Leopardi Centre, and Oxford University also opened a dedicated unit for Leopardi Studies in recent years, supporting the promotion of research on Leopardi and his European context, which has built on the growing interest in response to translations of his work.

Until relatively recently, critics who have tried to apply Leopardi's thinking to ecological thought have often been met with dismissal. A change in this regard has only begun to be perceptible, in part due to works such as the guest-edited special issue of the journal *Costellazioni*, titled 'Eco-Leopardi: Apocalyptic Visions and Critique of the Human in the Poet of Nature', which explicitly called for an examination of an 'Eco-Leopardi'. This issue, published in 2019, invited analyses of Leopardi's critique of Anthropocentricism and use of the rhetorical device of anthropomorphism, actively encouraging readings of Leopardi's work that brought him to bear on current ecological thinking, cultivating a new sense that such endeavours could be considered to be valuable, worthwhile and serious scholarship. In addition, as was mentioned in the original call for papers, the recent increase in ecocriticism, seen in works such as Brian Moore's *Ecological Literature and the Critique of Anthropocentrism* (2017), has helped to highlight the potential of taking Leopardi's careful engagement of critiques of anthropocentric modes of thinking seriously. Recent scholarship of this nature has helped to bring to light the richness of Leopardi's analysis of the often-overlooked literary history within which challenges to anthropocentric modes of thought were first set out in the works of ancient thinkers.

My work also owes a debt to older studies of Leopardi available to the English reader today that have not received the recognition they deserve. This includes Giovanni Carsaniga's 1977 book, *Giacomo Leopardi: The Unheeded Voice*, which I use in my account of the relationship between poetry and philosophy in Leopardi's thought. Another important text I draw on throughout is Daniela Bini's *A Fragrance from The Desert: Poetry and Philosophy in Giacomo Leopardi*, published in 1983, whose name is also a reference to the 'noble flower' of Leopardi's poem, which took root in the shadow of Mount Vesuvius, 'consoling the wilderness' while sending its 'waft of sweetest scent' into the sky.[32] More recent studies that have helped me to situate Leopardi's philosophical contributions include Nicholas Rennie's *Speculating on the Moment: The Poetics of Time and Recurrence in Goethe, Leopardi, and Nietzsche* (2005), Frank Rosengarten's *Giacomo Leopardi's Search for a Common Life through Poetry* (2012), Roberto Esposito's *Living Thought: The Origins and Actuality of Italian Philosophy* (2012), John Gray's *Soul of the Marionette* (2015), Fabio Camilletti's *Classicism and Romanticism in Italian Literature: Leopardi's Discourse on Romantic Poetry* (2015), Emanuela Cervato's *A System That Excludes All Systems: Giacomo Leopardi's «Zibaldone di pensieri»* (2017), Roberta Cauchi-Santoro's *Beyond the Suffering of Being: Desire in Giacomo Leopardi and Samuel Beckett* (2017), Martina Piperno's *Rebuilding post-Revolutionary Italy: Leopardi and Vico's 'New Science'* (2018), and the collection of essays *Mapping Leopardi: Poetic and Philosophical Intersections* (2019), edited by Emanuela Cervato, Mark Epstein, Giulia Santi and Simona Wright. I strive to amplify the significance of the contributions of these works throughout, and list them here in recognition that their sufficient acknowledgement is already overdue.

Unearthing the ways in that Leopardi's thought has shaped Modern European Philosophy in largely underrecognized ways, I aim to show that, in a present where we find ourselves deeply immersed within an array of converging crises, compounded by our damaged relationship with nature and one another, by returning to Leopardi's thought, we can find a reminder of the wealth of resources at our disposal to help us to overcome the theoretical impasses threatening to hold us back. This book is an attempt to demonstrate the underrecognized significance of Leopardi's theorization of community and the urgency of liberation. Taking up an invitation found in the work of Paul Gilroy to consider justice on a planetary scale, I attend to the question of what aspects of the ethics to be found in Leopardi's poetic work can be strengthened to support our contemporary struggles for justice, exploring how his lines of thought interact with today's movements and ideas, including those which are anti-racist, ecological, intersectional, feminist, queer and visionary in nature.[33]

Before turning to examine Leopardi's critique of the vices of humans, our trifles and what he saw as our proclivity for illusions in his theoretical work, I first wish to highlight the pertinence of a metaphor found in an essay by the theorist Rebecca Solnit. This observation, it seems to me, captures the latent potential of the insights found in the work of Leopardi, whose mental lucidity Arnold emphasised. In her essay 'The Slow Road to Sudden Change', written after the United States launched its war on Iraq, Solnit highlighted that mushrooms give us an apt metaphor for the way that what appears at first to be an overnight change in fact tends to arise from a long build up. Elucidating this idea *Hope in the Dark* (2016), the book which arose from this essay, Solnit wrote:

> Mushroomed: after a rain mushrooms appear on the surface of the earth as if from nowhere. Many do so from a sometimes vast underground fungus that remains invisible and largely unknown. What we call mushrooms mycologists call the fruiting body of the larger, less visible fungus. Uprisings and revolutions are often considered to be spontaneous, but less visible long-term organizing and groundwork – or underground network – often laid the foundation. Changes in ideas and values also result from work down by writers, scholars, public intellectuals, social activists, and participants in

social media. It seems insignificant or peripheral until very different outcomes emerge from transformed assumptions about who and what matters, who should be heard and believed, who has rights.[34]

Solnit's beautifully depicted observation highlights the significance of the long-term work of organising and laying a foundation, from which the fruits on ones' labour can start to arise. It is with this image in mind that I wish to turn to the works that were foundational to Leopardi's philosophical thinking, the *Zibaldone* and the *Operette*. As I will show, in these works, a destructive dichotomy between humanity and nature started to arise, which governed the shape of his later work. This paves the way for a critical examination of Leopardi's philosophical poetry within the *Canti*, in which I elucidate the significance of consolatory nature of Leopardi's thought, and where the themes of citizenship, strength and solidarity take centre stage.

1

Vices, trifles and illusions

Problematising works

Offering a satirical articulation of his critique of modernity in two of his central works, the *Zibaldone* and the *Operette*, Leopardi critically assessed the Enlightenment philosophy of the eighteenth century and the prominent themes of the Scientific Revolution. In the *Operette*, he subjects to ridicule what he sees as the detrimental and stubborn strength of the ego within Western Philosophy, which he counteracts with a staunch anti-anthropocentrism that throws into question modern assumptions that such critiques are a uniquely recent phenomenon. Relating his thought to that of Freud through recent work by Jacqueline Rose, I suggest that Leopardi's positioning of his later work in response to the biblical quote 'men love darkness rather than light' is of contemporary significance, particularly when considered through the lens of today's environmental crisis. Examining Leopardi's portrayal of his critique of modern attitudes, in the *Zibaldone* and the *Operette*, I reveal how his thought was shaped by the problematic of his time, which was informed by the ideas of Leibnizian metaphysical optimism, of which he was deeply critical, and to which Leopardi ultimately responds with a resolve to resist despair.

The Zibaldone: The seedbed of Leopardi's ideas

The name 'zibaldone' – which means a 'heap of things' or 'miscellany' in Italian – refers to so-called 'commonplace books' that described a register of continuous learning, which were used as a means of compiling information. One of the best-known examples of such a form is perhaps the *Zibaldone da Canal*, which was written in the early fourteenth century by a Venetian merchant and is now housed in the Beinecke Rare Book Library at Yale University. Composed as a collection of notes on various subjects, it came into the possession of Niccolò da Canal in the fifteenth century, from whom it took its name.[1] It is now considered to be the earliest extensive merchant's manual, providing minutely detailed repertoires of commercial information that are seen as important sources for the economic history of late medieval northern Italy. Leopardi's own *Zibaldone di pensieri*, commonly referred to solely as the *Zibaldone*, was his immense critical notebook, which he fondly referred to in his work:

> To a young man who, in love with his studies, said that you learn a hundred pages a day about how to live, and the practical knowledge of men, so-and-so answered 'but the book' (but this book) 'has 15 or 20 million pages'.
>
> [2588]

In fact, the *Zibaldone* spanned over 4000 pages, which Leopardi nurtured from 1817 to 1832, and wrote with particular fervour from 1821 to 1824, drawing up partial indexes to aid his cross-referencing. His entries were composed in a series of creative spikes, and covered a wide range of themes to which he would frequently return to in order to add, modify or correct his reflections on them.[2] Described by Harold Bloom as Leopardi's 'hodgepodge of thoughts', the *Zibaldone* is comparable to Nietzsche's collection of unpublished notes *Nachlass*, which formed the basis for *The Will to Power*, due to the ability it gave Leopardi to develop some of the ideas he would later reshape in the dialogues and experimental pieces he composed for the *Operette*.[3]

It has taken over 175 years since Leopardi's death for his notebooks to receive a full English translation, which was undertaken by a team of seven translators led by Michael Caesar and Franco D'Intino, who worked for seven years in order to see the work published in 2013. Although Leopardi didn't write the *Zibaldone* with publication in mind, his private meditations shed great light on the course of his thinking, and, thanks to the new translation of the *Zibaldone*, English readers can now trace how the theoretical basis of Leopardi's literary work developed. As Jonathan Galassi, whose translation of Leopardi's poetry in the *Canti* was published in 2012, has claimed, the *Zibaldone* was 'the seedbed of all of Leopardi's work', playing an integral role in his problematization of the concerns of modernity.[4]

Throughout the *Zibaldone*, Leopardi conveys his analysis of the origin of unhappiness, the 'corruption and decline of mankind', and the warnings he found had been unheeded from the 'most ancient sages', whose ideas he frequently sought to echo. According to his analysis, modern the state of humankind was one of decline, caused by our inability to appropriately metabolize our new knowledge:

> From my lengthy reflections ... one may infer ... that the corruption and decline of mankind from a better state is proved by a very remote, universal, consistent, and unbroken tradition, but that such a tradition and the records of the most ancient history and wisdom also prove that this depravity, corruption and decline of mankind from a happy state arose through knowledge, and through knowing too much, and that the origin of this unhappiness was the knowledge of both itself and of the world, and the excessive use of reason. This truth appears to have been known by the most ancient sages, and to have been one of the principal and crucial truths that they ... contented themselves with hinting at vaguely to the people.
>
> [2939–40]

While some of Leopardi's entries to the *Zibaldone* are brief jottings, others are full-length essays, portraying his lifelong concern with literature, philosophy and science, and multitudes of other themes, including, poetry, contemporary society, the ancients and barbarism.[5] Drawn together by an intricate web of references, in his work, Leopardi examines individual psychology and analyses the effect of scientific progress on metaphysics.[6] As Negri described in *Flower of the Desert*:

> In the enormous *Zibaldone* wherein he expressed his thought, occasionally interrupted and illuminated by prodigious poetic set

pieces, Leopardi constructed a philosophical and political discourse that is entirely open to time-to-come [*là-venir*]. Wherever pain and solitude become the real conditions of life, it is possible to open up a space of hope, to invent an active disutopia, and glimpse a constitutive praxis of a new world: in this way, Leopardi reappropriated his God. This reading of Leopardi helped me resist.[7]

Asking himself if his reading was 'adequate to the reality in which his poetry moved', Negri's work, as we will see, saw in Leopardi an important 'philosophical and political discourse' that addressed itself to the 'time-to-come' in ways that I assess throughout the course of this study. As I refer to the *Zibaldone*, I will give examples to show Leopardi's position in relation to the ideas I introduce, many of which reappear throughout Leopardi's oeuvre in one form or another, firstly in Leopardi's *Operette*, and later, as I show in my examination of 'La ginestra', in the *Canti*.

The Operette morali: Experimenting with 'weapons of ridicule'

We can find the first glimmerings of the *Operette morali* in 1820, when Leopardi wrote to his lifelong friend Pietro Giordani, on September 4: 'In the last few days, as though to take revenge on the world, I've devised and sketched some short satirical pieces in prose.'[8] This work gave Leopardi the opportunity to scrutinize the ideas which were central to both his time and our present times. Murphy alludes to this in his article from 2011: 'Flower of the Desert: Poetics as Ontology from Leopardi to Negri', where he describes 'Leopardi's untimely critique of progressive history', and writes: 'A generation before Nietzsche, almost contemporaneous with G. W. F. Hegel, Leopardi was already thinking in an "untimely" fashion on the basis of his own youthful studies in classical philology', highlighting the prescient nature of his thought.[9]

In 1824, Leopardi wrote the first twenty of the *Operette morali*, which included moral sketches and satirical and philosophical dialogues, and completed his 'Discorso sopra lo stato presente dei costumi degl'italiani' ('Discourse on the Present State of the Morals of the Italians'), which would not be published until 1906. Working in a continuous stint of daily labour starting in the middle of January and continuing to the end of November, and, completing his work in 1827, Leopardi gradually gave form to a collection of dialogues and short stories within which he prepared the groundwork for a philosophical treatise to come by bringing comedy to: 'the condition and general spirit of the age', 'the revolutions and circumstances of the world' and 'the vices and abominations not of men but of man' [1393].[10] Negri described these works as 'a kind of lightning rod in the interpretations of poetry and above all the philosophy of Leopardi' in his study, *Flower of the Desert*.[11] Here, comparing the *Operette* to the work of German idealists, the 'typical problems' of which he argues Leopardi attends to, Negri wrote:

> These *Operette* are German in the sense of the extraordinary technical adaptability that Leopardi attributes to the language of that people – which takes nothing away from the beauty of his Latin tongue. They are also German in the sense that they take up, with extraordinary consonance, the typical problems of classical German philosophy, critical and post-critical, to which they propose an original solution. A great speculative poetry confronts the European philosophical genius in its entirety. Permitting ourselves a paradox, we can conclude these remarks by observing that the theme of the Operette echoes Kant's answer to the question 'What is Enlightenment?'[12]

Arguing that the *Operette* has been too easily excluded from the considerations of classical Italian Leopardi criticism, including the work of Cesare Luporini, Mario Fubini, Giovanni Gentile and Walter Binni, Negri emphasised the materialism of the *Operette*, of which he wrote:

> Maturity of conception of the world, serenity of philosophical judgement, ironic progression in prose as in fable, and attention to literary form go hand in hand. I do not understand why there is such resistance to considering this materialist canto as an exceptional stylistic document precisely because of the extreme density of its materialist contents. Why should a rigorous materialism impede our poetic pleasure and deprive us of the joy of a truly corporeal style?[13]

Emphasizing the importance of the collection, Negri argues that Leopardi's essays and dialogues give expression to a Leopardian universe of 'high poetic originality and the singular philosophical force' through a wide range of mediums, from prose to fables and dialogues.[14] Within them, Leopardi reworked the principal themes he set out in the *Zibaldone*, framing his ideas in narrative form, while putting into practice his conviction that storytelling had the potential to both enlighten and unite.

The posthumous edition of the *Operette* work was edited by his friend Antonio Ranieri, with whom Leopardi lived in the last seven years of his life, staying in the Villa delle Ginestre, owned by Ranieri's brother-in-law Giuseppe Ferrigni, before his death on 14 June 1837.[15] Here, in the villa built shortly after the 16 December 1631 eruption of Mount Vesuvius, which it overlooked, Leopardi and Ranieri had hoped to gain refuge from the second world cholera pandemic, which spanned from 1826 to 1849.[16] Ranieri's edition of the *Operette* was published by Felice Le Monnier in 1845, which Nietzsche would later read, and included twenty-four operette, including fables, dialogues, essays and collections of aphorisms. His characters, among whom many were non-human, included protagonists borrowed from ancient texts and mythology, such as Hercules and Atlas. They often offered a perspective different to the norm of the centralised human, giving Leopardi the ability to reflect on humankind from a distance, and to consider subjects as wide ranging as the quest for human happiness, the function of poetry, astrology, self-destructive tendencies of people, who he criticised for their consistent lack of moral courage and, ultimately, nature.

By giving his work the title *Operette morali*, Leopardi purposefully situated his studies with respect to a rich and longstanding tradition. The work of Stoic philosopher Lucius Annaeus Seneca (4 BC–AD 65), which I consider in my examination of Leopardi's way of conceiving our relationship with death, includes his philosophical or moral essays, ten of which are traditionally called *Dialogues*, which spanned topics including the brevity of life within the ancient work, steadfastness and natural phenomena.[17] Another author of moral essays whose ideas are important when giving an account of Leopardi's philosophy, who I will refer in my account of Leopardi's notion of barbarism, is the poet and satirist Alexander Pope (1688–1744), whose *Epistles to Several Persons* were composed of four ethical poems, published 1731–5, which also informed Leopardi's thinking with regard to the powers of nature and the legitimacy of philosophical optimism.

Leopardi was also inspired by the work of the ancient Hellenized Syrian satirist 'Lucian of Samosata' (AD 125–AD 180), whose use of 'the weapons of ridicule' Leopardi located significant power in, which he was inspired by. Seeing Lucian's approach as a potential model for his own critique of the risks bound up with the excessive use of reason, Leopardi frequently returned in the *Zibaldone* to the appropriate deployment of comedy. In a letter he wrote to his friend Giordani on 27 July 1821, Leopardi wrote of his ambition prior to composing the *Operette*:

> For ridicule first to please, and second to give intense and lasting pleasure, that is, for its continuation not to be boring, it must be directed at something serious, something important. If it is directed at trifles, and things that are, I might almost say, beyond ridicule, apart from its giving no pleasure at all, it provides very little amusement and soon becomes boring. The more serious the object being made fun of, and the more important it is, the more amusing the ridicule, also because of the contrast, etc. In my dialogues I will strive to bring comedy to what hitherto has been characteristic of tragedy, that is the vices of the great, the fundamental principles of calamity and human misery, the absurdities of politics, the improprieties pertaining to universal morals and to philosophy, the condition and general spirit of the age, the revolutions and circumstances of the world, the vices and abominations not of men but of man, the state of nations, etc.
>
> [1393]

As we see here, Leopardi intended to use his dialogues to bring attention to what he felt was 'something serious, something important', such as 'the condition and general spirit of the age' and the 'the vices and abominations … of man'. His belief in the importance of amusement is also apparent here, in his reference to the 'intense and lasting pleasure' he endeavoured to give rise to. Giving an account of the benefits he saw in the 'weapons of ridicule' he found in Lucian, he went on:

> And I believe that the weapons of ridicule, especially in this utterly ridiculous and chilly age, and also, because of the power they naturally possess, will be in a better position to be useful than those of passion, feeling, imagination, eloquence, more even than those of reasoning, although these are very strong today. Thus to rouse my poor country and poor century, I shall find that I have employed the weapons of feeling and enthusiasm and eloquence and imagination in lyric poetry, and in whatever literary prose works I may write, the weapons of reason, logic, philosophy in the philosophical treatise that I am planning, and the weapons of ridicule in the Lucianic dialogues and novellas I am preparing.
>
> [1394]

In a later account of his considerations concerning the fables of Lorenzo Pignotti (1739–1812), it will become increasingly clear that a key feature of Leopardi's endeavour to 'describe certain vices of the social world' was his ambition to bring the thought of the ancients and the moderns into unison in a way that could benefit his own time. In turn, in my later analysis of 'La ginestra', I will return to the significance of this as I examine another passage from the same period to show how Leopardi brings his ambition to employ 'the weapons of feeling and enthusiasm and eloquence and imagination in lyric poetry', mentioned here, to life in his poem.

Leopardi's engagement with the dialogue form throughout the Operette is also significant. Michael Caesar, who contributed to the translation of the Zibaldone into English, examined this in his article 'Leopardi's Operette morali and the Resources of Dialogue'. According to him, Leopardi's dialogues, in which he finds the means to effectively set forth his own voice and views, constitute a key stage in the form's history, adding also to the history of the genre of satire. As Caesar observed, and as will become increasingly noteworthy, not only did

Leopardi engage with dialogues in Lucian's work directly, but he also attended to references to Lucian found in the work of thinkers closer to his own time; 'through the massive utilization of his work made by seventeenth- and eighteenth-century rationalists and men of letters, from Fontenelle to Voltaire and G. Gozzi among many others'.[18] This is examined in more detail later, where I also touch on the importance of dialogues for the communication of the scientific ideas in the thought of Copernicus and Galileo. Here, I allude to the way Leopardi drew inspiration from Galileo's *Dialogue Concerning the Two Chief World Systems* (1632), to help him ensure the *Operette* was accessible to a public audience.[19] Lastly, I highlight Leopardi's recourse to Voltaire's dialogues, and his admiration for Pignotti's talent for adjusting Aesopian fables and transforming them, making them 'of some use to grown men' [67] in a way he sought to emulate.

The imagination, philosophy and poetry

Leopardi was initially damning in his portrayal of modern philosophy, the sterile speculation, pure mechanical rationalism of which he repelled him.[20] Criticizing its lack of political potential, as he wrote in the *Zibaldone* in 1820:

> Even if philosophy paved the way for the French Revolution, it did not bring it about, because philosophy, especially modern philosophy, is incapable by itself of achieving anything. And even if philosophy itself had the power to start a revolution, it could not sustain it.
>
> [126]

For him, philosophy, which he associated with mathematical reasoning, was involved in a conflict against the emotions, which he saw philosophy as seeking to suppress. As Giovanni Carsaniga highlights in 'Poetry to Philosophy' from *Giacomo Leopardi: The Unheeded Voice* (1977), this changed when Leopardi discovered the work of Germaine de Staël, whose use of varied and diverse approaches in the service of improving society allowed her to overcome the rigid boundaries so frequently found between disciplines:

> A persuasive opponent of intellectual pigeon-holing and of rigid boundaries between the various intellectual disciplines, Madame de Staël, spent a great deal of her energies demonstrating how to use varied and diverse approaches, how to employ concepts and facts from different methods and sources to arrive at a better understanding of the history of ideas and the cultural development of mankind, with a view to improving the present state of society. In her treatise *De 'linfluence des passions sur le bonheur des individus et des nations* [On the Influence of Passions on Individual and Social Happiness, 1796], she had tried to solve the dichotomy between nature (emotions, sensitivity) and reason that was soon also to occupy Leopardi's mind.[21]

By virtue of his engagement with the work of de Staël, whose thought informed the development of his own regarding pleasure, happiness and experience, Leopardi found himself increasingly compelled to synthesize philosophy and poetry.[22] Describing the shift he observed in himself after reading her work, which prompted him to refer to himself as a philosopher with increasing frequency, Leopardi reflected in 1821:

> Dedicating myself entirely and with the utmost relish to literature, I despised and hated philosophy. The *thoughts* of which our age is so fond bored me. in accordance with the usual prejudices, I believed myself to be born for letters, imagination, feeling, and that it was altogether impossible for me to apply myself to a faculty wholly opposed to these, that is, to reason, philosophy, mathematical abstraction, and to succeed in it. I did not lack capacity for reflecting, for paying attention, for comparing, for reason, for combining, I did not lack profundity, etc. But it was only after having read some works by Mm. de Staël that I believed myself to be a philosopher.
>
> [1742]

De Staël's philosophical examination of the significance of the passions was transformative for Leopardi's thinking, enabling him to conceive of philosophy as something that can cultivate the imagination and facilitate social change in a way he had previously doubted was possible.[23] In another passage Leopardi wrote in the same year, he considered in further detail the generative potential of the combination of disciplines he had previously viewed as separated by a rigid boundary:

> Let us observe how much imagination contributes to philosophy (which yet is its enemy), and how true it is that in different circumstances the great poet could have been a great philosopher, promoter of that reason which is lethal to the genre professed by him, and how, conversely, a philosopher could have been a great poet. The ability to mine a rich vein of similes is proper to the true poet (Homer [the poet] is the greatest and most fertile model). In a state of enthusiasm, in the heat of any passion, etc. etc., the mind discovers most vivid resemblances between things. Even the most fleeting vigor in the body, if it exerts some influence upon the spirit, causes it to see relationships between very disparate things, to find comparisons, extremely abstruse and ingenuous similes (whether in serious or joking vein), shows it relations it had never thought of, in short gives it a marvellous facility to draw together and compare objects of the most distinct kinds, such as the ideal with the most purely material, to embody in a very vivid manner the most abstract thought, to reduce everything to image, and to create from it some of the most vivid images you could think of. And not only by means of direct similes or comparisons, but also by means of very novel epithets, very bold metaphors, words containing in themselves a simile, etc.
>
> [1650]

Here, he conveys his appreciation of what the imagination can contribute to philosophy, and how a great poet, who has developed the ability to mine similes, see relationships and find comparisons, hones the same skills as those required for practising philosophy. In doing so, he contributes to a debate that reaches back further than Plato's depiction of an 'old quarrel between philosophy and poetry' in the *Republic*, by arguing that 'All faculties of a great poet' equate to 'the philosopher through and through'.[24] For him, De Staël's appreciation of the benefits of utilizing concepts and facts from a variety of methods and sources, as well as her focus on the significance of the emotions was all instructive.

In her article 'With Rhymes about the Human Fate Philosophy in the Poetry of Giacomo Leopardi', published in 2020, Aleksandra Koman observes that Leopardi does not use traditional forms of philosophical expression. She notes that he 'experimented almost every form of literary expression', prompting ongoing discussions in the world of Italian critics about the relationship between Leopardi and philosophy in a way that suggests 'that the reflective lyrics of the famous poet from Recanati are a noteworthy case'.[25] Supporting this notion of the noteworthiness of his work, in the continuation of his reflections on the relationship between the imagination, philosophy and poetry, Leopardi he writes:

> All faculties of a great poet, and all contained in and deriving from the ability to discover relations between things, even the most minimal, and distant, even between things that appear the least analogous, etc. Now this is the philosopher through and through: the faculty of discovering and recognizing relations, of binding particulars together, and of generalizing.
>
> [1650]

Having changed the way he saw philosophy following his reading of De Staël, Leopardi sought to overcome rigid boundaries, often oscillating in his work between literature and philosophy.[26] As a result, throughout his oeuvre, to varying degrees, most of his considerations can be seen to relate simultaneously to literary and philosophical discourse.[27] Nonetheless, as Koman has referred to, there remain critics who reject the contention that Leopardi's work bridges the gap between poetry and philosophy. An example of this can be seen in an argument presented by Lowry Nelson in *Poetic Configurations* (2010). Here, Nelson argues:

> In the welter of books and articles on Leopardi recently published, one notes the insistent claims, *pace* Croce, for Leopardi's greatness not only as a poet but as linguist, existentialism, and philosopher – or at least *philosophe*. Such claims often seem lacking both in critical preciseness and proper international perspective. The studies in which they are set

forth may simply be exercises within the assumed parameters of Italian academic expectations and performance: a phenomenon familiar in most countries as part of a general inflation and overproduction of critical, academic discourse.[28]

Dismissing claims pertaining to the philosophical value of Leopardi's work as examples of the 'overproduction of critical, academic discourse' is misguided, and ignores comments to the opposite effect from Leopardi himself. Such a position has the effect of contributing to the neglect of Leopardi's contributions to philosophical problems relating to form, optimism, evil, nature, racism and barbarism, among other topics. Nonetheless, an increasing number of contemporary theorists, of whom Negri and Gilroy are examples, refer to Leopardi as a 'poet-philosopher' in appreciation of the significance of his fusion. In his work, Negri highlights the centrality of poetry to the development of materialism, arguing in 'Materialism and Poetry' that poetry gives significance to the world, and contains within itself the hope of a transforming it.[29] Writing in relation to Leopardi's poetry, the sensualist nature of which he emphasises, Negri states:

> His is a poetry ... that arises within materialism – sensualist materialism, worn out by too long a struggle for emancipation and yet nonetheless an instrument of revolutionary critique. It is a poetry of Enlightenment reason, in certain respects, but mitigated by a sense of the crisis of the revolution.[30]

Another example of Leopardi being described as a 'poet-philosopher' can be seen in Italo Calvino's work, especially *Six Memos for the Next Millennium* (2016), where he described Leopardi's ability to capture the 'realm of death' within modernity:

> The sudden agile leap of the poet-philosopher [who] raises himself above the weight of the world, showing that with all his gravity he has the secret of lightness, and that what many consider to be the vitality of the times – noisy, aggressive, reviving and roaring – belongs to the realm of death, like a cemetery for rusty old cars.[31]

Such a critique of the so-called 'vitality of the times' is particularly prominent in the dialogues that Leopardi wrote in 1824, which I shortly examine, to illustrate the way in which he attended, first to the poor state of the world, before turning his attention to the vitality he saw people as lacking. Following this, I show how Leopardi stringent critique of the limits of the Enlightenment in their inception ultimately paves the way for a unique ethical stance, in which Leopardi underscores the philosophical necessity of cultivating courage, solidarity and compassion as central components of our ways of life within modernity.

Barbarous times in the *Zibaldone*

Given the important place that the *Zibaldone* has in Leopardi's oeuvre, I wish to begin by introducing some of the key themes that traverse this work, earning him his reputation as one of history's 'greatest pessimists'.[32] Although Leopardi continues to be largely excluded from Anglophone philosophical scholarship, the prescience and depth of his critique of anthropocentrism speak directly to the narratives underpinning our role in the environmental crisis. As Negri argues in *Flower of the Desert*, his thought extends well beyond the borders of Italy, displaying 'the will, the tension, and the passion that were to come', and making us 'draw a deep breath of imagination, transgression, revival'.[33] As Negri argues in *Flower of the Desert*, his thought, which brings to the fore the experience of the defeat of the Enlightenment, Jacobins and the revolution, extends well beyond the borders of Italy, displaying 'the will, the tension, and the passion that were to come'. Moreover, in doing so, it makes us 'draw a deep breath of imagination, transgression, revival'.[34] Demonstrating the impact of his ideas on another contemporary thinker, in an interview where she discussed the influence of Leopardi on Nietzsche's work, Susan Sontag spoke of her endeavour to continue a tradition made up of: 'people like Emerson, Leopardi, Chamfort, Valéry and Barthes ...' who have established '... a way of writing that breaks down the genres as we usually think of them: it's the tradition of the artist-thinker that unites writers as disparate as Wilde, Nietzsche, Benjamin and Adorno.'[35] As I will demonstrate, much of Leopardi's work was shaped by his decisive attempts to make an intervention to a tradition that extends as far back as to the thought and work of the ancients, in ways that philosophers like Nietzsche and Benjamin would later pick up in their work.

Rejecting philosophical systems of optimism

Between June 1820 and January 1821, Leopardi used the term 'ultraphilosophy', in his consideration of the task of philosophy.[36] Whilst appearing only once in the *Zibaldone*, his neologism has been adopted by critics as a convenient label for his thinking, depicting the thinker's interest in bringing together seemingly disparate themes to show the significance of their relationship.[37] Distinguishing his proposed method from modern philosophy, Leopardi highlights how he understands ultraphilosophy's potential for attending to our growing alienation from nature in modern society. Highlighting how it can contribute to our regeneration, he set out the vision of his work, writing in the *Zibaldone*: '… our regeneration depends upon an ultra-philosophy, one could say, which knowing things completely and profoundly, brings us closer to nature. And this should be the accomplishment of the extraordinary luminaries of this century' **[115]**. Giving some examples of such 'luminaries', Leopardi highlighted the importance of the role of systems in such thinkers' works, writing on 14 April 1821:

> All thinkers, especially the greatest of them, have each had their own system, and have been either the shapers or the supporters, more or less passionate and committed as the case may be, of one system or another. Leaving the ancient philosophers to one side, consider the greatest of the moderns. Descartes, Malebranche, Newton, Leibniz, Lock, Rousseau, Cabanis, Travy, Vico, Kant, in short, every last one of them. There is not a single great thinker who does not belong in this list. And I mean thinkers of every kind: those who have been thinkers in the sphere of ethics, politics, in the science of man, and in

any of its parts, in physics, in philosophy of every kind, in philology, in antiquarianism, in critical and philosophical erudition, in the philosophy of history, etc. etc.

[946]

In recent years, there has been an increase in attention to the role of systemization in Leopardi's thought, evident in works such as Cervato's *A System That Excludes All Systems: Giacomo Leopardi's «Zibaldone di pensieri»* (2017), and the collection of essays *Mapping Leopardi: Poetic and Philosophical Intersections* (2019), which both attend to this theme. For Leopardi, the ability to understand themes in relation to each other was the mark of a great thinker, and he put this idea into practice, methodically drawing together his reflections in the *Zibaldone* with more than 2400 cross-references and 3300 bibliographic references, and multiple indexes. This vigilant cross-referencing has allowed for his work's transmutation into a digital Zibaldone Hypertext Research Platform, developed by Silvia Stoyanova and Ben Johnston, on which readers can navigate his work by theme.

Among those thinkers whose systemic thinking Leopardi recognized was the German philosopher Gottfried Wilhelm Leibniz (1646–1716), who Leopardi described as 'perhaps Germany's greatest metaphysician' [1857]. Although he did not have access to Leibniz's works, which he drew on from secondary sources, his philosophical work was marked by an appreciation of Leibnizian metaphysical optimism, which he also had access to through the work of Alexander Pope (1688–1744).[38] Giving his account of Leibniz's system of Optimism early on in the *Zibaldone*, Leopardi wrote:

> Every species ... and every individual to the extent that it conforms to the nature of its species, is perfect, and possesses perfection (relative perfection, that is: since there is no such thing as absolute perfection or a paradigm of perfection, no one being or species is more perfect than another). It possesses all the good that is good for [392] it, because everything else would not be good. It is as good as it can be, because for it there is nothing good that is outside its nature. Indeed, outside

of that everything is bad, because there is no absolute good. All this is true in both physical and moral terms. (8 December 1820.) I believe this is the system (Leibniz's, if I am not mistaken) known as Optimism.

[392]

As I will show in my analysis of Leopardi's dialogues in the *Operette*, the thinking of rationalists such as Leibniz shaped his considerations of how we might understand ourselves, particularly our fragility, in relation to nature.[39] In 'The Wager of Prometheus', composed for the *Operette* in April–May 1824, for example, Leopardi makes reference to the Leibnizian notion 'that this is the best of all possible worlds' in a conversation that occurs between Momos and Prometheus, where he also highlights his contention that civilisation is 'the opposite of barbarism', arguing that it 'is not possessed today except by a small fraction of the human race'.[40] Leibniz's doctrine was satirized by Voltaire in *Candide, ou l'Optimisme* (Candide, or Optimism), published in 1759, as I return to consider later. In addition to considering Leibniz's account of such themes, Leopardi also considered these in the work of Pope, whose influential 'Essay on Man', which Tom Jones describes in his introduction to the work as a 'philosophical poem', was first published in 1733, and was composed of four epistles.[41] According to Voltaire, who was nonetheless critical of the content of Pope's ideas, the work was 'the most sublime didactic poem ever written in any language'.[42] These ideas, which Leopardi appears to have encountered through Michele Leoni's 1819 translation of Pope's work, contribute to the development of Leopardi's ideas, particularly the way he thinks about nature, and our relation to both the universe and infinity.[43]

In Leopardi's thought, for thinkers like Leibniz and Pope, our ills are a necessary effect of our nature and the constitution of the universe. Reflecting on the optimistic position Pope encapsulated in the final line of Epistle I, where he wrote: 'One truth is clear, Whatever is, is right', Leopardi's perspective, in ways that I go on to illustrate, took into account the events of the Lisbon Earthquake of November 1755, which led him to issue as a counterpoint with his own contention that 'everything is evil'.[44] Bringing his cosmic viewpoint, which I introduce more fully with recourse to his dialogues, to bear on Pope's ideas, Leopardi argued:

> ... the complex of so many worlds that exist; the universe; is only a spot, a speck in metaphysics. Existence, by its nature and essence and generally, is an imperfection, an irregularity, a monstrosity. But this imperfection is a tiny thing, literally a spot, because all the worlds that exist, however many and however extensive they are, since they are certainly not infinite in number or in size, are consequently infinitely small in comparison with the size the universe might be if it were infinite, and the whole of existence is infinitely small in comparison with the true infinity, so to speak, of nonexistence, of nothing.
>
> This system, although it clashes with those ideas of ours that the end can be no other than good, is probably more sustainable than that of Leibniz, Pope, etc., that *everything is good*. I would not dare however, to go on to say that the universe which exists is the worst of possible universes, thereby substituting pessimism for optimism. Who can know the limits of possibility?
>
> [4174]

Here, Leopardi explicity situates his cosmic thinking in opposition to the philosophical ideas he finds dealt with in the work of Leibniz and Pope. By arguing that the reflection that the imperfection of our existence is 'literally a spot' that is 'infinitely small in comparison with the size the universe might be if it were infinite', Leopardi tempers the optimism he finds in the work of these thinkers with a contextualization of our role in the larger scheme of things. In doing so, he brings to bear on the philosophical questions of his time a reflective exercise suggested by the Stoic thinker, Marcus Aurelius, which I will later consider in relation to Leopardi's poems. With these reflections in mind, Leopardi brought to the fore the ideas around which he would continuously circle throughout the course of his writing life. In addition to the reference to infinity we find here, in the autumn of 1819, the same year that he described how he 'became a philosopher, from the poet he once was', Leopardi wrote 'L'infinito' ('Infinity'), the poem for which he is perhaps most well-known.⁴⁵ Here, he describes the experience of gazing beyond the unending landscape seen from the hill Monte Tabor, now referred to as 'Colle dell'Infinito', several hundred metres from the library in which he spent much of his life in his hometown of Recanati and on which a stanza of his poem is inscribed, the first line of which reads: 'Sempre caro mi fu quest'ermo colle'. Describing a feeling of 'almost fear' when he absorbs this view in 'L'Infinito', the poet-philosopher depicts how his mind sinks into the immensity of the 'endless stillness' and the eternal in those moments as he strives to comprehend the 'superhuman silences, and depthless calm' of such unending space.⁴⁶

The sugar you stir

While in some parts of his writing, Leopardi's thought circles around the question of our importance in relation to infinity, in others, he attends to the juxtaposition of progress and regress, reflecting on our 'barbarous times, from which we have *not yet entirely emerged*' [**4289**]. Optimism, which we have just seen Leopardi considers in relation to Alexander Pope's ideas, is a complex topic in Leopardi's thought, and parallels can be found between the writer's understanding of the relationship between optimism and pessimism, and his ideas concerning barbarism and civilisation. This consideration of barbarism, in particular, arose from Leopardi's engagement with the work of Voltaire, particularly his reflections on the Lisbon Earthquake of 1755, which I consider in full later, examining the impact it had on the role of nature in Leopardi's thought.

For Leopardi, barbarism is an inherent aspect of modernity. In the *Zibaldone*, he gives a full account of this idea, highlighting the moral bankruptcy of slavery, which he calls upon to illustrate the reliance of 'progress' and 'civilisation' on a cost extracted from half of humanity. As he wrote in June 1821:

> Observe how many men are required to suffer constant and unrelenting unhappiness, disease, death, slavery (either unpaid and violent, or mercenary), calamity, pain, suffering, and travails of every

kind, in order to procure for other men this instrument of civilisation and supposed means of happiness. Tell me then (1) if it is credible that nature had from the beginning put this price, namely, the constant unhappiness of one half of all men (and when I say a half, I have in mind not only this branch of supposed social perfection but also the others that cost the same price) on the perfection and happiness of men. Tell me (2) if these miseries of our fellow human beings are consistent with this same civilisation which they serve. It is well known how slavery is defended by countless political writers, etc., and retained in practice, even against the theories, as necessary.

[1172]

For Leopardi, the misery induced by obtaining sugar, coffee and other commodities through slavery hollows out the meaning of civilisation. Such a term, he argues, is false in theory since it subsists by virtue of circumstances that are 'are absolutely uncivilized', and 'barbaric in the true and full sense of the term'. As he reflected considering the trajectory of sought-after luxuries consumed in the West:

> … And what I say about money also goes for commodities that come to us from distant parts, by means of the same our similar miseries, slavery, etc., such as sugar, coffee, etc. etc., and are deemed necessary for the perfection of society …
>
> And you may see from this how it is that civilisation (as is the way with all false theories) contradicts itself in theory, too, and furthermore cannot subsists without circumstances that are opposed to its nature and are absolutely uncivilized, indeed barbaric in the true and full sense of the term. So that perfect civilisation cannot subsist without perfect barbarism, the perfection of society without the perfection (and imperfection in the same sense and kind in which perfection is understood), and if this imperfection were removed the roots of the supposed perfection of society would be cut.

[1173]

In his 1991 essay 'Old and New Identities, Old and New Ethnicities', Stuart Hall reiterated this point, bringing the idea of sugar and tea plantations to bear on the topic of identity in contemporary life in England, writing:

> People like me who came to England in the 1950s have been there for centuries; symbolically, we have been there for centuries. I was coming home. I am the sugar at the bottom of the English cup of tea. I am the sweet tooth, the sugar plantations that rotted generations of English children's teeth. There are thousands of others beside me that are, you know, the cup of tea itself. Because they don't grow it in Lancashire, you know. Not a single tea plantation exists within the United Kingdom. This is the symbolization of English identity – I mean, what does anybody in the world know about an English person except that they can't get through the day without a cup of tea.
>
> Where does it come from? Ceylon – Sri Lanka, India. That is the outside history that is inside the history of the English. There is no English history without that other history. The notion that identity has to do with people that look the same, feel the same, call themselves the same, is nonsense. As a process, as a narrative, as a discourse, it is always told from the position of the Other.[47]

Hall's analysis shows the much longer history within which contemporary considerations concerning identity are located. In his essay 'The Local and the Global', also written in 1991, he extends his argument, observing: 'we suffer increasingly from a process of historical amnesia in which we think that just because we are thinking about an idea it has only just started'.[48] Leopardi's critique of our human centredness, which he borrowed from the ancients, demonstrates this. Such considerations also arise in the work of Paul Gilroy, who challenges this historical amnesia with recourse to the philosophy of Leopardi in *Postcolonial Melancholia* (2004). I return to this work again later, in which it is worth noting now Gilroy's description of Leopardi's work, which reads:

> It reveals no misplaced faith in automatic progress and retreats from the world of formal or institutional politics into the areas of ethical

judgment where its theodicy can be revealed. The resulting collision spoke directly to the immoral institution of racial slavery and the dubious extension of European powers into the rest of the planet.[49]

He adds to this, in his article from 2018, "Where every breeze speaks of courage and liberty": Offshore Humanism and Marine Xenology, or, Racism and the Problem of Critique at Sea Level', writing: 'Racial slavery is one fleeting instance of the perfidy of human beings and the wholesale failure of their trifling ethical systems over which Leopardi's cosmic pessimism about our species is erected.'[50] As previously mentioned, the role of this cosmic pessimism will be an overarching theme in my account of Leopardi's *Operette*, and I will later return to Hall's idea of historical amnesia in relation to the poet-thinker's work, when I consider its pertinence with regard to contemporary critiques of anthropocentricism. Before discussing these themes, however, I wish to briefly consider examinations that relate to Leopardi's thinking, concerning the relationship between Christianity, scientific development and the concept of extractivism. Following this, I provide a brief account of the critique of Christianity we find in Leopardi's thought, highlighting how it relates to his critique of anthropocentric thinking.

Binding nature to our service

The image of man's dominion over nature, which reaches as far back as the Book of Genesis, reappeared as one of the leading images of the emerging 'new science', particularly in the work of Francis Bacon (1561–1626), where nature was frequently depicted with recourse to women. In the first story of creation recounted in the Book of Genesis, at the end of the sixth day of creation and having created man in his own image, God issued the instructions: 'Be fruitful and multiply, and fill the earth and subdue it; and have dominion over the fish of the sea and over the birds of the air and over every living thing that moves upon the earth' (Gen.1:28). Portraying us as separate from any other form of life on Earth in such a manner, humanity was thereby placed by God at the centre of the created universe.[51]

Bacon took the notion of subduing the Earth as the guiding principle of his new vision of practical knowledge, according to which the purpose of science was to extend: 'the narrow limits of man's dominion over the universe [to their] promised bounds'. As Peter Harrison has set out in his article 'Subduing the Earth: Genesis 1, Early Modern Science, and the Exploitation of Nature', published in 1999, Bacon's vision was integral to the rhetoric of the Royal Society, established in 1660. As its founding member, Bishop Thomas Sprat, proclaimed in 1667, the aim of the society was to: 're-establish dominion over Things'. This view was in turn supplemented by that of Joseph Glanvill, another leading figure in the society, who, arguing along similar lines, maintained that the new science provided: 'ways of captivating Nature, and making her subserve our purposes and designments'. These proclamations demonstrated the agreement among the Royal Society's earliest key figures with the view that nature's resources are there for the service of mankind.[52]

This early formulation of a modern scientific method encouraged the conceptualisation of nature as a machine, devoid of mystery or divinity whose component parts could be dammed, extracted from and remade with impunity. In her work examining the potential of a Green New Deal in the United States, *On Fire* (2019), Naomi Klein remarked of such positions: 'You don't get much more human-centered than the persistent Judeo-Christian interpretation that God created the entire world specifically to serve Adam's every need.' Referring to Bacon's instructions in 1623 that nature ought to be 'put in constraint, moulded, and made as it were new by art and the hand of man', Klein emphasised the strong connection between current practices of extraction and the development of the idea of the domination of nature, writing: 'Those words might as well have been BP's corporate mission statement' of Bacon's position.[53]

Another thinker to whom Klein refers in *On Fire* is Carolyn Merchant, who wrote *The Death of Nature: Women, Ecology, and the Scientific Revolution*, published in 1980. Here, Merchant examined the extent to which seventeenth century science could be implicated in the ecological crisis, the devaluation of women in the production of scientific knowledge and the domination of nature.[54] Clifford Conner took up Merchant's ideas in *A People's History of Science* (2009), where he examined the significance of the patriarchal imagery in Bacon's writings, demonstrating, with recourse to Merchant's study, how these reflected the social position of women at the beginning of the seventeenth century in England.

Highlighting key moments where Bacon's framing of nature appeared especially problematic, Conner demonstrated how Bacon portrayed Nature as a woman hiding her secrets, which, according to Bacon, were: 'locked in nature's bosom' or 'laid up in the womb of nature'. Going one step further, Bacon's writing also contained arguments that nature would have to be forcibly penetrated to coerce her into giving up such secrets. He wrote, for example: 'a man [ought not] make scruple of entering and penetrating into these holes and corners, when the inquisition of truth is his whole object'. Highlighting the feminized way in which Bacon pictured nature to be at man's service, Conner notes Bacon's declarations: 'I am come in very truth leading to you Nature with all her children to bind her to your service and make her your slave' highlighting how, for him, nature must be taken 'by the forelock'.[55] Contending with the meaning of this recurring theme in his work, Clifford argued:

> The sexual imagery of penetrating, torturing, and enslaving Mother Nature should not be dismissed as harmless figures of speech unrelated to the way seventeenth-century English gentleman scientists perceived the world. The subordination of women was an essential component of their worldview, which was entirely committed to maintaining male dominance in a patriarchal society. To believe that the early scientists' pronouncements were 'value-free' with regard to women or any other social matters would be extremely naïve.[56]

From these excerpts, we can see the extent to which the view that nature's resources existed to serve the benefits of man, which was a prominent theme of the scientific revolution, rested upon the degradation of women. Furthermore, Kathryn Yusoff highlights the antiblackness at the heart of extractivism in *A Billion Black Anthropocenes or None*

(2018), where she demonstrates how this framework of thinking relates not only to geologic resources, but also to personhood:

> The human and its subcategory, the inhuman, are historically relational to a discourse of settler-colonial rights and the material practices of extraction, which is to say that the categorization of matter is a spatial execution, of place, land, and person cut from relation through geographic displacement (and relocation through forced settlement and transatlantic slavery). That is, racialization belongs to a material categorization of the division of matter (corporeal and mineralogical) into active and inert. Extractable matter must be both passive (awaiting extraction and possessing of properties) and able to be activated through the mastery of white men. Historically, both slaves and gold have to be material and epistemically made through the recognition and extraction of their inhuman properties. These historic geologic relations and geo-logics span Europe, the Americas, Africa, and Asia through the movement of people, objects, and racial and material categories.[57]

Adding to the insights of Merchant and Clifford, we also have recourse to the work of Lynn White Jr, whose essay, 'The Historical Roots of Our Ecologic Crisis', first appeared in *Science* in 1967, and has long been a cornerstone in the environmental studies literature. Examining the role of extractivist thinking in relation to religious thought, White, who maintained that Christianity 'bears a huge burden of guilt for environmental deterioration', emphasised the anthropocentrism that supported it. According to White:

> Especially in its Western form, Christianity is the most anthropocentric religion the world has seen. As early as the 2nd century both Tertullian and Saint Irenaeus of Lyons were insisting that when God shaped Adam he was foreshadowing the image of the incarnate Christ, the Second Adam. Man shares, in great measure, God's transcendence of nature. Christianity, in absolute contrast to ancient paganism and Asia's religions (except, perhaps, Zorastrianism), not only established a dualism of man and nature but also insisted that it is God's will that man exploit nature for his proper ends.[58]

While Leopardi referred to Bacon on a handful of occasions in the *Zibaldone*, he never did so extensively. Instead he mentioned him in passing, largely to elucidate his broader claims. In one reference, Leopardi includes him in his consideration of English, French and Italian philosophers, who he contrasts against the Germans, who, he held: 'have an abundance of originality in every subject, more than every other literate nation' **[2618]**. He also mentions Bacon in relation to his contention that: 'To assume a natural difference in intelligence between the ancients and the moderns would be absurd', where he also notes how circumstances modify intellects in such a way that they are made to seem of a different nature **[1353]**. As I will shortly turn to give an account of, throughout the *Operette*, and particularly in its earlier dialogues, Leopardi was heavily critical of the anthropocentric ways of thinking we see as being central to Bacon's thought. While the examinations of Leopardi's dialogues in the *Operette* I will later introduce critically assess the concept of anthropocentricism, as I will make clear, later, however, ultimately, he finds himself falling back on the same 'dualism of man and nature' that has played such a dominant role within the history of Christianity in the Western tradition.

It is worth briefly introducing here Leopardi's critique of Christianity in the *Zibaldone*. This has informed arguments set out by the Italian philosopher Emanuele Severino, for whom Leopardi, who he described as 'a poet of nihilism', was a forerunner to Nietzsche, whose images and themes can also be found in Leopardi's work. For example, as Kathleen Marie Higgins has examined in *Comic Relief: Nietzsche's Gay Science* (2000), in *The Gay Science*, written in 1882, Nietzsche positioned himself as a madman, who cried:

> 'Where is God?' he cried; 'I'll tell you! We have killed him – you and I! We are all his murderers. But how did we do this? How were we able to drink up the sea? Who gave us the sponge to wipe away the entire horizon? What were we doing when we unchained this earth from its sun? Where is it moving to now? Where are we moving to? Away from all suns? Are we not continually falling? And backwards, sidewards,

forwards, in all directions? Is there still an up and a down? Aren't we straying as though through an infinite nothing? Isn't empty space breathing at us? Hasn't it got colder? Isn't night and more night coming again and again? Don't lanterns have to be lit in the morning?'[59]

As I will show to varying degrees, both Nietzsche's reference to the Earth's position in relation to the Sun and the notion of infinite nothingness were both prominent themes in Leopardi's work. In the poet's thought, Severino describes the significance of Leopardi's philosophical critique with recourse to an allegory of a game of chess involving two opponents: a White Player, who supports Western Civilisation, and a Black Player, who seeks to overthrow the entire metaphysical tradition, the latter of whom Leopardi embodied.[60] Writing with regard to Severino's analysis, Daniela Bini remarked on the contemporaneity of Leopardi's intuitions, when she claimed:

> Contemporary criticism of Leopardi has pointed out the modernity of his intuitions, placing them in line with the thought of Nietzsche, Heidegger, and Musil, and even anticipating some of the "new dialogue of man with nature undertaken by modern physicists". The philosopher Emanuele Severino identifies the acme and the end of Western thought with Leopardi.[61]

The aspect of Leopardi's thought that both Severino and Bini pick up on, concerning his critique of the Western metaphysical tradition, relates in part to the way the poet thought of illusions. Speaking of the attraction of these, in the *Zibaldone*, Leopardi wrote: 'No one understands the human heart at all who does not recognize how vast is its capacity for illusions, even when those are contrary to its interests, or how often it loves the very thing that is obviously harmful to it' [207]. According to Sebastiano Timpanaro, for Leopardi, illusions can draw us in with their beauty and ability to bring us comfort. In his analysis, as I show more later, Timpanaro shows how the itinerary of Leopardi's thought was 'born of the courage of truth' and involved a continual rejection of attempts to escape from harsh human reality and illusions that fail to serve us.⁶² Situating Leopardi's work in *On Materialism* (1970), which I will examine in greater detail, Timpanaro wrote:

> Leopardi too felt deeply, from the morrow of Napoleon's fall, what has been called the 'historic disappointment' which followed the collapse of Enlightenment faith in progress. However, unlike the greater part of the Italian and European bourgeois intelligentsia, he neither slipped back into religious positions nor into a 'reasonable' form of Enlightened thought, suitably castrated and purged of its subversive charge.⁶³

For Leopardi, one of the reasons that he, for the most part, avoided slipping back into religious thought, was the way in which he viewed the development of Platonism and Christianity, which he saw as increasingly revering knowledge in a way that facilitated the world's progressive devitalization.⁶⁴ As, John Gray has given an account of in *The Soul of the Marionette: A Short Enquiry into Human Freedom* (2015), for Leopardi, Christianity was detrimental to life's quality, contributing to a decline in happiness as a result of its prioritization of the spiritual realm over and above the natural world.⁶⁵ Writing in the *Zibaldone* on 13 September 1821, he claimed: 'Christianity has found no means of rectifying life other than by destroying it, regarding it as a nothing, even an evil.' Roberto Esposito has also addressed this idea in *Living Thought: The Origins and Actuality of Italian Philosophy* (2012), where he examines the impact of this destruction of life in Leopardi's work.⁶⁶ For Leopardi, whose ideas foreshadowed Adorno and Horkheimer's claim in 'The Concept of Enlightenment' that 'men pay for the increase of their power with alienation from that over which they exercise their power', for Leopardi, modern rationalization negates the primal force of life in its self-defeating quest to protect and fully control it.⁶⁷ In his thinking, as Timpanaro's comment suggests, a significant outcome of the French Revolution was the denigration of the natural realm and experience, which Leopardi felt to be important areas of life, which lose out to the amplification of the significance of rationality. Adding to Timpanaro's elucidation of the significance of the revolution, Esposito writes:

> The failure of the revolution, for Leopardi, was not due to subjective errors or factual circumstances that forced it out of its natural course, but the result of a long-term process of abstraction by which human life is at the same time protected and undermined. By stripping nature of its veil – by removing it from its latency in the furious search for a naked truth –the Enlightenment, which was a direct progenitor of the revolution, deprived humankind of its material roots. In this way, and in contrast with its own sensist ideology, it brought to completion that process of idealization initially set into motion by the Platonic and then Christian traditions, which view spirit as 'more perfect than matter'.[68]

For Leopardi, Christianity refocused the anthropocentric mindset established by many ancient Greeks and Romans, promoting human-centred views. In *The Soul of the Marionette*, Gray affirms the contemporary relevance of the critique Leopardi sets out, which I commence to detail, claiming: 'events have confirmed Leopardi's diagnosis'.[69] Depicting Leopardi as a 'delicate poet who was also a merciless critic of modern ideals', Gray elucidates Leopardi's position when he writes: 'Struggling to escape from the world that science has revealed, humanity has taken refuge in the illusion that science enables them to remake the world in their own image.'[70] As will become increasingly clear from my presentation of Leopardi's thought, he was deeply concerned by the lack of attention we pay to the cultivation of a good character and lives within which vitality can be felt, and issued a series of warnings that the consequences he outlined stood to become further entrenched, if they were left ignored.

I turn shortly to present an overview of such warnings, highlighting the multitude of ways that Leopardi drew on the work of the ancients to test the validity and thoughtfulness of the human-centred views that he saw as governing modern society. Prior to setting out my account of Leopardi's Anti-Anthropocentricism in the *Operette*, however, I want to take a brief detour to introduce the similarity between a recurring theme that traverses Leopardi's problematising works and a notion that recurs in Freud's thought, which Jacqueline Rose has demonstrated the contemporaneity of, by examining through the lens of the Covid-19 pandemic, to prepare the way for elucidating the contemporary significance of his work.

Upside-down sunflowers

Shortly after he arrived in London at the end of his life, Freud wrote a letter to the novelist Rachel Berdach, the author of *The Emperor, the Sages and Death*, published in 1938, describing her work, which she had sent him as a 'mysterious and beautiful book'. In her moving article, 'To Die One's Own Death', published in the London Review of Books in November 2020, Rose reflects on Freud's philosophy of grief, citing from Berdach's novel at the outset: 'I want to know why we, like upside-down sunflowers, turn to the dark side rather than the light.' As Rose explores in her article, Freud's exploration of the depths of the human psyche during a period shaped by the flu pandemic of 1918–20, which infected half of the human race, shares some pertinent parallels with the global situation we have endured in recent years.[71] In her examination of Freud's response to the untimely death of his daughter, Rose argued that recent disasters have uncovered the material and racial faultlines of society. According to her, the Covid-19 pandemic threw into sharp relief how those who died and those closest to them were robbed of the deaths they deserved:

> As our screens display the toll of the dead, it is hard not be overcome by the scale of a tragedy that has left people we love dying in isolation, funerals pared back beyond decency, the rituals of family commemoration that make death manageable, or almost manageable, outlawed. Not to speak of the interminable counting that reduces humans to abstractions, robbing us a second time of each individual loss.[72]

The experience of recent years, Rose argues, has revealed the pertinence of Freud's sense of the impact on our psyche of the awareness of the mind's relative weakness in the face of disasters.[73] As he recognized in *The Future of an Illusion*, written in 1920, when the human race is faced with an elemental disaster: 'These powers nature lines up against us, magnificent, cruel, relentless, reminding us of our weakness and of the helplessness we had thought our cultural activities would overcome.' As a result, Freud continues, the human race 'forgets its cultural muddle-headedness and all its internal problems and enmities and recalls the great common task of preserving itself against the superior might of nature'.[74] Freud also argued of the nature of people in the work: 'We need in my view to accept that destructive (i.e. anti-social and anti-cultural) tendencies are present in all human beings and that in a large proportion of people such tendencies are powerful enough to dictate their behaviour within human society.'[75] Freud's notion of people's strong destructive anti-social and anti-cultural tendencies is a significant theme in Leopardi's work, in which the thinkers repeatedly return to theme of misanthropy.

As I examine shortly, Leopardi's diagnosis of society in the *Operette* reveals the significance of the course of his relationship with a similar idea, which he found in the Gospel of John. This notion, which served as the epigraph of one of Leopardi's most important poems, reads: 'And men loved darkness rather than light, John 3:19.'[76] It presents one of the most central themes in his work, which examines a comparable aspect of the human condition to that considered by Berdach, who asked why people are like 'upside-down sunflowers', who 'turn to the dark side rather than the light', which was also a theme taken up by Freud. Given the theme's importance to Leopardi's philosophy, I return to in my later analysis of Leopardi's poetic work, where I also consider how, before Freud, Voltaire made similar claims regarding how nature's powers, shown by the Lisbon Earthquake, compare in relation to our own. As I show in my examination of the ethics that Leopardi established, this theme was also taken up by Leopardi, who, in the final instance, believed our unity resides in our common struggle against nature.

Returning first to Rose's examination of Freud, however, on 25 January 1920, following complications arising from the Spanish flu during her third pregnancy, Freud's daughter Sophie Halberstadt-Freud died. Due to the restrictions on transportation in place owing to the ongoing pandemic, neither Freud nor his wife was able to be with their daughter as she passed.

As Rose highlights, Freud's work bore the imprint of his personal grief, despite his refutations of the fact. In *Beyond the Pleasure Principle*, from the same year, he wrote: 'If we are to die ourselves, and first to lose in death those who are dearest to us, it is easier to submit to a remorseless law of nature, to the sublime ἀνάγκη [Necessity], than to a chance that might perhaps have been escaped.'[77] For Rose, the philosophy of grief that came about in response to his great loss, and his refusal to accept that it was impacted by his personal tragedy, reveals the mind's inability to take the measure of its own pain.

In her article, Rose highlights the significance of the philosophy of grief offered by Freud, framing and the important way in which it was informed by this previous pandemic, which wiped out millions across Europe since the first recorded case on 4 March 1918.[78] Building on Laura Spinney's *Pale Rider: The Spanish Flu of 1918 and How It Changed the World* (2017), Rose examines how, although the death toll of the Spanish flu came close to the combined toll of the two world wars, as she observes: 'The Spanish flu has turned out to be a silent stalker of history, barely included in lists of the world's modern afflictions.' The event was effectively rubbed out of history.

While Rose was originally expecting to deliver the Sigmund Freud Lecture in Vienna on 6 May 2020, due to the Covid-19 pandemic, it was rearranged to 23 September, the anniversary of the day Freud died in 1939. Considering the reflections this rearrangement brought about, she wrote:

> The switch seems apposite, resonant of the times, while also echoing the tension between affirmation and destruction, between life and death, that from 1919 onwards was increasingly at the core of Freud's work. It was no doubt in response to this pressing context that I found myself newly alert to the wretchedness of the hour as it closed around Freud's family in Vienna, around the walls of what is now the Freud

Museum, first during the First World War and its aftermath, and then on the cusp of the even more deadly Second World War. I became acutely aware of the way the disasters of history penetrate and are repudiated by the mind – including my own since, during a lifelong preoccupation with Freud, I had not fully grasped the scope of this reality before.[79]

Underscoring yet more evidence of the strength of the mind's will to repudiate, Rose highlights that this feature of Freud's thought, which recognizes the resistance with which the mind will respond to what it takes to be too substantial a challenge, is the very bedrock of the Freudian project. As she writes:

> Psychoanalysis begins with a mind in flight, a mind that cannot take the measure of its own pain. It begins, that is, with the recognition that the world – or what Freud sometimes referred to as 'civilisation' – makes demands on human subjects that are too much to bear.[80]

Finally, Rose examined Freud's account of the death drive in *Why War? Psychoanalysis, Politics and the Return to Melanie Klein* (1993), examining how the force which drives living creatures to strive for an inorganic state comes increasingly to stand for a contradictory repetition that is absolutely indifferent to any path it might take.[81] The perversity of this tendency of the mind, Rose suggests, is most evident in the mechanism's total disregard for whether the subject that experiences the effects of a conflict was its original source. As Freud wrote of this tendency of the mind in 'The Ego and the Id' (1923):

> It is found in erotic cathexes, where a peculiar indifference in regard to the object displays itself ... Not long ago Rank [1913] published some good examples of the way in which neurotic acts of revenge can be directed against the wrong people ... Punishment must be exacted even if it does not fall upon the guilty.[82]

In her essay examining grief in Freud's work, Rose expands on this strength and indifference of the death drive when she highlights how, in the 1930s, Freud speculated that the 'perfection of the instruments of destruction' was leading the human race towards its end by allowing enemies to exterminate each other. She portrays how, for him, the gulf which 'earlier periods of human arrogance had torn too wide apart between mankind and the animals' was our great failing. Further aspects of Freud's thought that are comparable to features of Leopardi's thought examined later in this study are also drawn out by Rose, who highlights that, despite it having been the subject of virtually no commentary: 'Freud's despair was global and multi-species' in its reach.[83]

Overall, Rose's examination of our collective historical treatment of the Spanish flu adds to insights that have previously made elsewhere by Hall, who has utilized Freud's concept of disavowal to demonstrate our propensity to put aside and ignore painful experiences and evidence. Rose's striking analysis shows us the contemporary significance of our predilection for rewriting our stories, whilst highlighting how difficult we find it to handle challenges posed to our familiar conceptions of ourselves.[84] As I go on to show, Leopardi's writing is shaped by a similar recognition, in which he considers our failure to hold space for narratives that threaten to diminish our importance, and acknowledges our difficulty in relating to death in Western societies outside of the framework of fear and trepidation. Drawing on the reflections of ancient thinkers, whose consideration of mortality he brings to bear on the present, Leopardi, I go on to show, utilises their insights, which he extends as he considers the impact of scientific revolutions on modern thought.

Prior to examining Leopardi's considerations of the way in which we fail to approach challenges to our esteem in a way that correlates with reason, I firstly want to introduce some works from the *Operette* that demonstrate the experimental ways in which he conveys his concern with life's decay. Looking at his early dialogues, where, as Freud did in the 1930s, Leopardi considered the idea of the end of the human race, I turn now to consider some examples of the illustrative way Leopardi presented his concerns, highlighting the experimental means with which he questioned the importance of our species by imagining postapocalyptic scenes, in which the extinction of humans was often the topic of conversation.

The general spirit of the age in the *Operette*

Given the ridicule with which Leopardi regarded the activities of humans, it may sound surprising that his thought would be presented as having potential as a resource to call upon as we question how to respond to our present crisis. However, his mockery of humankind is only one half of the story of his life's work. While his critique of Enlightenment ideals – perhaps most notably, the theme of the progress of humankind – was oftentimes severe, my ambition in the second part of this study, where I focus on his reference to the 'dreams and vision' of the future, and the theme of solidarity in his work, is to illustrate that his thought did not come to a halt having set out a criticism of modern life. Rather, as I will argue, the problems he set out laid the groundwork for a late poetic philosophy, in which his aim was to 'cure', by offering a remedy to humanity's inclination towards self-destruction.

As I have suggested in relation to the ideas of Merchant, Klein, White and Clifford, a key characteristic of Christianity in the Western world was the anthropocentricism at its heart, which rested upon the belief that 'God created the entire world specifically to serve Adam's every need'. In the *Operette*, Leopardi set out to reveal the fundamental principles of calamity and human misery. He tirelessly subjected this framework of thinking to critique, particularly in his dialogues, where he was frequently damning of the 'folly of men'. In the *Operette*, the thinker sought to bring comedy to the general spirit of the age. His dialogues gave him the means to set out his diagnosis of the cultural dearth of modernity, which included the devitalization of modern life, a prominent anti-anthropocentrism, and an examination of the Earth from a cosmological and non-human perspective. Reminding us of our status as one species among many, the scenes in his dialogues revealed his astute awareness of our tendency to centre ourselves within the universe and our overinflated sense of importance, allowing him to ridicule our tendency to find use for ourselves in everything external to us, which we so readily assume exists to serve us and to experiment with the idea of what the world would look like after our species have died out. In one dialogue, in which Leopardi considers the impact of the Copernican Revolution on metaphysics, we find an example of his frequent depiction of our cosmic fragility:

> [A]fter a few years, the seed of these poor animals will be lost: for when they have wandered a little while over the earth, groping about, seeking something to eat and to warm themselves with; at last, when everything that can be swallowed has been consumed, and the last spark of fire extinguished, they will all die in the dark, frozen like so many bits of rock-crystal.[85]

In such a manner, his work predates more recent literary experiments like the work of the palaeontologist Jan Zalasiewicz, a member of the Anthropocene Working Group, who suggests in his experimental text *The Earth after Us* (2008) that we might measure our actions through a geological lens, considering what legacy humans will leave in the rocks. In a scene from another dialogue, Leopardi gives a postapocalyptic description of a world that hardly appears to have noticed that humans have gone extinct: '… now that they've all vanished, the earth does not feel she is lacking anything, the rivers are not weary of flowing, and the sea, though it no longer has to serve for traffic and navigation, does not seem to be drying up'.[86] He continues this theme throughout his *Operette*, returning to it once again in 1825, in his 'Apocryphal Fragment of Strato of Lampsacus', where he captures an array of themes under the heading 'Of the End of the World':

> Of this present world of which men are a part, that is to say one of the species of which it is composed, how long has it lasted until now, we cannot easily say, just as neither can we know how long it is going to endure from now on. The laws that govern it appear immutable, and such they are believed to be, for they do not change but little by little and over an unimaginable length of time, so that their mutations scarcely fall within the knowledge, let alone the observation of man. Yet this length of time, vast as it may be, is nonetheless minimal compared with the eternal duration of matter. We see in this present world a continual perishing of individuals and a continual transformation of things, one into another; but as destruction is continually compensated

for by production, and the genera are preserved, it is thought that this world has not nor is likely to have in itself any cause by which it must or might be destroyed, and that it shows no signs of transience. Nevertheless we may well infer the opposite, and from more than one indication, and this among others.[87]

According to the cosmic pessimism Leopardi sets out in his works of the *Operette*, the world is a small and finite place, one planet situated among others on which a strictly limited supply of resources is allocated unequally, and our lives are mere an acid spot in time.

In his early dialogues of 1824, Leopardi depicts the shared condition of our species as a whole, in its cosmic fragility. As Negri notes in *Flower of the Desert*, his tendency to group together customary themes to compare them, and use his groupings to explore new paths from which he later sought to extract and describe a common web, was particularly present during this year.[88] The theme addressed in these works – of which I examine 'Hercules and Atlas', written 10–13 February 1824, 'Fashion and Death', written 15–18 February 1824, and 'An Imp and a Gnome', which dates from 2–6 March 1824 – was the degeneracy of life, firstly of the Earth, and subsequently of the life of humans, the dearth of which he largely blames on us. Following my account of how these dialogues exemplify his intention to ridicule problems of his age, I turn to consider his subsequent work 'The Dialogue of Nature and an Icelander', written in May 1824, to highlight the change in Leopardi's thought that we can begin to see in the work before I close my examination of Leopardi's critical analysis of Enlightenment thought with an overview of his 1827 work 'Il Copernico' ('Copernicus').

The degeneracy of life

In the seventeenth century, the idea of the 'Great Chain of Being', which could be found in the work of the ancient Greeks, including Plato and Aristotle, was revived, traversing the theodicy – the attempt to defend God in the face of evil – of Leibniz and Pope.[89] Leopardi's engagement with these ideas was shaped by his study of the work of the naturalist

Comte de Buffon (1707–88), a thinker who Darwin, who built upon his ideas with his *Origin of Species* (1859), described as an early author who treated evolution in a scientific spirit in modern times.[90] Buffon wrote the encyclopaedic *Natural History: General and Particular,* which spanned dozens of volumes written between 1749 and 1804, rejecting Carolus Linnaeus' method of classifying species in his 1735 work *System of Nature,* which would provide the roots of modern scientific racism.[91]

Buffon set out his disputed argument concerning the 'degeneracy of life' in *Natural History*, arguing that life in the New World was 'shriveled and diminished', compared to that of the Old World. In North America, this notion dismayed Thomas Jefferson, another author of 'commonplace books', who led the charge against Buffon's theory, going to great lengths to disprove it.[92] One such effort occurred when, while serving as minister to France, Jefferson obtained a seven-foot tall stuffed moose and arranged to have it transported to Buffon to demonstrate the vitality of the species in North America, in an attempt to persuade him to recant his ideas on degeneracy.[93] These ideas of the shriveled and diminished degeneracy of life, as I turn to some examples of now, reappear in Leopardi's writing, often in relation to less Earthly travels.

'Hercules and Atlas'

In 'The Dialogue of Hercules and Atlas', written 10–13 February, Leopardi examines the effect of the death of the old values that once gave humans worth and energy. Referring to an old Greek myth in which Atlas was condemned by Zeus to bear the weight of the heavens on his shoulders, Hercules remarks to Atlas of the state of the world: '… it's a long time now since the world stopped making any noticeable sound or movement; for my part I had the strongest suspicion that it must be dead, and expected it from day to day, to infect me with its stench.'[94] Comparing the world's destitution to its previous thriving state, he says: 'Last time I carried it, it throbbed hard on my back, like the heart of an animal; and gave forth a continuous buzzing, that it might have been a wasps' nest.'⁹⁵ The duo, resolving to try to remedy this unfortunate state of affairs, devise a plan to wake the earth up, but Hercules worries its frailty is too great: 'I'd give it a good thwack with this club: but I'm afraid this would crush it, and turn it into a sort of wafer; or that, seeing it's so light, its crust has got very thin, and would shatter under the blow like an eggshell.'⁹⁶ Drawing on Hellenistic and Roman depictions of Atlas straining to hold the globe on his shoulders, in 'Hercules and Atlas', Jove sent Hercules to check with Father Atlas the state of the world that he carried upon his back. Hercules was surprised to find Atlas describe the weight of the world on his shoulders as less than had been before, and his account of the world's diminished state:

> But the world has become so light that this cloak I wear to protect me from the snow weighs more heavily upon me; and if it were not the will of Jove obliges me to stand here motionless, with this little ball on my shoulders, I'd tuck it under my arm or in my pocket, or hang it from one of the hairs of my beard, and go about my business.⁹⁷

Later in the dialogue, Leopardi's characters wonder if the world might be asleep rather than dead. Considering if there is a way of waking the Earth in a manner that observed its delicacy, Hercules thinks out loud:

> I'd give it a good thwack with this club: but I'm afraid I would crush it, and turn it into a sort of wafer … seeing it's so light, its crust has got very thin, and would shatter under the blow like an eggshell. Nor am I at all sure that men, who in my time used to fight with their bare hands against lions, and now against fleas, would not all perish in a flash from the impact. It's best for me to put down my club and you take off your cloak, and we'll play ball together with this wee sphere. A pity I didn't bring the armlets or rackets that Mercury and I use when we play at Jove's house, or in the garden; but our fists will do.⁹⁸

Through this conversation, Leopardi introduces a theme that was to become increasingly prominent in his work, where he increasingly turned away from considerations of the frailty of our planet, which is depicted here as comparable in delicacy to 'an eggshell', and towards the notion of the biological frailty of humankind, which helps to determine the shape of his ethics.

'Fashion and Death'

One important dialogue in which Leopardi continued his examination of the diminished state of life, considering this in relation to the lives of people whose misery and lack of bodily wellbeing he attended to was 'The Dialogue of Fashion and Death', where he considered the theme of the degeneration of experience. Here, Leopardi depicted a view comparable to that which Max Weber would later express in his 1919 lecture 'Science as a Vocation', where Weber deployed Friedrich Schiller's phrase concerning the 'disenchantment of the world', arguing that 'the fate of our times is characterized by rationalization and intellectualization'.[99] Written 15–18 February 1824 in 'Fashion and Death', Leopardi portrays Fashion's endeavour to convince Death of her destructive credentials. Setting out to highlight to her sister that while she is more methodical and discreet than her, she is similarly destructive, Fashion insists:

> I was saying that our common nature and custom is to continually to change the world, though you from the very start went for people and blood, while I content myself for the most part with beards, hairstyles, clothes, furniture, fine houses and the like. But in fact I have not failed, and do not fail, to play a few tricks that could be compared with yours, as for instance to pierce ears, lips and noses, and to rip them with the knicknacks I hang in the holes.[100]

Testing the dialogue as a suitably accessible means of expression, Leopardi uses Fashion to highlight peoples' willingness to endure pain to fulfil their aspirations, even when it proves to be their detriment:

> In fact, generally speaking, I persuade and force all civilized people to put up every day with a thousand difficulties and a thousand discomforts, and often with pain and agony, and some even to die gloriously, for the love they bear me. I don't wish to mention the headaches, the colds, the inflammations of every sort, the quotidian, tertian and quartan fevers that men get in order to obey me, being willing to shiver with cold or swelter according to my wishes, covering

their heads with woollen cloth and their breasts with linen, and doing everything my way even when it is harmful to them.[101]

Picking up Leopardi's theme of the degeneration of experience, at the outset of his consideration of the World Exhibition in The Arcades Project, written between 1927 and 1940, Walter Benjamin cites Fashion's cry to Death, utilizing Leopardi's thought in the service of his critique of the commodification of culture.[102] Benjamin cites from the dialogue on a series of occasions throughout his work, bringing it into relation to commodity fetishism. With reference to Leopardi's dialogue, Benjamin writes:

> For fashion was never anything other than the parody of the motley cadaver, provocation of death through the woman, and bitter colloquy with decay whispered between shrill bursts of mechanical laughter. That is fashion. And that is why she changes so quickly; she titillates death and is already something different, something new, as he casts about to crush her.[103]

Today, the insights of Leopardi and Benjamin evoke the destruction wrought by the 'ultra-fast fashion' industry, made up of companies like SHEIN, Boohoo and PrettyLittleThing. This facet of the multi-billion-pound global fashion industry delivers increasing quantities of anticipated landfill, fulfilling both philosophers' depictions of fashion's capacity to titillate death through its capitalization of deadly working conditions and low wage labour in the name of maximizing profits.[104]

This early piece in Leopardi's oeuvre allows the writer to convey his perception of the lack of vitality within modern life, which he blames on people, mocking our failure to curtail the negative consequences of our customs. Fleshing out his presentation of his era as 'the century of death', Leopardi argues, thinking once again of the 'leisured class', that those labours and exercises that do good to the body have been increasingly consigned to oblivion:

> Little by little, but mostly in recent times, I have assisted you by consigning to disuse and oblivion those labours and exercises that

do good to the body, and have introduced and brought into esteem innumerable others that damage the body in a thousand ways, and shorten life. Apart from this I have put into the world such regulations and customs that life itself, as regards the body and the soul, is more dead than alive so that with perfect truth this century might be called the century of death.[105]

Leopardi's dialogue allows him to revisit the comparison he frequently drew between the ancients and the moderns, which traversed the *Zibaldone*, in which he observed how the ancients were more in touch with their vitality, which was 'much higher' than people of modern times:

> They retained vigor, health, etc. etc., at an age at which they are not retained nowadays. At each and every age they were, relatively speaking, hardier, healthier, in short, more full of vitality than the moderns, better adapted to the functions of the body and physically more powerful.
>
> [1333]

As Leopardi shows here, during this period he believed that in his time, the body and the soul were in a state of deterioration, and the norms of life themselves had become detrimental to it.[106]

The relationship between the ancients and the moderns is a recurring theme in scholarship on Leopardi, the importance of which resides in its ability to highlight how his vision corresponds to his admiration for the ancients. As Emanuela Cervato examines in her study *A System That Excludes All Systems; Giacomo Leopardi's Zibaldone di pensieri* (2017), for Leopardi, the supremacy of enmity and hatred in modern societies contrasts starkly with the importance of the role of citizenship and love towards one's companions of the ancient times.[107] In *Living Thought*, Esposito notes Giambattista Vico's influence on Leopardi's work, arguing that the French Revolution jeopardized its own project by undermining human life through its subordination of the body to rationality for Leopardi.[108] As Esposito contends and I have already alluded to, the poet-thinker saw the Enlightenment as depriving 'humankind of its natural roots', and, as Leopardi argued in the *Zibaldone*, as a consequence, we have come to consider spirit as 'more perfect than matter' [**1615**].[109] Providing further clarification on this aspect of Leopardi's thought, Esposito explains:

> But to define a part – and only one part – of the living being as perfect means at the same time to take value away from the other part, making it subordinate to the first. It literally snaps human life into two, placing one of its dimensions, the biological one of the body, under the dominion of the other, defines as personal, spiritual, and rational.[110]

Reflecting on the relationship between rationality and sensuality in Leopardi's work, Esposito argues that, for him, the final outcome of modern civilisation is that it: 'claims to heal people by inoculating them with a poison that, in the long run, is lethal to them'.[111] By negating life's primal force, he shows, Leopardi finds the disenchantment of the world to be counterproductive, because it weakens precisely what it set out to nurture.[112] This can be seen in Leopardi's consideration of the theme of bodily wellbeing in relation to the development of reason, which he recorded in the *Zibaldone* in 1821, when he wrote:

> The development of reason, and the civilisation that derives from it, seems to us a perfection proper not only to the human mind, but also to the body, that is, in short, to man as a whole. So my question is: are illnesses, debility, failing strength, frailty, and extreme sensitivity perfections of the human body and of man? Is it not obvious that nature intended us to be good and healthy, and robust? Everything can be doubted, but not the fact that nature has always looked to the physical well-being of its creatures. This is a truth that may be intuited, and there is therefore no need to prove it. Nature placed a thousand obstacles in the way of the development of reason, etc., but favored the full development of our bodily faculties, and the vigor of the body, etc. etc., in every respect. Men have needed many centuries to arrive at this development of reason, but the development of the human body was perfect from the start, and, on the contrary, has deteriorated as time and civilisation have advanced.
>
> [1600]

Esposito reviews Leopardi's analysis of the indissoluble bond between body and life examined by Niccolò Machiavelli and Vico. He highlights Leopardi's interest not solely in subjecting the anthropocentric inflection he found in Enlightenment culture to critique but also in extending Giordano Bruno's radical critique of personalist humanism through his consideration of the infinity of the universe and the centrality of the animal world.[113]

Examining the 'moving references to the animal world in Leopardi's work', Esposito describes the poet as part of a line of thinkers, including Nietzsche, who contribute to a tradition, which: 'opens up a hitherto unknown or emarginated possibility in modern philosophy'.[114] Referring to works such as 'Dissertation on the souls of animals', 'The war of the mice and the crabs' and 'The song of the wild cock', Esposito brings Leopardi's admiration for animals to the fore. He examines how Leopardi saw a similarity between human and non-human animals in both their biological destiny and their capacity to adapt to external stresses, while simultaneously highlighting what Esposito describes as Leopardi's conviction that: 'in some ways animals are even superior, for their ecstatic vitality and intraspecies compassion which humans have lost'.[115] Considering animals' capability to represent the embodiment of joy and vitality of the ancients that Leopardi believed we have lost, Esposito examines this point further when he writes:

> But this positive attitude toward the animal world should not be limited to his critique of anthropocentricism. The animal is not only humans' neglected and marginalized other. It is also our 'before.' The animal is what infinitely precedes the human, because it is still rooted in the natural dimension from which the human species detached itself when it entered into the alienating regime of history. Not by chance, in the emotional tonality of the poet, the animal is associated with the primordial figures of the child, the savage, and the ancient world, united by their constitutive relationship with the origin.[116]

This is a theme I return to later, in my consideration the importance of vitality in Leopardi's thought, which I examine in relation to his late philosophical poetry.

'An Imp and a Gnome'

In another work from this period, 'The Dialogue of an Imp and a Gnome', written 2-6 March 1824, Leopardi continues to expand on his theme of the poor condition of the world and the life within it, which he aligns with death, assigning blame for this on the 'folly of men'.[117] Set in a world in which humans have become extinct, the Imp and a Gnome belatedly stumbling upon this discovery consider not only that our species is lost, but that this has been of little consequence.[118] Before learning that people had all died out, the Gnome, the son of Sabazius, who according to the abbot of Villars was one of the most ancient of the Gnomes, asks Leopardi's Imp to shed light on what 'those rascally men are plotting', given it had been some time since they had last caused trouble.[119] Citing in response the closing line of Zaccaria Valaresso's 1724 parody of a Greek tragedy, the Imp responded: 'you wait for them in vain, they are all dead', explaining that people, who he described as 'urchins', had died out by bringing about their own demise:

> Some [died] by warring amongst themselves, some on the high seas, some by eating each other, quite a few by killing themselves, some by rotting in idleness, some by racking their brains over books, some by debauchery and a thousand kinds of disorderly behaviour; in fact by studying all possible ways of going against nature and coming to a bad end.[120]

This work, which Negri described as 'a happy, scintillating dialogue' directed against human presumptuousness', fully displays Leopardi's inclination to blame humans for our misfortunes.[121] Depicting the extinction of our species as an event of little consequence which was able to come to pass unnoticed, **Leopardi's** protagonists struggled to come up with positive examples of the legacy of our species.[122] They noted how the Sun continued to rise and set, and how they could tell the date by the Moon in the absence of calendars, expressing relief at their inability to count the years, which came with the perk of allowing those remaining species to forever pose as young, and worry less about their impending death.[123]

'The Earth and the Moon'

The final dialogue from 1824 I want to consider before moving on to examine Leopardi's presentation of his way of thinking about nature in the *Operette* is that of 'The Earth and the Moon', in which, Leopardi continues his attack on the anthropocentric viewpoint we find in his previous dialogues. Extending this, Leopardi borrows tropes from Lucian of Samosata's 'Icaromenippus, An Aerial Expedition', as a means of mocking us, highlighting the narrowmindedness that our habit of thoughtlessly believing ourselves to be at the centre of the universe creates, while introducing the theme that critics have come to refer to as his 'cosmic pessimism'.[124] In this work, Leopardi paves the way for his more explicit attack in 'Copernicus', which I return to consider following my examination of the role of nature in 'The Dialogue of Nature and an Icelander', in order to pave the way for a consideration of the impact that Leopardi's insights in 'Copernicus', written in 1827, and the thought of Rousseau had on the shape and style of 'La ginestra'.[125]

The second-century work of Lucian, which has been referred to as an early example of speculative fiction, includes the dialogue 'Icaromenippus' within which the central protagonist Menippus depicts the Earth's scientists as 'a lot of shameless imposters', highlighting the limits of our knowledge and the extent to which our theories can override what came before.[126] Noting 'the grimness of their expressions, the paleness of their faces, and the luxuriance of their beards', Menippus, having derived that he was speaking with those at the top of their profession, ridiculed the inability of these seemingly clever men to prove any theory other than their own could be true.[127] Leopardi picks up ideas from Lucian's dialogue, in which the Moon is depicted as being inhabited, deploying them to criticize the presumptuousness with which we assume that humans are more important than other living beings in the cosmos, helping him to prepare the groundwork for his consideration of the philosophical consequences of the Copernican Revolution. In Leopardi's dialogue, having learned that the Earth was inhabited by living creatures, the Moon is irritated by the Earth's assumption that he would also be inhabited by men:

> Forgive me, Lady Earth, if I answer you rather more freely than might become a subject of yours, or a serving-maid, as I am. But the fact is that is seems to me more than a little vain of you to think that all things in every part of the universe are just the same as yours; as if nature had no other aim but to copy you precisely in every place. I say I am inhabited, and you jump to the conclusion that my inhabitants must be men. I tell you that they are not; and though you allow that they are different creatures, you do not doubt that they have the same properties and ups and downs as people do; and you quote me some physicist and a telescope.[128]

Construing 'Lady Earth' as a dull-witted character, here, Leopardi ridicules the ease with which our human-centred tendencies compel us to forget that we live amongst a rich variety of life. In such a way, this dialogue serves as one example of many of what Esposito has described as Leopardi's constant reminder that the Earth is 'rotating anonymously in a sky that is remote and indifferent to the fate of human beings', reducing our planet to one of an infinite number.[129]

As my examination of the early dialogues in the *Operette* has shown, Leopardi was vocal in his criticism of the vices, arrogance and folly of people. He focused particularly stringently in his such works on the degeneracy of life, which he moved between depicting on a planetary scale, and with greater focus on the habits of people. Although the themes from 'Earth and the Moon' are extended in 'Copernicus', before elucidating this, it is important to attend to an important way in which his thinking changed before he wrote his later dialogue in 1827, particularly with regard to what Leopardi identified as the greatest source of our suffering.

Exonerating humanity

In the recent book *Mapping Leopardi: Poetic and Philosophical Intersections* (2019), Rossella Di Rosa asks in her essay 'From Nature to Matter: Leopardi's Anti-Anthropocentrism and Inchoate Proto-Ecological Thinking' how Leopardi conceives of nature in relation to humanity. With reference to the Italian poet and critic Sergio Solmi, giving an account of his ideas, she writes:

> First, Solmi observes that ... 'two faces of nature' coexist in Leopardi's thought, as proved by coeval entries in *Zibaldone* that refer to both images of nature. Second, Solmi resolves the apparent contradiction of the definition of nature by claiming that Leopardi is not ambiguously conceiving two different natures. Rather, Solmi contends that the term 'nature' has two different meanings. In one, nature refers to the principle of existence – 'principo informatore dell'essenza' – but, in the other, it connotes a cosmic machine (una macchina cosmica; Solmi 90–1)[130]

Presenting her account of the significance of Solmi's observations, Di Rosa argues: 'Solmi's contribution to Leopardi scholarship is invaluable: it helps scholars to go beyond the traditional idea of a change in Leopardi's conception of nature, as well as to resolve the impasse of nature as "mother" vs "stepmother"'.[131] With regard to this point, it is worth noting here the way in which nature continues to take on the feminine form found earlier in the influential work of Bacon and others, in Leopardi's imaginary.[132] Increasingly referred to using negative maternal imagery, Leopardi frequently describes her as 'hostile', portraying her as a mother or stepmother, who bears and nourishes in order to kill, and 'suddenly destroys what has been created'.[133] In these instances, his feminine depictions correlate with Adriana Cavarero's illuminations regarding the role of feminine imagery in *Horrorism: Naming Contemporary Violence* (2008). They find their place among the misogyny of a patriarchal imaginary which assigns the female form to images of horror, as in the infanticidal mother Medea, who extends back to the ancient Greek world.¹³⁴ For example, Nature is accused of infanticide in 'The Dialogue of Nature and an Icelander', which I introduce next, when the Icelander confronts her:

> I have therefore resolved to conclude that you are the declared enemy of men, of the other animals, and of all your works; that now you ensnare us, now you threaten us, now you attack us, now you sting us, now you strike us, now you rend us, and at every moment you hurt us or persecute us; and that, by custom and institution, you are the butcher of your own family, and so to speak of your own flesh and blood.¹³⁵

Returning, however to the two different natures that Di Rosa discusses, she provides one example of many of the way that Leopardi depicts nature in the first sense, in which it conveys 'life' and 'existence', highlighting a remark from the *Zibaldone*, where Leopardi writes: 'Nature calls me to live, as it does all created or possible beings – not only my nature but the general nature of things, the absolute idea and shape of existence' [2383]. As D'Intino argues in the introduction to the *Zibaldone*, Leopardi's model here is 'a pre-Platonic Socrates, whose philosophy remains close to nature'.¹³⁶ In the first sense, Leopardi's references to 'going against nature' align with the views of the Roman Emperor, Aurelius, for whom nature comprises the nature of all things, and where going against nature meant being unwilling to do the work of a human being by failing to act as a rational being and good citizen.¹³⁷ In the introduction to his translation of Aurelius' *Meditations*, Gregory Hays helps to elucidate this connection between the thought of Aurelius and that of Leopardi, in which he claimed:

> Marcus himself more than once compares the world ruled by *logos* to a city in which all human beings are citizens, with all the duties inherent in citizenship. As human beings we are part of nature, and our duty is to accommodate ourselves to its demands and requirements – 'to live as nature requires,' as Marcus often puts it.¹³⁸

We find echoes of Aurelius' sense of a duty 'to live as nature requires' throughout Leopardi's work, including in the *Zibaldone* and the

Operette, in which, in his dialogue 'An Imp and a Gnome', he gives an account of how we all came to die out 'by studying all possible ways of going against nature', while failing to realize 'that the world was in rebellion'.[139] According to the second meaning of the term that we find in Leopardi according to Di Rosa and Solmi, it refers to a cosmic machine, and appears in works like Leopardi's 'Apocryphal Fragment of Strato of Lampsacus', written in the autumn of 1825, where he focuses on the different modes of existence of matter. For example, he writes: 'But inasmuch as the said force never ceases to work on and modify matter, so those creatures which it continually forms, it likewise destroys, shaping new creatures from their matter.'[140] This materialist theme traversing his work also appears in 'Nature and an Icelander', where Nature calls for the Icelander to consider:

> ... that the life of this universe if a perpetual cycle of production and destruction, the two so bound together, that each continually serves the other, and the preservation of the world; which as soon as one or the other of these ceased to be, would likewise be dissolved. For which reason it would be detrimental to you if there were anything in the world free of suffering.[141]

Solmi and Di Rosa's observations concerning the different, and oftentimes coexisting ways that Leopardi depicts nature are compelling. However, my argument rests on the contention that acknowledging this does not undermine the extent to which, at increasingly consequential moments in Leopardi's thinking, his philosophy upholds a problematic depiction of nature as hostile and inimical to the lives of non-humans and humans alike. In relation to Di Rosa's suggestion that the significance of Solmi's insight lies in its ability to transcend the traditional idea of change in Leopardi's conception of nature, I suggest that both thinkers' observations can inform a nuanced appreciation of nature in his work without it being necessary to completely do away with the valid recognition of the change in his attitude towards nature. To give an account of my claim that such notions of a shift in his thinking are compelling, firstly, I introduce Leopardi's dialogue of 'Nature and an

Icelander', after which I give an example of the traditional notion of change in Leopardi's thought that Di Rosa refers to.

'Nature and an Icelander'

On 21, 27 and 30 May 1824, Leopardi wrote 'The Dialogue of Nature and an Icelander', in which the theme of the ability of people to damage ourselves begins receding, giving way to Leopardi's increasing belief that nature is the greatest source of humanity's suffering. Having 'traversed the greater part of the world, and 'sojourned in many different countries', Leopardi's representative of humankind, the Icelander bumps into a looming figure: 'a most enormous torso; which at first he thought must have been made of stone, like those colossal herms seen by him many years before on Easter Island' as he was rounding the Cape of Good Hope. This figure, it transpires, is 'Nature herself'. Having drawn closer, she demands from the Icelander an explanation for his unexpected appearance: 'Who are you? And what are you doing in these parts, where your species was unknown?'[142] Responding to Nature's enquiry, the Icelander, who is motivated by Leopardi's thinking regarding misanthropy in a way that will become clearer later, explains his resolution to flee from society. Describing to Nature how his efforts to be free of the suffering were caused by his neighbours, the Icelander tells Nature of his attempts to protect himself from the 'folly of men' 'Even in my earliest youth ...', he begins:

> ... with little experience, I was convinced and clear about the vanity of life, and the folly of men; who fighting continually amongst themselves to acquire pleasure which give no delight, and possessions which do them no good; putting up with and justifying to one another infinite cares and infinite evils, which weary them and in fact are harmful; find themselves further and further from happiness the more they seek it.[143]

Untrusting of his peers, the Icelander determined to focus on keeping himself free from suffering, striving to separate himself from the community around him in the hope of avoiding harm.[144] Having done this, while he finds himself free 'from the molestation of men', he discovers that he is still unable to avoid suffering:

> I learnt for certain how vain it is to think, if you live among men, that you can, as long as you hurt no one, in turn escape from being hurt by others ... But from the molestation of men I freed myself early, keeping myself apart from their society and retiring into solitude ... This accomplished, and living almost bereft of the least shadow of pleasure, I was still not able to keep myself free of sufferings.[145]

The Icelander's intention to retire into solitude is a decision that goes against one of the central tenants of Stoic thinking concerning 'the life according to nature'.[146] According to the thought of Aurelius, humanity is conceived of as part of a single constitution of rational animals for whom social development is important.[147] For him, humans are rational and naturally political animals, for whom the good lies in community.[148] The Icelander's decision to turn away from social interaction, and attempt to live in his solitude, allows Leopardi to reiterate a Stoic point about the consequences of our modern rejection of ancient ideals that are founded on community.[149] However, having blamed the Icelander and mocked and ridiculed people in his previous dialogues, gradually, Leopardi's attention turns towards the role nature plays in the suffering of people. His understanding of nature somewhat splits in two, with the emphasis he places on the evil of nature becoming the groundwork of his ethics. Whilst up until now, we have seen that Leopardi is deeply critical of the habits of humans, blaming us for our folly and egoistic desires, ultimately nature 'herself' transforms into becoming the primary source of our pain in Leopardi's thought.

Confirming nature's guilt

One of the early influences on the adjustment that took place in Leopardi's thought came in 1818, when the young poet was devastated by the premature death of his beloved childhood friend Teresa Fattorini, who he used to watch embroidering from the window he worked by in his father's library. The untimely death of his neighbour, at the age of only twenty-one, was one of the early prompts for Leopardi's considerations on the unfairness of life and the innocence of those he witnessed suffering under nature's violence. Indicating this in his 1828 poem dedicated to Teresa 'A Silvia' ('To Silvia'), where he described her as the 'dear companion of my innocence', Leopardi gave expression to the shift that would increasingly dominate the way he viewed people and nature in relation to innocence and guilt. Raging against nature, he described his inconsolability over the loss of his 'much-lamented hope', empathizing with humanity as he asked: 'Is this man's fate?'[150] Slowly and iteratively, these ideas began to strengthen in Leopardi's work. He ultimately captured this transformation in January 1829 in the *Zibaldone*, when, elucidating the consequences for his philosophy, he wrote:

> My philosophy makes nature guilty of everything, and by exonerating humanity altogether, it redirects the hatred, or at least the complaint, to a higher principle, the true origin of the ills of living beings, etc. etc.
> [4428]

Examining this change in Leopardi's thought, Timpanaro finds another source for the discernible shift in Leopardi's engagement with the ideas of optimists like Voltaire and Pope. As Timpanaro brings to our attention, Leopardi considered these thinkers responses to the philosophical consequences of our fragility in the wake of the earthquake that struck the Portuguese city of Lisbon on 1 November 1755, reducing the city to ruins in less than ten minutes, at length. Reflecting on the complexity of the role of nature in the development of Leopardi's ethics of solidarity, the critic observed a change in the philosopher-poet's thought, which he found to be particularly prominent in the dialogue of 'Nature and an Icelander'. Presenting what Di Rosa described as 'the traditional idea of a change in Leopardi's conception of nature', in *The Freudian Slip* (1974), Timpanaro describes the two movements he observes in Leopardi's work:

> In a first movement, [Leopardi's pessimism] opposes a good nature to a corrupt civilisation, and then, in a second movement, it identifies

nature as the enemy of man and founds a new morality on the solidarity of men in their struggle against it.[151]

He goes on to identify an important problem at the heart of Leopardi's thought: '[The problem] encompasses the object of pessimism itself (is Nature man's enemy in the Leopardian sense, or is "human nature" evil?'[152] Referring to the way that such questions in turn impacted the shape of Timpanaro's Marxism, in *Spectrum: From Right to Left in the World of Ideas* (2005), Perry Anderson examines this, reformulating Timpanaro's observation when he writes:

> Nature, to which so many eighteenth century thinkers had appealed as the beneficent force by which the tyranny of prejudice and artifice of custom stood judged, gradually changed shape in [Leopardi's] vision, becoming the malignant stepmother whose cruelties – illness, infirmity, senescence, death – ultimately condemned all human being to helpless misery.[153]

Here, Anderson refers to the ideas of eighteenth century thinkers like Leibniz and Pope, who he argues saw nature as the means through which God delivered his plan, and also notes the gradual change of shape that of the concept of nature in Leopardi's vision. This shift provides another layer of complexity through which to consider the role of the concept of nature in Leopardi's thought. It helps to illuminate the way in which the innocence of people was increasingly brought to the fore in Leopardi's work, as he veered between thinking of nature as indifferent to us in a way that we perceive to be hostile as a symptom of our anthropocentric inflection and considering nature to be outright malign. Capturing this aspect of Leopardi's thought perfectly, Creagh has observed:

> Early in his career Leopardi believed in a beneficent Nature, the purveyor of innocence, imagination, activity, fruitful illusions, etc, betrayed by man in favour of Reason. This attitude changed in the course of writing the *Operette*, and by the time he composed *Eleander*, Nature, Fate, the gods, the immortals and so on are all ranged together as the implacable enemies of mankind. The next stage in Leopard's thought, ultimately embodied in *La ginestra*, was to call on human solidarity in the face of this monstrous alliance.[154]

In the 'Dialogue of Timander and Eleander' written in June 1824, which Creagh refers to here, and which Leopardi saw as serving as a sort of preface to the *Operette*, Leopardi noted his surprise that, where he expected to arrive at hatred, he instead found compassion for the unhappiness of humanity in the face of its own fate.[155] Leopardi's ideas in this work consider the same topic as that assessed by Rebecca Solnit, who asserted in *Hope in the Dark* that changes in ideas and values result from work passed down by writers, scholars, public intellectuals and social activists. In the dialogue, Leopardi similarly considered the capacity of writing, 'especially moral works' and their capacity to contribute to endeavours to benefit our species.[156] Relating such a notion to poetic works, Eleander suggests:

> If any book of an ethical nature might do good, I think that poetical books might do the most: I say poetical, taking this term in a broad sense; that is, books intended to move the imagination; and I mean no less in prose than in verse. Now I have a low opinion of that kind of poetry which when read and meditated on, does not leave the reader's mind so noble a sentiment, that for half an hour it prevents him from entertaining a base thought, or performing an unworthy act. But if the reader breaks faith to his best friend an hour after that reading, I do not on this account condemn that particular poem: for otherwise I would have to condemn the most beautiful, the most passionate and the noblest of poems in the world.[157]

Returning to the theme of Leopardi's changing ways of conceiving nature, one theme that became increasingly prominent as his work progressed, which I later assess in relation to its consequences for Leopardi's call for solidarity, was his depiction of an opposition between people and nature. In his writing, he increasingly referred to nature with ecological processes and events in mind, particularly those which bring strife upon people. This can be seen, for example, when the Icelander conveys to Nature the fruitlessness of his journeys, which he undertook for the purpose of seeking the tranquillity of life:

> But I have been seared with heat between the tropics, shrivelled with cold near the poles, afflicted in the temperate zones by the

changefulness of the air, and troubled everywhere by the commotion of the elements. Many are the places I have seen where not a day goes by without a storm: which is to say that every day you assault and do regular battle against the inhabitants of those places, who are guiltless of any injury towards you.[158]

The Icelander describes the 'frequent occurrence of earthquakes', the 'multitude and fury of volcanoes', and the 'ferocious winds and hurricanes' by means of a way of conveying the indifference of Nature to humans, who always has 'a mind to things quite other than the happiness of men or their unhappiness'.[159] The way that Leopardi depicts the afflictions that we experience at the behest of nature foreshadows a remarkably similar passage from Freud in *The Future of an Illusion*, mentioned earlier, where he details the danger of the natural elements we remain subject to, and our comparable 'weakness and helplessness', writing:

> [N]o one is under the illusion that nature has already been vanquished; and few dare to hope that she will ever be entirely subjected to man. There are elements, which seem to mock at all human control: the earth, which quakes and is torn apart and buries all human life and its works; water, which deluges and drowns everything in turmoil; storms, which blow everything before them; there are disease, which we have only recently recognised as attacks by other organisms; and finally, there is the painful riddle of death, against which no medicine has yet to be found, nor probably will be. With these forces nature rises up against us, majestic, cruel and inexorable; she brings to our mind once more our weakness and helplessness, which we thought to escape through the work of civilization. One of the few gratifying and exalting impressions which mankind can offer is when, in the face of an elemental catastrophe, it forgets the discordances of its civilization and all its internal difficulties and animosities, and recalls the great common task of preserving itself against the superior power of nature.[160]

Noting these similarities in Freud's passage, Timpanaro remarks how Freud's notion of 'man's oppression by Nature' is among the finest in his writings, and: 'displays surprising, though certainly quite accidental, affinities to Leopardi'.[161] Like Leopardi, Freud highlights nature's ability to bury 'all human life and its works' and examines the philosophical significance of 'the painful riddle of death'. In 2016, such a threat loomed over Leopardi's own works, including his 1819 poem 'Infinity', when, following the earthquakes that shook Visso in the Marche Region, his manuscripts had to be moved to an archive in Bologna in response to concerns for their safety.

By pointing out the innocence of the inhabitants of places affected by what Leopardi took to be Nature's 'regular battle', we can begin to see what Timpanaro refers to as the 'second movement' of Leopardi's thought, which 'identifies nature as the enemy of man'.[162] This shift, as Timpanaro argues, prompts Leopardi to establish a new morality, based on solidarity among humans. I examine this theme a little later, when I refer to what critics have come to call the 'solidarity stanza' in 'La ginestra'. Firstly, I delve deeper into a topic mentioned by Timpanaro, who, discussing the change he finds in Leopardi's thinking about nature, remarks: 'its sources (in its second stage) must be sought in the anti-providentialism of Voltaire's poem on the *Lisbon Disaster*'.[163] I examine how Leopardi's engagement with Voltaire's work helped to shape his own, before highlighting the pertinence of the theme of consolation in a letter written by Rousseau to Voltaire, offering an idea which Leopardi went on to develop.

Voltaire's 'cruel piece of natural philosophy'

As I elucidated in my account of the significance of the relationship between systems and philosophy in Leopardi's thought, for thinkers like Leibniz and Pope, and other eighteenth-century optimists, our ills, including when we are struck by disease, floods, earthquakes and other disasters, are a necessary effect of our nature and the constitution of the universe. This optimism, which was rife in the eighteenth century, and took on a new lease of life in the name of 'progress' in Leopardi's time, appalled him.[164] As Timpanaro has suggested, the way that Leopardi ultimately understood nature was also shaped by his engagement with Voltaire's work. This was deeply intertwined with philosophical debates concerning optimism and became particularly prominent in his attempt to make sense of events like the Lisbon Earthquake.

Considering the theme of evil within such frameworks of thought, in *Nature's Evil: A Cultural History of Natural Resources* (2021), Aleksandr Etkind examines such ideas through the prism of how we acquire, use, value and trade natural resources. As he demonstrates, and as Leopardi was particularly attuned to, the Age of Enlightenment culminated in the Lisbon disaster, which threw into question many of its essential beliefs.[165] Inviting a comprehensive re-evaluation of evil by challenging previously held notions of the trust to be placed in an omnipotent or good God, it generated a range of popular literature drawing moral conclusions from the destruction, in the form of newspaper discussions, books, essays, poems, eyewitness accounts and theatre presentations.[166] Of these, Voltaire's letter to his acquaintance Jean Robert Tronchin on 24 November 1755 is perhaps the most significant example, due to the reappearance of Voltaire's ideas within it in Leopardi's late philosophical poetry. In his letter, Voltaire drew an analogy between the earthquake's victims and 'ant-heaps', trapped beneath the debris of the disaster:

> This is indeed a cruel piece of natural philosophy! We shall find it difficult to discover how the laws of movement operate in such fearful disasters in the best of all possible worlds–where a hundred thousand ants, our neighbours, are crushed in a second on our ant-heaps, half, dying undoubtedly in inexpressible agonies, beneath debris from which it was impossible to extricate them, families all over Europe reduced to beggary, and the fortunes of a hundred merchants – Swiss, like yourself – swallowed up in the ruins of Lisbon. What a game of chance human life is! What will the preachers say – especially if the Palace of the Inquisition is left standing! I flatter myself that those reverend fathers, the Inquisitors, will have been crushed just like other people. That ought to teach men not to persecute men: for, while a few sanctimonious humbugs are burning a few fanatics, the earth opens and swallows up all alike.[167]

Leopardi took Voltaire's conviction that the Lisbon Earthquake 'ought to teach men not to persecute men' seriously, incorporating Voltaire's conclusion that we should restrain from fighting amongst ourselves into his late poetry. He also drew from Voltaire's use of the form of the dialogue, drawing particularly heavily from his 'Dialogue between the Philosopher and Nature', which appeared in his *Philosophical Dictionary*, first published in 1764.

In this dialogue, Voltaire depicts a conversation between a Philosopher and Nature, during which the Philosopher seeks clarity from Nature regarding her essence, thereby providing a model for Leopardi's work. Voltaire's Philosopher, for example, asks Nature whether a 'supreme intelligence' presides over her operations, which leads him to discover how small and insignificant he is in the eyes of Nature, who responds:

> I am water, earth, fire, atmosphere, metal, mineral, stone, vegetable, animal. I feel indeed that there is in me an intelligence; you have an intelligence, you do not see it. I do not see mine either; I feel this invisible power; I cannot know it: why should you, who are but a small part of me, want to know what I do not know?[168]

His depiction of Nature highlights her lack of interest in humankind, who she considers inconsequential in the broad scheme of things. This was later echoed by Leopardi, corresponding to Piperno's observation in 'Forgery as a Form of Leopardi's Authorship' that his work often performed an 'active intervention' on those texts whose insights he wished to reiterate.[169] In fact, he had been an expert in literary 'forgery' since he composed 'Inno a Nettuno' ('Hymn to Neptune') entirely in Ancient Greek in 1816, fooling literary critics into thinking that it was an original Greek classic.[170]

As Fubini has pointed out, in 'Nature and an Icelander', Leopardi's depictions of 'the threats and rumblings of Mount Hekla', a volcano in Iceland – where the eruption of Eyjafjallajökull in the Spring in 2010 cost the European aviation industry an estimated $250 million per day – drew from Voltaire's work the 'Histoire de Jenni' ('The History of Jenni').[171] It appears to have laid the foundation for Leopardi's decision to bring together his final ideas regarding nature by referring to Mount Vesuvius, which overlooked his home in Naples, where he wrote 'La ginestra' in 1836, during an outbreak of cholera. We can also see the germ of Leopardi's materialist interest in the cyclical creation and destruction of sentient life within nature in Voltaire's work, where the Philosopher asks:

> Would not non-existence be better than this multitude of existences made in order to be continually dissolved, this crowd of animals born and reproduced in order to devour others and to be devoured, this crowd of sentient beings formed for so many painful sensations, that other crowd of intelligences which so rarely hear reason. What is the good of all that, Nature?[172]

Returning finally to Leopardi's dialogue between Nature and his Icelander, the suggestion that human life is inconsequential for Nature is reformulated by the writer, whose protagonist reminds us: 'I have not, as you believe, made certain things or performed certain actions to give you pleasure or to do you good. And finally, if I happened by chance to blot out your whole species, I would not be aware of it.'[173] Responding to the Icelander's accusation that Nature is inimical to humankind, Nature ridicules the notion that she cares for the activities of human beings, setting the record straight when she comments:

> Did you perhaps imagine that the world was made for your benefit? Let me tell you that my handiworks, in my arrangements and my operations, except very seldom, I always had and always have a mind to things quite other than the happiness of men or their unhappiness. When I hurt you in some way and by whatever means, I do not even notice it, except very rarely: just as normally, if I please or benefit you, I do not know it.[174]

Similar in form and in style to Voltaire's work, we see here how Leopardi's depiction of Nature as somewhat indifferent to our lives had its roots in his dialogue between the Philosopher and Nature.

To improve our sense of the impact of Voltaire's work on Leopardi, I turn now to briefly consider Voltaire's depictions of the results of the disaster in Lisbon, where he offered a potent critique of the attempts to justify the evils of human existence by the philosophical optimism found in the work of Leibniz and Pope.[175] In *Candide, ou l'Optimisme* (*Candide, or Optimism*), Voltaire extended his notion of the senselessness of the cruelty of nature that he also set out in his 1755 'Poème sure le désastre de Lisbonne' ('The Lisbon Earthquake'), in which he critically assessed the maxim 'Whatever is, is right'. In *Candide*, Voltaire's protagonist, a survivor striving to make sense of the aftermath of the Lisbon Earthquake, considers the teachings of his family philosophy tutor Dr Pangloss, who Voltaire used to satirically champion such optimism. Conveying such a position with respect to the disaster, Dr Pangloss explained to Candide:

> Things cannot be other than they are. For, since everything is made for a purpose, everything must be for the best possible purpose. Noses, you observe, were made to support spectacles: consequently, we have spectacles. Legs, it is plain, were created to wear breeches, and are supplied with them. Stone was made to be quarried, and built into castles: that is why his lordship has such a fine castle – for the greatest baron in the province must also be the best housed. Pigs were made to be eaten: so we eat pork all year round. It follows that those who say that *everything is good* are talking foolishly: what they should say is that *everything is for the best*.[176]

Throughout *Candide*, Voltaire traces his protagonist's attempts to weigh up Pangloss' claims in light of the earthquake that struck Lisbon, evaluating the legitimacy of metaphysical optimism. What finally prompts Candide to question this received wisdom is an encounter, which occurs towards the end of the work in Chapter 19, where Voltaire described Candide's encounter with a Black man in the Dutch colony of Surinam. This man, who had been enslaved by Mynheer Vanderdendur, had had his left leg and right hand cut off. Sharing his story, he told Candide:

> [I]t is the custom here. They give us a pair of linen breeches twice a year, and that is all our covering. When we labour in the sugar works, and the mill catches a finger, they cut off a hand. When we try to run

away, they cut off a leg. I have suffered both these misfortunes. This is the price at which you eat sugar in Europe.[177]

These ideas, which I return to a final time later on with reference to critics who point out the anti-Black sentiment found within Voltaire's writings, contributed to Leopardi's thinking about the relationship between civilisation and barbarism in the wake of the Enlightenment. In Voltaire's work, using Candide, the writer challenged the notion put forth by Leibniz and Pope that 'Whatever is, is right'. Expressing this with Candide's refusal to endorse Dr Pangloss' conclusions in light of the testimony of the slave he encountered in Surinam, the protagonist declared: 'Ah, Pangloss! ... you never guessed at such an abomination! This is the end. I must renounce your optimism.'[178] Examining in his 1979 essay 'The Pessimistic Materialism of Giacomo Leopardi' Maria Sirocchi's 1962 comparative analysis between Leopardi and Voltaire's work, Timpanaro drew together several threads that traversed the poet's thought, writing:

> Christianity, for Leopardi, is not genuine primitiveness, inseparable from a proclamation of man's inherent need for happiness, but barbarie, i.e. corrupted civilisation, which aggregates within itself the ills of the excess of civilisation which preceded it (distance from nature, mortification of hedonistic impulses) and those of ignorance and superstition. This demand for a return to nature, against a society which claims to educate the spirit while neglecting the body, Leopardi maintained to the end. But, first spasmodically, later with increasing vigour, there developed in his thought another line, which derived not from Rousseau but rather from the Voltaire of the Poème sur le désastre de Lisbonne.[179]

Timpanaro – whose work Anderson has argued was shaped by the theme he took from Leopardi of 'the inevitability of the ultimate victory, not of man over history, but of nature over man' – appears to have missed the significance of what Leopardi derived from Rousseau's contribution to these debates, however, which I will illuminate in my analysis of 'La ginestra'.[180]

Rousseau's letter

Famously, Rousseau complained to Voltaire in a letter dated 18 August 1756, that whilst he mocked the source of consolation he found in Pope's *Essay on Man*, Voltaire's outlook only gave him reason to despair.[181] In Rousseau's words:

> You reproach Pope and Leibniz for insulting our ills by holding that all is good, and you so crowd the picture of our misery that you aggravate our sense of it: in place of the consolation for which I'd hoped you do nothing but afflict me; [...] Pope's poem alleviates my ills and brings me to patience, yours sharpens my pains, excites me to complaint and leaving me nothing but a shaken hope, it reduces me to despair. 'Man, be patient,' Pope and Leibniz tell me, 'your ills are a necessary effect of your nature and the constitution of the universe. The eternal and beneficent being who governs it wanted to protect you from them: of all possible economies he chose that which brought together the least ill and the most good, or to say the same thing still more plainly, if it is necessary, if he didn't do better it's because he couldn't do better.[124]

As Tom Jones has highlighted in his study of Pope's work, for Rousseau, the positions held by Pope and Leibniz present a world that is entirely open to causal explanation, in which what strike us as disasters are caused by human actions:

> Rousseau makes the point that the Pope-Leibniz view he prefers does not necessitate blaming God for natural evils. Even things like earthquakes, when they strike us as disasters, are caused by human actions: people choose to live in Lisbon, in close proximity to one another, in high stone houses. Those choices are as much the cause of their death as the earthquake.[182]

Such a view, which appreciates the increasingly significant and influential effects of human behaviour on the damaging effects of such events, aligns with the contemporary, albeit more secular appreciation of current scholarship relating to the Anthropocene, which takes as its starting point the acknowledgement that human activity, rather than natural progress, is the primary cause of central tenets of the environmental crisis. Today, greater understanding of the effects of living within the Anthropocene has led to it being more widely recognized that the increasing magnitude of disasters often described as 'natural' is exacerbated by the choices of people, who have caused weather patterns to be less predictable and affected the balance of ecosystems supporting life and biodiversity.[183]

Returning to Rousseau's letter however, as we can see, he accused Voltaire of aggravating the misery he depicts. Voltaire, according to Rousseau, fails to alleviate humanity's woes, instead bringing pain and despair to a place where he could otherwise have provided consolation. Espousing the view according to which natural events occur at the behest of an 'eternal and beneficent being', Rousseau's ideas, whose influence on Leopardi has been well documented in other regards, underline a sense of the human yearning for the alleviation of our ills.[184] As Christophe Litwin has observed in his examination of the relationship between metaphysical optimism and the role of consolation in Rousseau's thought in 'Rousseau and Leibniz: Genealogy vs. theodicy' (2019):

> What he admired in Pope's poem was not its metaphysical optimism, but the consoling power of its praise of virtue in the Fourth Epistle. Virtue did not prevent pain or bring any actual cure for it, but allowed us to enjoy and taste a secret and sweet contentment even as we suffered: 'virtue handed over to pain still enjoys more contentment than vice amongst the pleasures' (*CC* 1: 140). While this theme of consolation and the sweet contentment of the virtuous life, independent of one's pain, would find significant echoes in Rousseau's 1756 'Letter to Voltaire,' in 1742 the consoling virtue of Pope's poem was unrelated to 'optimism.' Thus, before his exchange of letters with the Leibnizian thinker and naturalist scientist Charles Bonnet (who wrote under the pseudonym 'Philopolis') in the wake of the publication of the *Discourse on Inequality*, Rousseau had not expressed interest in the *Theodicy*. He had briefly engaged with Leibniz on other subjects discussed in the Desmaizeaux collection of letters and essays. He had neither proved eager to take sides in the quarrel of 'optimism' nor pictured this system as a consolation.[185]

In my examination of Leopardi's philosophical poem 'La ginestra', written in 1836 at Torre del Greco, which I examine shortly, I consider how Leopardi's work relates to the notion that works of art can aid with the alleviation of suffering by empowering us to resist the temptation to be reduced to despair. In this upcoming section, I highlight the similarities between Rousseau's recognition for the need to provide a form of consolation in response and that of Leopardi, who provides a response which finds its own unique shape and is underpinned by the poet's conviction of the importance of cultivating moral strength within ourselves.

My account of Leopardi's *Operette* has allowed me to provide examples of Leopardi's extensive criticism of the anthropocentric tendencies of human beings and the development of Leopardi's conceptualisation of nature. I have shown how, in many of his dialogues, Leopardi was demonstrably critical of expressions of instrumental thinking, which narrow-mindedly place human interests at the heart of the universe, without accounting for what is lost with such a manoeuvre. Ultimately, however, the extent to which Leopardi considers nature as evil, which is influenced in particular by his engagement with the work of Voltaire and Pope, engenders the limit of his critique. In ways I go on to show, by setting up a battle between humanity and nature, his philosophy is limited by the significant ways that it succumbs to narratives of opposition with roots in the Judeo-Christian tradition he so fiercely critiqued. As I examine a little later, it is according to this tradition that the narrative that continues to shape our present, which supposes that in order to flourish we must control and dominate nature, was accorded its power. Before this, however, I turn next to examine the effect that the Copernican Revolution had on Leopardi's thought.

The dethroning of the Earth

In his 1543 work *On the Revolutions of the Heavenly Bodies*, the Renaissance polymath Nicolaus Copernicus dedicated his preface to Pope Paul III. Here, he expressed his concerns regarding the potential impact of his scientific discovery, which would shake our understanding of the role of humanity within the universe, by transferring to the Sun many of the astronomical functions previously attributed to the Earth.[186] Anticipating the reception of his arguments, Copernicus reflected:

> I can readily imagine, Holy Father, that as soon as some people hear that in this volume, which I have written about the revolutions of the spheres of the universe, I ascribe certain motions to the terrestrial globe, they will shout that I must be immediately repudiated together with this belief. For I am not so enamored of my own opinions that I disregard what others may think of them. I am aware that a philosopher's ideas are not subject to the judgement of ordinary persons, because it is his endeavor to seek the truth in all things, to the extent permitted to human reason by God. Yet I hold that completely erroneous views should be shunned. Those who know that the consensus of many centuries has sanctioned the conception that the earth remains at rest in the middle of the heaven as its center would, I reflected, regard it as an insane pronouncement if I made the opposite assertion that the earth moves. Therefore I debated with myself for a long time whether to publish the volume which I wrote to prove the earth's motion or rather to follow the example of the Pythagoreans and certain others, who used to transmit philosophy's secrets only to kinsmen and friends, not in writing but by word of mouth, as is shown by Lysis' letter to Hipparchus.[187]

In the body of the text, describing his endeavour to comprehend the longstanding confusion in the astronomical traditions concerning the motions of the universe's spheres, Copernicus wrote:

> I began to be annoyed that the movements of the world machine, created for our sake by the best and most systematic Artisan of all, were not understood with greater certainty by the philosophers, who otherwise examined so precisely the most insignificant trifles of this world.[188]

Leopardi's lifelong fascination with the 2000-year-old history of astronomy led him to closely examine the intertwinement of scientific and literary development, in order to replicate aspects of the history in his own writing. By 1813, when he was only fifteen, Leopardi had written the *History of Astronomy*, a 300-page work tracing the development of astronomy over two millennia and several ancient languages. Leopardi's history referred to almost 2000 astronomers, philosophers, poets and other authors, often in the original language.[189] In 2011, the Italian astrophysicist Margherita Hack published the second new edition of his work, *Storia dell'astronomia. Dalle origini ai giorni nostri*, where she built upon Leopardi's study, adding translations from Greek that Leopardi had not provided, on the assumption his readers would not need them. Beginning where Leopardi ends, Hack extends Leopardi's work, which made use of the most advanced research of the time available to him in his father's famous library and traces a new trajectory into perspectives opened up in the twenty-first century by the most recent conquests.

Copernicus was a central thinker within Leopardi's cosmic framework, in whose writings the philosopher found an excellent literary model, which he made use of to support his ambition to evolve an Italian literary language capable of expressing philosophical and scientific ideas clearly.[190] Seizing upon and dramatizing the language and images that Copernicus employed throughout *On the Revolutions*, Leopardi for example built upon Copernicus' reference to the Earth's motion being 'created for our sake', and philosophers' otherwise precise examinations of the 'most insignificant trifles of this world'.[191] Like Copernicus, who argues 'that completely erroneous views should be shunned', Leopardi holds a similar belief, observing the obstacles which stand in the way of relinquishing false views throughout his writing. Although Copernican themes traverse Leopardi's work, they feature particularly prominently in the *Zibaldone* and the *Operette*. In an entry in the *Zibaldone*, written in late 1819, for instance, Leopardi set out his understanding of the significance of the Copernicus' system:

> One proof in a thousand of how much purely physical systems influence intellectuals and metaphysicians, is the case of Copernicus, who for the thinker completely changes the idea of nature and man as conceived by and natural to the ancient system known as Ptolomaic, reveals a plurality of worlds, shows man not to be a unique being, as the position, the motion, and the destiny of the earth are not unique,

and opens up an immense field of reflections, concerning the infinite number of creatures which according to all laws of analogy must inhabit the other globes analogous in all respects to our own, and also those which although we do not see them must surround the other suns, which is to say the stars; it belittles the concept of man, and exalts it, reveals new mysteries of creation, of the destiny of nature, of the essence of things, of our own being, of the omnipotence of the creator, the purpose of creation etc. etc.

[84]

In Leopardi's thought, the revelations of Copernicus marked an end of human uniqueness, shaping his cosmic sensibility, and encouraging him to increasingly commit to conveying a sense of the triviality of human life. This positioning, which Gilroy describes in *Postcolonial Melancholia* as 'the same inconsolable, tragicosmic sense of human triviality', has its own consequences for how we can position Leopardi's thought in relation to environmental activism today, which I will consider later.[192] For Leopardi, the revelations of Copernicus marked the end of human uniqueness, shaping his cosmic sensibility and encouraging him to increasingly convey a sense of the triviality of human life. According to him: 'The system known by the name of Copernicus' could be regarded as 'a great discovery and innovation, even as regards metaphysics' [**1857**], and alongside Copernicus, 'Descartes, Galileo, Newton, Locke, etc.,' also 'truly changed the face of philosophy' [**1857**]. For him, the metaphysical consequences of the Copernican revolution were monumental, and adding to his entry in the *Zibaldone* from 1818, he also included his insights in 'An Imp and a Gnome', where he echoed Copernicus' reference to 'the most insignificant trifles of this world', subjecting our presumptuousness that the human race alone could be deemed to have value to ridicule:

> IMP: Is that so surprising? When they not only persuaded themselves that the things of the world had no purpose other than to serve them, but reckoned that everything else put together, compared with the human race, was a mere trifle. And therefore their own adventures they called world revolutions, and the histories of their peoples, histories of

the worlds; although even within the confines of the earth one could count perhaps as many species, not simply of creatures in general but just of animals, as there were living men. And yet these animals, who were made expressly for their use, never realized that the world was in rebellion.[193]

As I will return to, Leopardi's reflections on the trifles of our world in turn later reappear in Nietzsche's work, where, in *On Truth and Lies in the Nonmoral Sense*, he utilises Leopardi's mockery of the notion of describing the 'histories of the worlds', when in fact one means to speak of the history of humanity.

In his 1827 dialogue 'Copernicus', which was included in the posthumous edition of the *Operette*, Leopardi brought together the ideas he had developed in the *Zibaldone* and in previous dialogues from the *Operette*, to formulate his thoughts regarding the consequences of the Copernican Revolution. Adopting a style reminiscent of Galileo's in *Dialogue Concerning the Two Chief World Systems, Ptolemaic and Copernican* (1632), Leopardi elucidated the various ways the revelations of Copernicus entailed a radical shift in 'the idea of nature and man'.[194] By making use of the literary word and the imagination to combine precision, evidence and lyricism in the hope of reaching a wider audience, Leopardi drew out the ramifications of this for human beings, anticipating some of the central concerns of posthumanism in doing so. His appreciation of the significance of the Copernican Revolution underpinned his departure from widely held assumptions that viewed humans as entitled sovereigns, anticipating some of the central concerns of posthumanism in doing so. At one point in his dialogue, Copernicus is positioned as unsuccessfully pleading with the Sun to move around the Earth, which the Sun describes as a tiny 'handful of mud', upon which are scattered 'half a dozen beastlings'.[195] Here, Leopardi explains the philosophical significance to the newly dethroned status of the Earth, which had previously sat centred motionless at the heart of the universe, considering herself to its 'empress':

> The Earth until now has held the first place in the universe, which is to say the middle; and (as you know) she herself being motionless,

with no other occupation than to look around her, all the other globes of the universe, the greatest no less than the smallest, and similarly the brightest along with the most dim, have gone rolling over and under and beside her without ceasing; with a haste, a bustle, a frenzy astonishing to think of. And so, all things appearing to be busy in her service, it seemed that the universe was of the nature of a court; in which the Earth sat as on a throne; and the other globes around, in the manner of courtiers, guards and servants, attended some to one office and some to another. So that, in effect, the Earth has always thought herself empress of the universe: and in truth, things being as they have been in the past, one can hardly say she reasoned badly; indeed I would not deny that this opinion of hers was well founded.[196]

Drawing out the various ways Copernicus' discovery belittles the 'concept of man' in this manner, Leopardi describes the 'worthlessness of the human race', mocking our sense of grandeur and exceptionalism, while teasing out the impact of the disruption caused by the Copernican worldview on the way people could think of themselves.[197] Describing the shock to be expected as a result of the Sun not moving around the Earth, through Copernicus, Leopardi beseeched:

[I]t will upset the degrees of the importance of things, and the hierarchy of beings; it will alter the purposes of creatures; and so doing it will cause a vast upheaval even in metaphysics, indeed in everything that touches the speculative part of knowledge. And it will come about that men, even supposing they are able and wish to consider things sensibly, will discover themselves to be quite another thing, from what they have been so far, or have imagined themselves to be.[198]

With recourse to the Sun's point of view and the testimony of Copernicus, Leopardi highlights our unwillingness to fully appreciate the change away from ideas which rest upon the geostatic system handed down from the Greek astronomer Ptolemy, according to which the Earth sat at the heart of a set of nested, transparent spheres, which Copernicus threw into question.[199] Responding to Copernicus in the dialogue with a certain lack of interest, the Sun retorts by observing that, if it bore the potential to offer some consolation, people would be likely to argue in the face of evidence regardless:

> [M]en will have to content themselves with being what they are: and if they don't like it, let them go reasoning back to front, and arguing in the face of the evidence of things; as they will most likely do; and in this way they will go on thinking of themselves as whatever they wish, barons or dukes or emperors or anything else they case to be: and so they will be more consoled, and these opinions of theirs will give me not the slightest displeasure.[200]

In passages such as these, Leopardi examined the blow to humankind issued by his discoveries of Copernicus that were later supported by Galileo, which wounded human narcissism before both Darwin and Freud compounded this injury.[201] In her essay 'From Nature to Matter' Di Rosa examines this aspect of Leopardi's work, showing how it casts doubt on the basic assumptions that have underpinned Western culture, thereby enabling a critique of anthropocentric culture through a critical analysis of the alleged superiority of human beings.[202] Dennis Looney has also observed the significance of this dialogue, which he described in 'Leopardi's "Il Copernico" and Paradigm Shifts in Art', published in 2005, as 'an ironic and comical tour de force'. For Looney, Leopardi's piece signalled a compositional change in his writing, where, shifting away from the Lucianic model for the philosophical prose of the *Operette*, Leopardi takes up a renewed commitment to philosophical poetry, which culminates in the late poem, 'La ginestra'.[203] I return to this idea in my examination of the work, where I assess the ways in which Leopardi's piece takes seriously the need for consolation while simultaneously highlighting the importance, of developing a strong sense of character, by learning to face the light of those harsh truths we might wish to turn away from.

I have highlighted Leopardi's arguments in 'Copernicus' because they seem to me to bring home the significance of our capacity, or lack of, to keep pace with the changes demanded of us by shifts in paradigms in society. Although reading Leopardi's work from this perspective suggests that a lot is left to be desired, knowing this to be the case equips us with a sense of the weaknesses we need to be aware of, which can help to guard against their exploitation by those who, benefitting from the status quo, seek to preserve it. A recent example highlighting the pertinence of Leopardi's insights can be seen in the lack of our proportional response to the environmental crisis following a warning, issued by the majority of living Nobel laureates in the sciences, and more than 1700 independent scientists, known as the 'World Scientists' Warning to Humanity', published in 1992. This letter, which detailed how 'a great change in our stewardship of the Earth and the life on it is required, if vast human misery is to be avoided', was met with radio silence in comparison to the scale of change it called for. As a result, in 2017, the 'World Scientists' Warning to Humanity: A Second Notice' was issued, calling again for sufficient recognition of humanity's central part in pushing the Earth's ecosystems beyond its capacities to support the web of life. As its authors noted, 'humanity has failed to make sufficient progress in generally solving these foreseen environmental challenges' and, as a result, 'alarmingly, most of them are getting far worse'.[204] Numerous similar examples could be provided to highlight the degree to which the tendency that concerned Leopardi – that we fail to adjust our thinking in a timely manner, regardless of the evidence to suggest that we should – has significant consequences for how we respond to the environmental and political challenges facing us.

Importantly, in 'Copernicus', Leopardi brought his insights concerning the way we deal with change to bear on the way we manage resources when he considered the potential effects that the Sun's refusal to move would have on the access to light of the Earth's inhabitants. In the dialogue, before Copernicus had been called upon to converse with the Sun, Leopardi depicted a conversation between the Sun and the First Hour of the day, who had approached the Sun with horses ready to move her around the Earth. Alarmed by her insistence that the Sun was 'not budging' and finding herself therefore unable to bring the day into being, the First Hour pleaded against the Sun's resolve that: 'if men want to see any light, they should keep their fires burning, or provide it some other way'. As the First Hour appealed:

> And what way does Your Excellency think the poor wretches might find? And having to fuel their lamps, or provide enough candles to burn all through the day, will be an exorbitant expense. If they had already discovered that kind of air that can be used for burning, and to light their streets, rooms, shops, cellars and everywhere, and all at little expense; then I would say that the case was not so bad. But the fact is, we have three hundred years to go, more or less, before men discover that remedy: and in the meanwhile they will run out of oil and wax and pitch and tallow; and they will have nothing more to burn.[205]

The first well-recorded instance of a streetlight being powered by gas was a demonstration that took place in Pall Mall, London in 1807, only two decades before Leopardi wrote his dialogue.

Nonetheless, he was able to bring into unison his understanding of the inadequate pace of attitudinal change and the way in which we treat finite resources as though they are infinite.[206] His work includes a number of estimations of how soon we would have meaningful discussions about the way we separate ourselves from nature, and how long it would take us to address the problem of depleting expensive and finite resources. In the *Zibaldone* in 1820, he guessed that it would be another hundred years before people would start talking about 'the progression of excessive civilization', whilst in 1827 Leopardi predicted that 'we have three hundred years to go', more or less before we would find a way to light everywhere without an exorbitant expense. These guesses have ended up being relatively accurate. For example, according to an article published in March 1912 in 'Popular Mechanics', displayed an appreciation of the essentials of anthropogenic climate change, warning about the potential consequences of excessive consumption. According to the author, Francis Molena: 'The year 1911 will long be remembered for the violence of its weather.' He goes on to clarify what effects the combustion of coal scientists predict will have on the climate in the future, writing:

> The furnaces of the world are now burning about 2,000,000,000 tons of coal a year. When this is burned, uniting with oxygen, it adds about 7,000,000,000 tons of carbon dioxide to the atmosphere yearly. This tends to make the air a more effective blanket for the earth and to raise its temperature. The effect may be considerable in a few centuries.[207]

A positive exception to the accuracy of Leopardi's timeline today is that a hundred years before Leopardi expected, we have already discovered the technology to transition from non-renewal to renewable energy consumption. In terms of that 'kind of air' that he suggested might help to address the 'exorbitant expense' of burning fossil fuels, we already have the means of wind farms to utilize wind energy, one of the cheapest sources of electricity, to generate power for lighting. However, our ongoing reliance on fossil fuels continues to be the primary source of carbon emissions driving climate change, while the removal of trees from forested land, in part to meet demand for timber, soy, beef, palm oil, all contribute to making Leopardi's forewarning that we will one day find ourselves with 'nothing more to burn' so pertinent. Making use of the means we have to utilize those renewable resources that nature can replenish can minimize the unnecessary carbon emissions driving climate change and air pollution, thereby helping to minimize nature and biodiversity loss, issues which, taken together, make up today's triple planetary crisis.

As I will return to examine, in recent decades, scholars of Leopardi have highlighted that, despite his deep engagement with ideas that were still in their inception, he failed to sufficiently foresee the negative impact of the political and commercial forces working against environmental justice. Today, political and corporate barriers impede infrastructural change, playing the most significant roles in preventing, delaying and challenging societies' attempts to move away from overreliance on finite resources and towards the use of renewables. Some of these are significant enough to run the risk of impeding our ability to adopt new practices in sufficient time to prevent us from crossing the threshold of tipping points, which could easily initiate a series of cascading disastrous and unnecessary effects.[208]

Conclusion

In his consideration of the Copernican Revolution, Leopardi elucidates his view of people's tendency to fail to consider things sensibly, a proclivity he saw as being particularly strong when ideas deemed to threaten one's importance or worth were involved. Today, we can consider Leopardi's appreciation of our unwillingness to change our thinking to meet new paradigms in science or society and apply it to how we engage with the consequences of the environmental crisis. According to Christiana Figueres, the former UN Executive Secretary for Climate Change and Tom Rivett-Carnac, a senior political strategist for the 2015 Paris Agreement, our task today, as they wrote the *Future We Choose: Surviving the Climate Crisis* (2020), is to 'let go of the old world': 'To meet the challenges of the climate crisis and preserve all that we hold dear; to retain democracy, social justice, human rights, and other hard-won freedoms in the future, we must part ways with that which threatens to destroy them.'[209] As Leopardi illustrated in 'Copernicus', the challenge of changing people's minds in such ways, to encourage them to align with changes in the world is significant and worthwhile, even though it will likely involve coming up against our tendency, identified by the Sun in Leopardi's dialogue, to 'go reasoning back to front, and arguing in the face of the evidence of things'.[210] The thought of Copernicus and Leopardi reveals themselves to be resources we can draw from, as we meet the task we find ourselves challenged with today, which involves needing to make profound shifts in how we live, work and relate to one other. As I turn to consider next, extending a line of thought found in Looney's article, Leopardi's later work gives significant examples to show ways of meeting the challenge of facing the need to change in ways that benefit society.[211]

I have introduced some of the central themes in Leopardi's critical diagnosis of modernity in the *Operette* and the *Zibaldone*, such as the role of dialogues, which allowed him to critique the vices of the social world, the use of ridicule and humour, the folly of humanity, the persistence of barbarism, and what he took to be the violence of nature. Next, I turn to consider how the writer resolves to meet the challenge of reviving our vitality, by weaving together philosophy and poetry in one of the final works to be written for his collection of poems, the *Canti*. In my following assessment of the value of the conception of a better society depicted in 'La ginestra', written in 1836, I examine the Leopardi's appreciation that, when faced with a choice between fear and hope, the ease with which we forget that, as well as bringing the possibility of danger, certain events also 'bring a probability of good' [66]. Considering the 'new mysteries of creation' that Leopardi believed were revealed by the new Copernican system, I take seriously his reflection on what is lost when we are too readily inclined to fear, tracing solutions to this tendency in a range of more recent thinkers, including Vandana Shiva and Rebecca Solnit, whose work is pertinent in highlighting the potential opportunities available to us as we meet the challenge of the environmental crisis.

In my earlier examination of Jacqueline Rose's essay, which considered Freud's thought concerning grief and death in relation to pandemics, I highlighted the significance of Rose's consideration of the poignancy today of Freud's recognition of the mind's response to its own limits. Referring to Rose's recourse to Laura Spinney's comprehensive examination of the impact of the Spanish flu in *Pale Rider*, I noted her thesis that Freud's insights can perhaps help us to reach a greater understanding of our collective forgetting of the events of the Spanish flu, which, despite causing more fatalities than both world wars combined, remains an example of the historical amnesia that Stuart Hall has highlighted, in his own utilization of Freud's concept of disavowal.

As I have sought to show in my account of Leopardi's consideration of the challenges to our self-perception brought about by the Copernican revolution, the poet's work was marked by a similar sensitivity.[212] Adding to existing recognition of the strength of his critique, next, I turn to highlight how Leopardi issues a crucial yet too readily overlooked response to the problems he diagnosed. This is most pronounced in 'La ginestra', a work that was shaped by Leopardi's acknowledgement of the significance of the theme – highlighted by Rousseau in his letter to Voltaire – of consolation. His late work, as I go on to illustrate, bears the fruit of the poet-philosopher's sustained engagement with the question of how the resources of literary history can contribute to the creation of works of art that bear the potential to cultivate a 'time of strength', while simultaneously assuaging despair.

2

Dreams and vision

A philosophy that aims to cure in the Canti

The bleak, cosmic repudiation of Enlightenment thought that traverses Leopardi's *Operette*, *Zibaldone* and other works alters slightly throughout the development of Leopardi's writing as we can see in his poems in the *Canti*, where he attends to the problems that he previously elucidated. In his late philosophical poem 'La ginestra', also commonly referred to as the 'Flower of the Desert', the poet made his intention to resolve the earlier tensions he had set out in his work clear, through his inclusion of a reference to John 3:19 from the New Testament, transcribed in Greek and translated into Italian, at the opening of the work.[1] Beginning with the line: 'And men loved darkness rather than light', Leopardi situated his poem, demonstrating his intention to attend to his reflections in the *Zibaldone* and the *Operette* through a different lens, for which he sought resolution.

Responding to accusations that his critique of humanity makes him a misanthrope, as Eugene Thacker has observed in *Infinite Resignation: On Pessimism* (2018), on 21 May 1829, Leopardi examined the notion, which he had previously explored in 'Nature and an Icelander', that misanthropes are found among people in the world, writing:

> Anyone who has few dealings with people is unlikely to be a misanthrope. True misanthropes are not to be found in solitude but in the world. They praise solitude, yes indeed; but they live in the world. And if such a person withdraws from the world, he loses his misanthropy in solitude.

This entry was the note to another, recorded on 2 January 1829, in which Leopardi resolved that his philosophy would serve as an active intervention on misanthropic thought, by seeking to resolve the ill humour felt towards fellow humans:

> My philosophy not only does not lead to misanthropy, as might seem to anyone who looks at it superficially, and as many accuse it of doing, but by its nature it excludes misanthropy, by its nature it aims to cure, to extinguish that ill humor, that hatred (not systematic but nevertheless real hatred) which very many people who are not philosophers, and would not wish to be called or thought of as misanthropes, feel in their hearts nonetheless toward their fellow humans, either habitually, or in particular circumstances, by reason of the ill which, rightly or wrongly, like everyone else, they receive from other people. My philosophy makes nature guilty of everything, and by exonerating humanity altogether, it redirects the hatred, or at least the complaint, to a higher principle, the true origin of the ills of living beings, etc. etc.
> [4428]

As we can see here, Leopardi's intention, which has been too readily overlooked, was to extinguish the 'ill humour' that he believed so many people feel either habitually, or on certain occasions, towards their neighbours. With this in mind, as I will set out, it becomes possible to see how Leopardi endeavoured to resolve the tension he had built up in his earlier dialogues, particularly within 'Nature and an Icelander' and 'Copernicus'.

Throughout the rest of this study, I examine the consequences of the complaint that Leopardi issues against nature, which allowed the poet to build an ethics of solidarity, demonstrating the significance of his intention not solely to diagnose, but also ultimately to cure. While previously, I sought to give an account of what Calvino has described as the 'ceaseless discourses on the unbearable weight of living' in Leopardi's critique of modernity, what follows is an examination of those noble, affirmative and consolatory aspects of his philosophy.[2] As I go on to illustrate, this occurs through Leopardi's apparent resolve to create work that corresponds to his depiction of a 'work of genius' in the form of lyric poetry, which attends to despair through the cultivation of enthusiasm. As part of my evaluation of the strengths of his ethics, I will relate his work to contemporary ecological thinkers, suggesting potentially fruitful connections, first by exploring how the ideas of several critics might contribute to extending Leopardi's thought, and finally to see how his work in turn can contribute to contemporary discourse. Before turning to such examinations, it would be useful to begin by reviewing how, with 'La ginestra', Leopardi brought together the themes of evil, optimism, form, solidarity, nature, humanity, guilt, innocence and others into his later poetic work, which I begin by introducing.

Drawing inspiration from Petrarch's *canzoniere*, Leopardi's *Canti* (*Songs*) established his reputation as Italy's most important Romantic poet.[3] His work, which is widely considered to be one of the great achievements of Italian poetry and one of the most influential works of the nineteenth century, was made up of forty-one compositions, with evolving experiments in style and thematics.[4] Leopardi saw the *Canti* as a 'reliquary' for his ideas, feelings and deepest preoccupations, encompassing a vast range of tones and material, including early personal elegies and idylls, philosophical satires, and radical public poems on history and politics. It contained the first truly modern lyrics and allowed Leopardi to evoke his private suffering and grief, and posit his beliefs about human life, forming 'crystallizations in poetic form of Leopardi's thought'.[5] His classicist inclination is apparent in the collection, where Leopardi expresses his severe criticism of a world marked by the comforts of religion and self-deluding faith in the ability of scientific knowledge to ameliorate the tragic nature of life is. Six of Leopardi's poems from the *Canti* are known as the *Idilli* ('The Idylls'), were written from 1819 to 1821 and include: *Il sogno* ('The dream'), *L'Infinito* ('The Infinite'), *La sera del dì di festa* ('The evening of the feast day'), *Alla Luna* ('To the Moon'), *La vita solitaria* ('The solitary life') and *Lo spavento notturno* ('Night-time terror'). In these works, Leopardi introduces themes such as the transience of things, the intuition of universal pain, the oppressive weight of eternity and the blind power of nature.

'La ginestra' is the longest poem in the *Canti*, which Leopardi wrote towards the end of his life in 1836, bringing together the philosophical, emotional and autobiographical theories and ideas which, as Creagh has written had been: 'a long time in wood before being bottled'.[6] The poem is also known as 'The Broom', which refers to a plant, a gorse-like shrub, known by its Latin name *planta genista*. It is said that Geoffrey of Anjou, also known as 'Plante Genest', of the Plantagenet family, who held the English throne from 1154 to 1485, would wear a sprig of the yellow blossom in his helmet to give him courage and strength, and prior to going into battle, he plucked the plant from a steep bank, and declared: 'this golden plant, rooted firmly amid rock, yet upholding what is ready to fall, shall be my cognizance. I will maintain it on the field, in the tourney and in the court of justice.'[7] In Leopardi's poem, the Broom serves as similarly a poignant symbol, reminding us of the inner strength we have recourse to in the face of the threat of expressions of the power of nature. His work installs in us a sense that we can respond to calls to action from a place of courage, instead of fear. Drawing together his response to the critiques of post-Enlightenment thought he set out in the *Zibaldone*, the *Operette* and elsewhere, which is too regularly overlooked, throughout the piece, Leopardi encourage us to come together in unity. He proposes positive ways we can respond to the challenges we often face, which he centres on figures like the noble Broom and poor farmer, to whom we can turn to for inspiration as we enhance our capacity to bring about meaningful change.

In his account of Negri's 'poetic turn' in his 2011 article 'Flower of the Desert: Poetics as Ontology from Leopardi to Negri', Timothy Murphy demonstrates the significance of Negri's focus on Leopardi's 'Broom' as forming the basis for much of his work on immaterial labour and network resistance.[8] According to Murphy, who describes Leopardi's poem as 'laying out the broad outlines' of what he calls 'Leopardi's anticipatory Nietzscheanism': 'Leopardi's last great poem, "La ginestra, o il fiore del deserto" ("The Broom; or, The Flower of the Desert"), ... serves as the culmination of Negri's account of the poet's poetic, political, and philosophical project.'[9] In her examination of the significance of the poem, set out in *A Fragrance from the Desert: Poetry and Philosophy in Giacomo Leopardi*, Daniela Bini highlights the role of the imagination at the core of Leopardi's philosophy of life:

> The value of the imagination goes beyond its synthetic activity. Its major asset is its creativity, which is not merely a reproduction of reality. The beauty of created images lies in their being only approximately close to their models, in their vagueness, their lack of definition. These qualities stimulate the imagination of those who perceive them, and thereby serve to continue the creative process.[10]

As Bini notes here, the force of feeling that Leopardi conjures through his work gives it its potency, helping to instil in Leopardi's audience a conviction that they too can foster the nobility his Broom represents.

According to Timpanaro, Leopardi established a 'new morality on the solidarity of men', that is based on an appreciation of the significance of neighbourly love, and a concern for the welfare of others. Today, a comparable moral foundation would support the optimism of the will that Gramsci described and help us to apply the necessary pressure on those contributing most to the environmental crisis. Leopardi's 'La ginestra' allows the poet to express his philosophical thought and arises out of the transformation in his judgement concerning who or what is to blame from the dearth of vitality experienced in modern times. His work helps us recognize the opportunity we can seize and bolsters our confidence in the power of imagining a radically different/new future for ourselves and the Earth. Beginning from a place of recognition, he demonstrates how it can help us overcome the fears which have hitherto controlled us, hindered our opportunities to grow and prevented us from recognizing the hope with which we might relate to our future.

Leopardi's ethics of solidarity

For theorists such as Severino, Leopardi can be understood as an underrecognized forerunner to Nietzsche. Whilst critics have examined the extent to which Nietzsche can be thought of as an affirmative philosopher who draws from the ancients the ideal that living well is of the highest value, there has been little work of this nature undertaken in English in relation to Leopardi's thought. Those who contributed to the book *Nietzsche as Affirmative Thinker* (1985), including Robert Solomon, for example, have examined the 'Nietzsche's affirmation' from a range of different perspectives. In his article 'A More Severe Morality: Nietzsche's Affirmative Ethics', Solomon explored how Nietzsche's moral philosophy contains 'an ethics that is considerably more than nihilism'.[11] According to him, although Nietzsche talks about creating new values, what often most concerns him is a return to an old and neglected set of values.[12] Urging us on in the desperate state of affairs, Solomon highlights the way in which, for Nietzsche, it is doing, not willing, that is of moral significance: 'morality does not consist of principles but of practices'.[13] He finds in Nietzsche's work an attempt to recollect a 'morality of nobility', which, in his emphasis on character and the virtues, makes him resemble Aristotle.[14] Extending this line of thinking in *Living with Nietzsche: What the Great 'Immoralist' Has to Teach Us* (2003), Solomon also writes that the philosopher recaptures 'what is best in Western ethics' through his revisitation of the ancients in this way.[15] With a consideration of Solomon's observations concerning Nietzsche's inclinations in mind, I wish to argue that not only the same can be said of Leopardi, but also that he may have influenced Nietzsche in this regard.

As I go on to show, Leopardi drew, in particular, on the thought of Aurelius and Seneca, as well as on more contemporary thinkers, like the naturalist and precursor to Darwin, Comte de Buffon. Through his recourse to these thinkers, particularly those who reach back to the ancient tradition, I argue that Leopardi reflects on how we can confront our fear of death in a manner that embodies the notion of consolation he finds in Seneca. As has been the case with Nietzsche, I will highlight the various ways in which Leopardi's final position is less pessimistic than it is frequently presented as, and how contrary to what his damning analysis of human folly in the *Operette* would suggest, his philosophical thought is in fact defined by a love for humankind. Ultimately, I argue that we can find a care for how we might learn to confront our mortality and aspire to die with dignity, following a life well lived. Since such a reading will be seen as contentious by some, I present my analysis in relation to a reading set out by Timpanaro, which is later restated by Anderson. In relation to these, I argue that, by refusing to grant the significance of the Stoic themes in Leopardi's late poem, Timpanaro in particular runs the risk of missing an essential component of Leopardi's consolatory philosophy. Before turning to my account of Timpanaro's reading of Leopardi, however, I first set out a brief sketch of one of the ways Nietzsche was influenced by Leopardi's work.[16]

According to the archivist Max Oehler, who directed the Nietzsche Archive in Weimar, Nietzsche's library contained the Le Monnier version of Leopardi's *Operette*, edited by his friend, Ranieri.[17] Nietzsche's familiarity with Leopardi's work prompted him, in the aphorism 'Prose and poetry', in the *Gay Science*, to express his admiration for the poet-thinker:

> In this century, four very strange and truly poetic persons attained a mastery of prose, for which this century is otherwise not made – out of a lack of poetry, as I have suggested. Excluding Goethe, who may fairly be claimed by the century that produced him, I see Giacomo Leopardi, Prosper Merimee, Ralph Waldo Emerson, and Walter Savage Landor, the author of *Imaginary Conversations*, as worthy of being called masters of prose.[18]

Previously, in 1874, the composer Freiherr Hans Guido von Bülow – known for his support of the careers of Richard Wagner and Johannes Brahms – had sought to encourage Nietzsche to translate Leopardi into German, recognizing Nietzsche's affinity with Leopardi's thought. Speculating about the hypothetical translation's potential, Bülow suggested to Nietzsche that it would introduce 'Schopenhauer's great Latin brother' to the nation, and in doing so might reach similar levels of significance to Schlegel's translation of Shakespeare on the dissemination of the latter's work.¹⁹ In his response, dated 2 January 1875, Nietzsche wrote:

> I felt much too delighted and honored by your letter not to think tenfold about the proposal you are making me regarding Leopardi. Of course, I know only bits and pieces of his prose writings; one of my friends, who lives with me in Basel, has often translated individual passages from them and read them to me, always to my great surprise and admiration; we have the latest Livornese edition. (By the way, a French work on Leopardi has just appeared, by Didier in Paris, I forget the name of the author – Boulé? I know the poems from a translation by Hamerling. I myself don't understand enough Italian and although I'm a philologist I'm unfortunately not a linguist (the German language annoys me enough).²⁰

Nietzsche's work echoes Leopardi's comic style, ridiculing, for example, the arrogance of 'world history' in *On Truth and Lies in a Nonmoral Sense*, written in 1873, where Nietzsche suggests comparing the history of humanity to a fable, as Leopardi's did in 'The History of the Human Race' the work with which he opens the *Operette*. Considering the arbitrary essence of the human intellect when considered within nature, the vastness of which Leopardi had emphasised in 'Infinity', while recalling the 'eternities' during which our intellect did not exist, Nietzsche too hints at the futility of human life, when he writes:

> Once upon a time, in some out of the way corner of that universe which is dispersed into numberless twinkling solar systems, there was a star upon which clever beasts invented knowing. That was the most arrogant and mendacious minute of 'world history,' but nevertheless, it was only a minute. After nature had drawn a few breaths, the star cooled and congealed, and the clever beasts had to die. One might invent such a fable, and yet he still would not have adequately illustrated how miserable, how shadowy and transient, how aimless and arbitrary the human intellect looks within nature. There were eternities during which it did not exist.
>
> And when it is all over with the human intellect, nothing will have happened.²¹

Taking up Leopardi's mockery from 'An Imp and a Gnome' of our use of the term 'world history', in which the Imp took issue with the presumptuousness of the human race, Nietzsche amplifies Leopardi's reference to Copernicus' depiction of the trifles of our world, with his suggestions that 'nothing will have happened' when it is all over with the human intellect.[22] Recalling too Leopardi dialogue 'An Imp and a Gnome' Nietzsche echoes the considerations of the interlocutors who consider that 'men are all dead, and the race is lost' in the *Operette*, he brings attention to a central theme of Leopardi's thought, concerning what sense we are to make of living in the face of the inevitability of our mortality, particularly in the context of the astrological revelations initiated by Copernicus' discoveries.[23]

Leopardi's considerations of these themes have important consequences for efforts to extrapolate from his thought about whether we can meet the environmental crisis and its intersecting crises with dignity, and how to work towards this, if so. In my view, there are important examples in which presentations of Leopardi's thought in this regard have been skewed. I examine one of these shortly, in my assessment of Sebastiano Timpanaro's analysis of the 'final formation' of Leopardi's philosophy, which I consider after a short consideration of the way in which the poet responded to metaphysical optimism in 'La ginestra'.

Renewing forgotten ancient moral practices

While as Solomon argues, Nietzsche returns to neglected values pertaining to the noble character in ancient thinkers, as I described earlier, Leopardi also believed that we need to recover some practices from ancient civilisation that have been forgotten. For Leopardi, who Anderson described in *Spectrum*, as 'a direct interlocutor of antiquity', such work would support efforts undertaken in the name of social improvement, which seek to support our emergence from 'barbarous times'.[24] As he writes in the *Zibaldone*: 'The current *progress* of civilisation is still a *revival*; it consists, for the most part, in *recovering what has been lost*' [**4289**]. One of the ways we see this conviction influencing the shape of 'La ginestra' is in the opportunities Leopardi takes to revive both the moral and the political practices of the ancients, as well as in the attention he paid to their works of art. This is particularly evident in Leopardi's references to ideas such as the exercise of the 'view from above', Stoic attitudes to death and a renewed enquiry into citizenship in the form of his advocacy for a 'just society of citizens' in which 'right and piety will take root'.[25] These ideas, which he seeks to deliberately bring back to the fore, contribute to the work of uncovering in order to revive those practices that will support the recovery of life's lost vitality, which he explored so thoroughly in his dialogues.

Voltaire's rejection in *Candide* of the optimistic view of the world set out by Leibniz in his *Theodicy*, written in 1709, was taken up by Leopardi, who ridiculed notions of 'preestablished harmony' that had taken on a new lease of life in the name of progress during his time.[26] In October 1821, Leopardi explicitly attacked Leibniz's ideas, including his idea of the 'monad' in the *Zibaldone*, arguing that the philosopher's optimistic notions amounted to 'fables and daydreams'. In a passage where he described Romanticism as 'a system utterly false in theory', Leopardi questioned:

> What do the great discoveries of Leibniz, perhaps Germany's greatest metaphysician, and certainly a very profound speculative thinker respecting nature, a great mathematician, etc., amount to in this regard? Monads, optimism, preestablished harmony, innate ideas. Fables and daydreams. What do those of Kant, the leader of a school, etc. etc.? I believe that no one knows, not even his disciples. Through their profound speculations regarding the general theory of the arts, the Germans have recently given us the romance of Romanticism, a system utterly false in theory, in practice, in nature, in reason, in metaphysics, in dialectics, as shown in several of these thoughts.
>
> [1857]

He returned to consider systems of optimism again in Bologna on 19 April 1826, where he wrote even more forcefully in the *Zibaldone*:

> *Everything is evil. That is to say everything that is, is evil; that each thing exists is an evil; each thing exists only for an evil end; existence is an evil and made for evil; the end of the universe is evil; the order and the state, the laws, the natural development of the universe are nothing but evil, and they are directed to nothing but evil. There is no other good except nonbeing; there is nothing good except what is not; things that are not things: all things are bad. All existence; the complex of so many worlds that exist; the universe; is only a spot, a speck in metaphysics. Existence, by its nature and essence and generally, is an imperfection, an irregularity, a monstrosity. But this imperfection is a tiny thing, literally a spot, because all the worlds that exist, however many and however extensive they are, since they are certainly not infinite in number or in size, are consequently infinitely small in comparison with the size the universe might be if it were infinite, and the whole of existence is infinitely small in comparison with the true infinity, so to speak, of nonexistence, of nothing.*
>
> [4174]

This claim, which Giovanni Carsaniga rightly cautions too much has already been made of, nonetheless captures the force of Leopardi's rejection of the idea of preestablished harmony popular in his time.[27] Explicitly relating his views to those of 'Leibniz, Pope, etc', Leopardi positing his own system, continued:

> This system, although it clashes with those ideas of ours that the end can be no other than good, is probably more sustainable than that of Leibniz, Pope, etc., that everything is good. I would not dare however to go on to say that the universe which exists is the worst of possible universes, thereby substituting pessimism for optimism. Who can know the limits of possibility?
>
> [4174]

Here, Leopardi suggests that he considered true pessimism to be the direct opposite of optimism, extending this in his typically cosmic fashion to refer to 'the worst of possible universes'. His return to the notion that 'this is the best of all possible worlds', which he also depicted in 'The Wager of Prometheus', takes on a universal perspective, referring to our existence as 'a spot, a speck in metaphysics', in reference to the ideas of thinkers like Seneca and Aurelius.

Demonstrating his keen awareness of the separation between his thought and that which enjoyed contemporary popularity, Leopardi rejected the idea that it necessarily followed that his views were wrong. Instead, he suggested that those who demonstrated noble values during his age were too readily dismissed. In fact, for Leopardi, the optimistic thinking he saw as prevailing in his time was an expression of a form of cowardice, an expression of a deep-rooted desire for 'thought to be enslaved again', which arose out of a refusal to confront reality's harsh conditions.[28] He expressed this position in the 1831 poem 'Il pensiero dominante' ('The Dominant Idea'), which was inspired by Fanny Targioni Tozzetti and written in Florence as an exaltation of the idea of love. In the piece in the *Canti*, Leopardi once again attacked metaphysical optimism, expressing disdain for his 'prideful age', which he accused of being 'in love with slogans', and feeding itself 'on empty hopes'.[29] He returns to this theme again in 'La ginestra', where he lamented his 'proud and foolish century', deriding those whose 'resurgent thought' relinquished the 'way forward' and 'call it progress', and describing the instant offence he took to 'each unworthy act' of 'cowards and ungenerous, mean spirits'.[30] For him, far from providing a form of consolation which could be truly sustainable, the slogans set out by eighteenth century optimists encouraged a reliance on empty hopes that strip us of our agency while preventing us from facing what he described as the 'bitter fate' of our mortal human condition.[31] In contrast to this, as Pamela Williams has observed: 'whatever other characteristics human nobility has in *La ginestra*, it certainly means facing and admitting the truth'.[32] In *A Fragrance from The Desert: Poetry and Philosophy in Giacomo Leopardi* (1983), Daniela Bini makes a similar observation, arguing that Leopardi's work was motivated by a moral duty to state and spread the truth.[33]

This duty appears to have been taken up by Nietzsche, whose work was motivated by a similar ambition to undermine false truths.[34] Nietzsche's depiction of himself as a madman in recognition of the fact that his ideas were not aligned with the dominant thought of the time shares areas of commonality to the person in Leopardi's work who accepts 'the truth about the bitter fate' of the human condition, who is misconstrued as being a coward.[35] Kathleen Marie Higgins' reflections on Nietzsche's stance in *Comic Relief: Nietzsche's Gay Science* (2000) highlight this when she writes: 'Unfortunately, the madman's audience is made not of honest men but of smug "modern" men who enjoy deriding him.'[36] Before returning to consider examples of nobility in Leopardi's poem, which he deemed to be a counterexample to the unsustainable and false consolation to be found in the cowardice of philosophical optimism, I briefly consider the role of darkness and light in his advocacy for admitting the truth.

In the article 'Materialist and Poetic Humanism in G. Leopardi', published in *Life: The Human Quest for an Ideal* (1996), Emilio Di Vito examines the theme of light in 'La ginestra', seeking to understand the significance of Leopardi's decision to refer to the tendency of people to veer towards darkness at the outset of his poem. Describing how Leopardi changes the meaning of 'darkness' and 'light' from its biblical context, in which 'the "darkness" of sin is contrasted with the "light" of God's grace', Di Vito argues that: 'in "La ginestra" the "darkness" of religious faith is contrasted to the "light" of reason'. He continues: 'The quotation from St. John's Gospel "and men loved darkness more than light", which inspired La ginestra (The broom) ... attains the light of truth by passing through it', referring to the challenge of accepting the harshness of our human condition.[37] In his poem, Leopardi contends that those who find difficulty in accepting our fateful condition turned their backs 'like cowards on the light that made it clear', drawing a relationship between those who are referred to as loving darkness in St. John's Gospel and the state of his age as he saw it.[38] In contrast to such 'cowards', he praised those who embodied a 'great spirit' by confronting our reality.[39] By developing this notion, Leopardi paved the way to providing his own form of consolation, which he hoped, by virtue of its accordance with the truth, would be more resilient, and could fulfil his ambition of setting forth a philosophy that aims to cure.

The miserable condition nature handed to us

Timpanaro examined the consequences of the biological frailty Leopardi highlights in his work in his study *Sul Materialismo* (*On Materialism*), translated in 1975. Here, he considered how Leopardi's ideas could help overcome difficulties encountered in studies of the relationship between structure and superstructure in Marxist thought. Suggesting that his writing could help to encourage acknowledgement of 'the persistence of certain biological data even in social man', Timpanaro contends:

> This does not at all mean that one can 'explain what capital is by taking man's biological constitutions as one's point of departure'. Rather, it means that one can regard, for example, certain features of literary, philosophical and religious phenomena as determined not only by a given socio-economic situation but also by reflection on certain general characteristics of human existence. On the whole, I think that one can see how every failure to give proper recognition to man's biological nature leads to a spiritualist resurgence, since one necessarily ends by ascribing to the 'spirit' everything that one cannot explain in socio-economic terms.[40]

Timpanaro had Leopardian pessimism in mind when he referred to philosophical and literary work that reflects on 'certain general characteristics of human existence', describing this in greater detail in his preface, where he wrote:

> ... Leopardian pessimism, precisely because of the materialist and hedonistic basis which is most explicit in its final formation, is immune from the Romantic and existentialist dross which gravely contaminates the thought of Horkheimer and Adorno – and even the later works of Marcuse, despite their far more political and secular character.[41]

This reference to the 'final formation' corresponds to the final stanzas of 'La ginestra', where Leopardi examined how we are to make sense of the biological frailty given to us by nature. Here, as Timpanaro writes, Leopardi attends to giving: 'proper recognition to man's biological nature'.[42] More specifically, his exemplary Broom embodies a dignified stance in the face of its destiny to return 'to the place it knew before'.⁴³ Leopardi's portrayal of the plant's posture in relation to the fragility of her life allows the poet to contrast her nobility against those cowards he derides, whose morality he deemed to be founded on 'vain mythologies', and who presumed that fate or themselves had made them immortal.⁴⁴ Acknowledging that we will all ultimately be obscured by oblivion, he depicts the Broom as a 'hopeless abject supplicant', bowing her 'blameless head', while succumbing to the 'cruel power of subterranean fire', and 'returning to the place it knew before'.⁴⁵ Exemplifying an alternative means of relating to the conditions of our lives to those adopted by those he accused of cowardice, he uses both the plant of the wilderness, and the farmer caring for his family to demonstrate the possibility of adopting a noble stance in the face of such challenges. In doing so, he reminds us of the inherent value of living and dying well. He shows us that, rather than bringing shame on ourselves by living in denial, or lashing out at our neighbours, there remain latent opportunities to uncover the possibility of moving beyond the fearfulness, senseless pride, hate and anger that he saw as pervasive. This, he believed, would help us resist the lure of that 'darkness' that he associated with false beliefs, and which he saw people as being so inclined towards.

Leopardi also gives the example of such a stance in human form, when he depicts the character of a poor man, whose appreciation of the finitude of our lives is examined. Demonstrating his tenderness, Leopardi describes how this noble farmer 'nurtures poorly in these fields' and their 'scorched and poisoned earth', remaining constantly prepared to collect his wife and children and flee their longtime nest, which 'was their one defense from hunger', and to watch it fall prey to 'the burning flood', which, unending and unstoppable, will one day advance. Describing additionally how the man 'still lifts his anxious eyes ....' to the fatal peak of the tremendous mountain, which threatens ruin for his family and their mean possessions. Even in the face of uncertain danger, Leopardi presents his farmer as readying himself to protect his wife and children, holding fast to the spirit of familial love he is demonstrably prepared to live by until the moment of death, there establishing him as another exemplar of the noble nature.[46]

This poor man, 'bending to his vines', which he nurtured in the scorched and poisoned earth embodies, for Leopardi, a person with nobility of spirit, who 'dares to lift his mortal eyes', to confront and admit the pain in our destiny. In spite of his awareness of his own fragility, the man still resolves to live according to 'honest words' that 'subtract nothing from the truth', revealing Leopardi's ongoing commitment to facing the truth.[47] Writing in the *Zibaldone* of Niobe, who is often aligned with a stance of nobility in his thought, Leopardi refers to her role in Ovid's *Metamorphoses* where '… after her misfortune, it is said, if I am not mistaken, that she cursed the Gods, and admitted herself defeated, but not compliant', to suggest that he saw refusing compliance as an appropriate way we might resolve to relate to our own conditions [505]. In the poem, he also evokes the vast span of time of nature, who 'stays evergreen'. Highlighting her ignorance 'of man and of the age', Leopardi describes how she travels 'such a long road' that she might as well be standing still, issuing a sobering but resonant reminder of our ongoing vulnerability despite what we take to be advances in civilisation.[48] It is such aspects of Leopardi's late poem that underpin Timpanaro's claim that Leopardi gives full recognition to our biological fragility, although his reading differs from my own.

While Timpanaro's examination of the significance of Leopardi's depiction of the theme of mortality in his poem is compelling, his overall analysis is diminished by the way he dismisses the work's consolatory importance.[49] Describing the 'various romantic-existentialist pessimisms which the European bourgeoisie has given birth to over the last two centuries', which he is keen to differentiate Leopardi's work from, he explains the reasons underlying his position, when he writes: 'With regard to socio-political oppression, a millennial philosophical tradition (represented in ancient times primarily by Stoicism, and in more recent times by idealism) has proffered "inner freedom" as recompense.'[50] This notion is later echoed by Anderson in *Spectrum*, who, prior to introducing Timpanaro's work on Leopardi, emphasises the 'titanism' in Leopardi's call for universal solidarity when he writes:

> ... the temper of Leopardi's pessimism was not stoic: it recommended no renunciation of the passions remaining loyal to what pleasures could be found in the world. Nor did its conclusions have anything in common with Schopenhauer's later metaphysic of misanthropic resignation. Leopardi's response to the weakness and insignificance of human life in the cosmos was the opposite – a 'titanism' calling for universal solidarity in the battle against nature, that every life must lose.[51]

Picking up on Timpanaro's emphasis on 'the materialist and hedonistic basis' of Leopardi's work, Anderson also argues that Leopardi's pessimism was not Stoic because it remained loyal to the pleasures to be found in the world. In fact, Timpanaro argued this point at length, maintaining that Marxism refutes examples of '*consolation philosophiae*' – whether Stoic, Romantic, existential or idealist in kind – in part because 'so-called inner freedom is a poor substitute for true freedom'. In doing so, he brought Leopardi's work to bear on a broader discussion of the complex relationship between existentialist thought and Marxism that I cannot examine here. This refutation, Timpanaro argues Leopardi's thought helps to show, also applies to our biological nature:

> The man of culture is always free, even if he is subject to enslavement or torture, because he lives in a world of ideas over which external restrictions have no power. Marxism represents the most decisive and coherent refutation of this *consolation philosophiae*. It contends that, except in those cases where the notion of inner freedom represents an extreme defensive posture designed to hold out the prospect of a future resurgence, so-called inner freedom is a poor substitute for true freedom, which cannot exist apart from man's actual emancipation from oppressive social relationships. But this refutation, if it is correct, is also valid for 'physical ills'. One cannot reject *consolation philosophiae* as illusory in relation to socio-political oppression and at the same time regard it as completely valid and sufficient unto itself in relation to nature's oppression of man.[52]

The difference between the two scenarios Timpanaro described here is that, while with regard to socio-political oppression, the goal is to obtain actual emancipation from oppressive social relationships, we will never be able to escape our nature as mortal beings. As Leopardi elucidates in his work, all that is in our power in such a regard is to adopt a stance in relation to this reality that allows us to live in a way we can look back on with contentment. Timpanaro however extends his comparison between socio-political oppression and our biological nature, arguing that citing 'the heroic calm with which so many men have confronted suffering and death' as a counterargument to the 'objective fact' that 'old age, sickness, etc. are causes of unhappiness for the great majority of persons afflicted with them' means that one has not considered the high price paid for the attainment of such calm.[53] With such a reading, he misconstrues Leopardi's late philosophy, overlooking the fact that his resolve to portray a 'heroic calm' formed part of his endeavour to build on the strengths of the ancients, from whom he sought guidance in adopting a noble stance in relation to our mortal nature in the cosmos. Consequently, Timpanaro's analysis overlooks the importance of Leopardi's appreciation of our psychological need for consolation, which became a central part of his endeavour to provide a philosophy that set out to cure. Such positions of classical theorists like Timpanaro too readily overlook Leopardi's commitment to navigating how we ought to respond to the fear we feel in the face of the reality of our mortal nature, which he gives examples to show we can approach with grace and humility.

Timpanaro's depiction of recognitions of the attention Leopardi paid to how we ought to stand in the face of death as 'existentialist dross' is unhelpful, and his insistence on refuting *consolation philosophiae* does a disservice to the compositional change to be found in the poet's writing.[54] As Dennis Looney's article helps to reveal, in his late work, Leopardi moved away from his usual method of employing ridicule, and towards centering pity, sympathy and consolation, which became key for his philosophical approach. Timpanaro's intention to negate the significance of the influence of Stoicism for Leopardi's work overlooks this, and Anderson's account of the critic's position betrays its weakness: 'Leopardi's pessimism was not Stoic: it recommended no renunciation of the passions, remaining loyal to what pleasures could be found in the world.'⁵⁵ Whilst it is important to highlight the significance of Leopardi's hedonistic motivation, this approach that Timpanaro adopts and Anderson has echoed reveals a failure to sufficiently consider the poet's method. This can be seen, as I have previously shown, in relation to his praise of Pignotti, where he approves of the fabulist's method of taking what he found to be useful in works he engaged with, and using them to portray 'certain political maxims, certain fine qualities of the human character'. This practice, as Timpanaro appears to fail to consider, allowed room for Leopardi to leave behind those aspects of the work of thinkers that did not align with what Leopardi set out to convey in his own.⁵⁶

Considering this theme of the role of the passions, hedonism and pleasures in Leopardi's thought, we saw earlier how, for him, modern life is marked by its separation from its natural roots. As Negri argues, extending his consideration of the 'Spinoza-Leopardi relationship' in relation to sensism in 'Between Infinity and Community: Notes on Materialism in Spinoza and Leopardi' (1989), and writing in *Flower of the Desert*: 'The whole of Leopardi's thought developed in the search for an exaltation of sense, the recovery of the truth of passion, the liberation of imagination.'⁵⁷ As he wrote in [2415] 'Life is by nature made for living, and not for death. That is to say it is made for activity, and for all that is the most vital in the functions of living creatures.' Leopardi also argued that 'Things are made for mutual love', and for him, such love was 'the enlivening principle of nature', which could counteract the 'destructive principle' [59] of that 'real hatred' he found residing at the core of misanthropy [4428]. The way in which Leopardi conceptualises the relationship between the nourishment of the body and that of the soul has also been examined by critics, who have attended to his notion that vigor is necessary for survival and the enjoyment of life. For example, in his article 'Nourishment and Nature in Leopardi', published in 2016, Dario Del Puppo highlighted how: 'to nourish meant, for Leopardi, to engage with nature', and argued that food, taste, smell and nutrition were central to Leopardi's conception of what it meant to live life well.[58]

I also examined earlier, with recourse to Roberto Esposito's arguments in *Living Thought*, the way in which considered with a certain envy animals' aptitude for joy as he reflected on how we live. For example, as he wrote in the *Zibaldone* on 12 February 1821:

> [T]he happiest creature possible is the one who is most distracted from the mind's tendency toward absolute happiness. Such are the animals, and such was man in nature. In them the desire for happiness, being turned into desires for a this or that happiness, or goal, and above all deadened and dissipated by continuous activity, by present needs, etc., did not and does not have sufficient strength to render the living being unhappy. Hence activity in particular is the surest *possible* means to happiness.
>
> [649]

This notion further demonstrates Esposito's previously considered claim that Leopardi's positive attitude towards the animal world should not be limited to his critique of anthropocentricism.[59] As Esposito has suggested, it also serves as a representation of humans' 'before'; that time in which we were, in Esposito's words '… still rooted in the natural dimension from which the human species detached itself when it entered into the alienating regime of history', and yet to find ourselves cut off from our own prospects of vitality.[60]

The property of works of genius: Should laughter or pity prevail?

One of the important ways Leopardi dealt with our difficulty in appreciating our finitude and biological limits was through his utilization and revitalization of the practices of the ancients. For instance, we can trace Leopardi's approach in his later work back to his engagement with Germaine de Staël's writing, where he observed her analysis of 'works of genius', the potential consoling power of which he sought to develop. One example of this was his consideration of the expression of pain in ancient times, particularly in statues, such as the prototype of the bereaved mother, whose fourteen children were slaughtered, Niobe, who Staël's referred to in *Corinne, ou l'Italie* (Corinne, or Italy), published in 1807.[61] Here, Leopardi notes Staël's observation that the expression of Niobe, rather than being utterly distraught, 'retains its beauty even in despair', prompting her reflection, in Leopardi's words that: 'what touches us so deeply in works of genius is not misfortune itself but the power over this misfortune that the soul retains'. For Leopardi, who associated works of genius with those of the ancients, such an observation was a 'fine condemnation of the Romantic system', which he believed 'eschews all nobility' [87]. One of the reasons Leopardi was critical of Romanticism was because their 'works of the mind' failed to arouse the admiration and deep feeling that ancient works conjured. According to Leopardi:

> As a result, their works of the mind bear no trace of this great feature of their origin, and, as a pure imitation of truth, like a rag statue with a wig and a wax face, etc., have much less effect than an imitation that, with simplicity and naturalness, preserves the ideal of beauty, and transforms the common into the extraordinary, that is, shows in its heroes a great soul and a dignified attitude, arousing admiration and deep feeling through the power of contrast. In the Romantic system, on the other hand, you cannot be moved except in the way you are moved by the everyday events of life. The Romantics express them faithfully, but without imparting to them anything of the extraordinary and the sublime, which elevate the imagination and inspire deep meditation, and intimacy, and lastingness of feeling.
>
> [87]

These considerations informed Leopardi's conclusion that: '... once again, it can be seen that the ancients left more for thought than they expressed, and the impression of their works was more long-lasting' [88]. From such comments, we are able to get a sense of Leopardi's appreciation of the power of particular works of art to leave long-lasting impressions, by virtue of their ability to evoke a dignified attitude and depth of feeling. For Leopardi, the conclusions, imagery and narrative tools of the ancients are a resource to draw upon to help us understand our place within the cosmos.[62] He believed that 'we need still to *recover* much from ancient civilisation', writing:

> The tendency over these recent years, more than ever before, toward social improvement, has brought about, and continues to do, the *renewal* of many ancient practices, both physical, and political and moral, which had been abandoned and forgotten during barbarous times, from which we have *not yet entirely emerged*.
>
> [4289]

Observations of this nature traverse the *Zibaldone*, where his endeavour coincides with Hall's suggestion in *Questions of Cultural Identity*, for us to examine resources from history that can help us to 'reinscribe the past, reactivate it, relocate it, *resignify it*' as a means of strengthening our position in the present.[63]

We can find an example of Leopardi's idea of such a renewal and reactivation of the past in the *Zibaldone*, which pertains to the work of the eighteenth century fabulist Lorenzo Pignotti. In an entry from 1819, Leopardi considered Pignotti's work, which included *Favole e novelle* (*Fables and Short Stories*), published in 1782, describing Pignotti's writing as an example of works that were 'reduced from their original Aesopian model' to be 'of some use to grown men'.[64] Demonstrating his admiration for the eighteenth century fabulist, who was among many who used the form as a vehicle for social and political satire in Italy at the time, and who he saw as repurposing the devices of the ancients to make them suitable for a contemporary adult audience, Leopardi wrote:

> In most of Pignotti's fables (and perhaps in others as well), the purpose of the fable, which is to use sweetness, simile, etc., in order to teach children, etc., has vanished and does not remain even in appearance (as in didactic poetry), for they are intended to describe certain vices of the social world, certain political maxims, certain fine qualities of the human character that are neither of concern to children nor

possible for them to recognize and understand – for example, the one about the donkey, the horse, and the ox. Rather, these fables have been reduced from their original Aesopian model to not inurbane little satires, or pure games of wit, that is, pleasant comparisons or little stories, of some use to grown men, like Marmontel's Contes moraux and other works of that kind, except that in this case they describe animals, plants, etc. etc.

[67]

By recognizing the potential of using these rhetorical devices to conduct a social or political intervention by guiding ones' moral judgement in the service of ethical instruction, Leopardi considered how Pignotti's description of the 'fine qualities of the human character' arose through a process of reduction from their 'original Aesopian model'. This depiction of praiseworthy qualities of the human character later comes to the fore in Leopardi's work, firstly in the Broom central to 'La ginestra', in a demonstration of Leopardi's sustained commitment to reminding us that our notion of being at the centre of the universe has been undermined, and secondly in the qualities of the poor farmer. We also find in his philosophical poetry his method of taking what he deemed to the most significant attributes of practices from the past and reworking them in the service of social improvement, and as a means of conveying 'certain political maxims' and responding to the 'vices of the social world', which he had previously set out so vividly.

Initially, as I previously examined in my dicussion of the role of Lucian's work in shaping Leopardi's writing, as Leopardi wrote in 1821, he had resolved to use the 'weapons of ridicule' to rouse his 'poor country and poor century' [1393]. Whilst many scholars have noted how, during the development of his ideas, Leopardi's depiction of people softened, what has received less critical attention is the way this shift impacted the form of his work. This change, whereby Leopardi steadily withdrew the blame he had previously ascribed to humanity was, as I have already shown, prompted in part by his reflections on the devastation caused by the Lisbon Earthquake. In 'La ginestra' Leopardi echoed Voltaire's depiction in his letter to Tronchin of the disaster as a 'cruel natural philosophy', describing nature as our 'cruel nurse', who 'with the slightest movement in a moment' partly destroys. In a stanza towards the end of his poem, he borrows again from Voltaire, this time deploying his imagery to highlight our fragility, which he compares to 'the sweet nests of a multitude of ants', emptied and buried in an instant, by 'a little apple, falling from a tree'.[65] This description is comparable to that of Voltaire, who depicted the Lisbon Earthquake in 1755 in his correspondence, writing of:

> ... a hundred thousand ants, our neighbours ... crushed in a second on our ant-heaps, half, dying undoubtedly in inexpressible agonies, beneath debris from which it was impossible to extricate them, families all over Europe reduced to beggary, and the fortunes of a hundred merchants ... swallowed up in the ruins of Lisbon.[66]

Whilst Timpanaro and others have rightly demonstrated the shift in Leopardi's thought concerning the relationship between people and nature, what they too frequently miss is how this shift led to an adjustment in the means through which Leopardi communicated his ideas. This change prompted a move away from the dialogue as a form and, perhaps in recognition of Rousseau's praise for the consolatory offering of Pope's philosophical poem 'Essay on Man', towards Leopardi's own work of consolation – 'La ginestra'.

Highlighting the function that laughter had previously fulfilled in his work, in his dialogue 'Timander and Eleander', Leopardi suggested that ridiculing our woes could be a source of comfort, when he wrote:

> By laughing at our woes, I find some comfort; and I seek to bring some to others in the same way. If this is not granted me, I still hold it certain that laughing at our woes is the only profit we can gain from them, and the only remedy to be found in them, you must not think that I have no compassion for humanity. But not being able to cure it by any effort, any art, my labour, any compromise; I consider it far more worthy of man and of manganous despair, to laugh at our common woes, than to set myself to sighing, weeping and screeching along with the rest of them, or encouraging others to do likewise.[67]

In 'La ginestra', he grapples again with such ideas, asking how we should respond to our foolish inclinations when he asks: 'mortal unhappy race, what notion of you finally assails my heart?', answering: 'it's hard to say' whether '... it's laughter or pity that prevails'.[68] Such a resolve to reconsider his assumption that laughter and ridicule should take precedence as a suitable response had consequences for the form that his later work would take, and motivated a move away from ridiculing dialogues, towards a form of poetry that offers a momentary sense of hope. Moreover, the shape of this poetry corresponds to that previously outlined in Eleander's description of poetic works that 'move the imagination', which leave noble sentiments in the reader's mind. In doing so, this aspect of this work marks a departure from Leopardi's earlier choice to 'rouse [his] poor country and poor century', making use of the Lucianic 'weapons of ridicule' in his dialogues, and an arrival at his consolatory poetry, 'La ginestra' [1393].

Next, I highlight the importance of enthusiasm, dignity and strength for Leopardi, whose insights arose out of his engagement with the work of Staël. Leopardi's late philosophical poetry was shaped by his admiration for works of art whose impressions are long-lasting, by virtue of the 'dignified attitude and depth of feeling' in a way this is demonstrable. Like those ancient works he praised, in 'La ginestra', he sought to arouse enthusiasm by depicting a 'great soul and a dignified attitude', hoping to initiate deep feeling by portraying not only 'misfortune itself' but, also, crucially: 'the power over this misfortune that the soul retains'. In the case of the farmer, his misfortune was his continuing vulnerability in the face of 'the progress of the fearful boiling' from 'the inexhaustible womb' of Mount Vesuvius, while the power over his misfortune he evoked was his resolve to refuse to comply with nature's appetite for destruction in the meantime, by attending to his family, nest and field with unwavering love.[69] Considering the property of 'works of genius', which Leopardi believed could counteract 'a state of extreme dejection' and provide a kind of restoration of ones' spirit by deploying the weapons of feeling and enthusiasm, in a manner that 'opens and revives the heart' in the *Zibaldone*, Leopardi wrote in 1820:

> It is a property of works of genius that, even when they represent vividly the nothingness of things, even when they clearly show and make you feel the unhappiness of life, even when they express the most terrible despair, nevertheless to a great soul that finds itself in a state of extreme dejection, disenchantment, nothingness, boredom, and discouragement about life, or in the most bitter and *deathly* misfortune (whether on account of lofty, powerful passions or something else), such works always bring consolation, and rekindle enthusiasm, and, though they treat and represent nothing but death, they restore, albeit momentarily, the life that it had lost. And so, while that which is seen in the reality of things grieves and kills the soul, when seen in imitation or any other form in works of genius (e.g., in lyric poetry, which is not, properly speaking, imitation) it opens and revives the heart.
>
> [260]

This reflection gives us an appreciation of Leopardi's views on how to make sense of nothingness and seeming indifference, the theme he articulates particularly strongly in the final stanza of 'La ginestra'. It is true that, as Timpanaro focuses on in his analysis, 'La ginestra' depicts 'the most terrible despair', closing on a note of disenchantment, nothingness and discouragement about life, a despair in which he describes may also relate to 'the most bitter and *deathly* misfortune (… on account of lofty, powerful passions or something else)'. However, Timpanaro's reading fails to give due accord to Leopardi's equally significant aspiration to imitate works of genius, that, when read and meditated on, 'always bring consolation, and rekindle enthusiasm' by reviving our passions and opening our hearts.

Considering the desirable effects of works of genius, Leopardi held that such works had the power to help us overcome indifference and insensibility. Arguing in late 1820 that 'all greatness is itself a kind of beauty and greatness that fills the soul when it is conveyed by a work of genius', Leopardi described how they seem to 'enlarge the reader's soul, to raise it up and to make it take satisfaction in itself and its despair' **[260]**. Exploring this topic further, Leopardi continued:

In addition, the feeling of nothingness is the feeling of something dead and deathly. But when this feeling is vivid, as in the case I am describing, its vividness prevails in the reader's mind over the nothingness of the thing that it makes him feel, and the soul receives life (if only fleetingly) from the very force with which it feels the perpetual death of things, and its own death. For no small effect of knowing the great nothing, and no less painful, is the indifference and insensibility that it very commonly inspires, and must naturally inspire, toward nothingness itself. This indifference and insensibility is removed by the reading or contemplation of a work of genius: it makes us sensitive to the nothingness of things, and this is the main cause of the phenomenon I have discussed.

[261]

In this light, the vividness of Leopardi's portrayal of the inevitability of the destruction in time of our lives, loves and even civilisations, which so struck Timpanaro, illuminates his success in inspiring a feeling of nothingness. However, more attention is due to Leopardi's commitment to ensuring that the contemplation of his work, whose acquaintance with works of genius I strive to reveal and has also been examined by Emanuele Severino, removes 'indifference and insensibility'. In short, Leopardi's response to the faults he finds with these features of his age is to strive, with his lyric poetry, to encourage enthusiasm through his depiction of nobility and strength of character.

One of the ways in which we can see how Leopardi's considerations of Staël's examination of 'works of genius' shaped his work is in the way he depicts a 'great soul and dignified attitude'. In his portrayal of a noble stance adopted in the face of mortality, Leopardi depicts a dignified attitude that corresponds to the idea of strength that he admired in artists, which applies equally to those seeking to strengthen their characters. Writing in early October 1820, Leopardi reflected on the power of a strength that is calm:

> You need a time of strength, but a strength that is tranquil, a time of actual genius rather than of actual enthusiasm (that is, an act of genius rather than of enthusiasm), the influence of past, future, or habitual enthusiasm rather than its presence, and we might even say its twilight

rather than its midday. Often, the best time is the moment that follows the experience of enthusiasm or feeling, when the soul, though calm, goes back and rides the waves once more after the storm, and recalls with pleasure that past sensation. This is perhaps the most suitable and most frequent time for the conception of an original subject, or the original parts of a subject.

[258]

Here, Leopardi elucidates his ambition to evoke enthusiasm in order to later facilitate a 'strength that is tranquil'. The value he ascribes to such a strength affirms Staël's alignment of nobility, peacefulness and 'the true image of tranquillity in strength' that he found in *Corinne*. Here, this is portrayed in Staël's description of two Egyptian statues of lions at the foot of the Cordonata in Rome and the equestrian statue of Marcus Aurelius on the Capitoline Hill, works of art which embodied the virtues that would become central to his depiction of a quietly strong and dignified attitude in 'La ginestra'.

Shortly, I turn to look more closely at the way Leopardi drew from Seneca, Aurelius and other, more recent thinkers, to forge the consolatory philosophy that marked his departure from the mode of satire he found in the dialogues of writers ranging from Lucian to Bruno to Voltaire.[70] Before doing so, I firstly wish to highlight an important passage in the *Zibaldone* that helps to illuminate the degree to which Leopardi considered the notion that the way in which consolation is offered can have an important impact on whether its recipient is likely to respond with resolve or apathy. Here, the theme of consolation reappears, which he also dealt with in 'Copernicus', where the Sun mocked people's tendency to argue in the face of evidence 'so they will be more consoled'. Early on in the *Zibaldone*, in 1819, Leopardi recorded an observation concerning his mother's attempt to ease the distress of his younger brother, Pietrino, who had lost the stick he was playing with out of the window:

> Once my mother said to Pietrino, who was crying because Luigi threw his little stick out of the window: 'Don't cry, don't cry, because I would have thrown it out myself.' And he was comforted by the

thought that he would have lost it anyway. Observations about this very common reaction in people, and about a related reaction, namely that we are comforted and pacified by convincing ourselves that the particular good could not be obtained, or that the evil in question could not be avoided, and we therefore try to convince ourselves of that and are desperate when we fail, even though the evil remains the same in every way. See p. *188*. See in this respect Epictetus's *Handbook*.

[65]

In this passage, it is noteworthy that Leopardi considers the pacificism that arises from the common reaction in people, who are 'comforted … by convincing ourselves that the particular good could not be obtained' and resolve to conclude that 'the evil in question could not be avoided'. This observation helped to shape his philosophical thinking, elucidating the nature of the relationship between believing in the inevitability of bad things happening and the way this so easily leads to an abandonment of any hopes of bringing about change. By bringing home the negative effects of responding this way to our aversion to suffering, such a reflection underlines the importance of attending to our need for consolation thoughtfully.

Regarding his reference to the Stoic philosopher Epictetus (l.c. 50 – c. 130 CE), whose *Handbook* Leopardi translated in 1825, Mario Fubini, Pamela Williams and others have pointed out the significance of Leopardi's engagement with his ideas, which can be seen, for example in the ending to 'Parini, or Concerning Fame', found in the *Operette*.[71] According to Epictetus, philosophy was deeply immersed in life, and there is a clear distinction to be drawn between teaching about life and life itself. Explaining this notion in his short handbook of ethical advice the *Handbook*, Epictetus argued:

> A carpenter does not come up to you and say 'Listen to me discourse about the art of carpentry', but he makes a contract for a house and builds it … Do the same thing yourself. Eat like a man, drink like a man … get married, have children, take part in civic life, learn how to put up with insults, and tolerate other people.[72]

As the Neoplatonist Simplicius claimed, for Epictetus: 'One must produce the actions that are taught by discourses. The goal of discourse is actually actions.'[73] Echoing this notion in 'Parini', written in 1824, Leopardi wrote:

> And truly, if the principal subject of literature is human life, and the first object of philosophy to guide our actions, there is no doubt that action is much worthier and more noble than meditation and writing, as the end is more noble than the means, and as affairs and things matter more than words and discourses. Indeed, no mind is created by nature to study; nor is man born to write, but only to act.[74]

Similarly, as I will go on to demonstrate, Leopardi also drew inspiration for regarding the importance of taking part in civic life as a good citizen from Aurelius, who served as Emperor to Rome.

A philosophy of consolation

Appreciating the need for consolation that Rousseau expressed in his letter to Voltaire, Leopardi sought to provide this in his work in a way that invoked enthusiasm for action as a guard against inclinations to resign ourselves to inaction, believing we cannot secure better lives for ourselves. An important critic who has examined the role of consolation in 'La ginestra' is Williams, who helped translate the *Zibaldone* into English, and whose 1998 article 'Leopardi's Philosophy of Consolation in "La ginestra"', highlighted the significance of the third stanza of Leopardi's poem, known as the 'solidarity stanza'.[75] According to Williams, 'La ginestra', written the year before his death in 1837, should be read as an embodiment of the maturity of his thought, and considered as his 'last will and his testament'. It is here, she argues, where Leopardi delivers his final verdict concerning our relation to nature.[76] Leopardi's work, as I have shown, developed in light of ongoing debates concerning the Lisbon Earthquake, which he transposed on to 'the terrifying mountain, Vesuvius the destroyer', which loomed above him as he wrote.

Against the reading of critics like John Alcorn and Dario Del Puppo, Williams underscores the importance of 'the combative spirit of the poem' which she argues 'is clearly predicated on the blindness and folly of Christian revivalism' contending that it is misleading to refer to motives that include maxims of the Christian faith to highlight the way in which Leopardi depicts noble relations between individuals within society. Whilst in the final stanza of his poem, Leopardi considers the noble attitude to the human predicament on a personal level, the third stanza allows Leopardi to extend Voltaire's contention that a lesson to take from the Lisbon Earthquake, which Leopardi applies to the eruption of Mount Vesuvius, 'ought to teach men not to persecute men'. In his 'solidarity stanza', Leopardi emphasises the commonality of our struggle, arguing that to 'take up arms' against, 'set a trap' or 'make trouble for his neighbor' seems as stupid as to 'battle fiercely with your friends', 'threatening them with your sword', and inciting them to run when 'surrounded by hostile soldiers', 'during the heaviest fighting on the field'.[77]

Highlighting Leopardi's intention to write works in which he would try to re-establish the principles that should form the basis of society to profit to his readers Williams refers to a letter the poet wrote to the secretary to the Prussian Ambassador in Rome, Karl von Bunsen, in which he underscored this ambition. Williams also brings the theme of solidarity to bear on the biblical epigraph of Leopardi's poem, in her analysis, in which she writes:

> The combative spirit in La ginestra derives from the blindness and folly of human beings who will not accept the circumstances of life, the terms on which we have been asked to live. Leopardi's use of the Biblical epigraph of the poem, 'E gli uomini vollero piuttosto le tenebre che la luce', refers to the view without illusions, which is the light, set against the dark false hopes of Christian revivalism, which followed the destruction of so much sophistry and illusion during the Enlightenment. Leopardi's writings had been criticised as narrowly self-interested, negative, and unresponsive to the needs of society in general (see Palinodia, 11. 227–39); his reply is here to state in the solidarity stanza how human beings should stand in relation to one another.[78]

For Williams, 'the solidarity stanza [is] Leopardi's final word on how, given the human predicament, human beings should stand in relation to one another'.[79] His voice, she contends, is a lone one, 'against a facile, evasive, unreflecting optimism', which is at odds with the reality of the human situation while remaining pervasive: 'He is incensed by the lie at the centre of such optimism, in particular by the self-addiction implicit in anthropocentric illusions'.[80] Crucially, Williams underscores that, within Leopardi's condemnation of human conceit, the thinker sets out a moral framework without reference to existing political institutions or specific social reforms, but rather based on the shared nature of our pain.

Arguing that 'La ginestra' can be seen as an extension of Leopardi's endeavour in translating Epictetus' *Handbook* to help others in the way Epictetus' work had helped him, Williams argues that his poem 'is an inducement not to harm other people and thus to reduce their suffering'.[81] Importantly, she contends that, for Leopardi, the moral framework of his work rests upon the universal principle of suffering. 'The foundation for social cohesion', she writes, 'is each individual's capacity for suffering'.[82] Evoking this point further, she highlights the multitude of ways that the images of his poem emphasize the dangers and the distress of individual's experience, which are enhanced by their pointlessness and changelessness. Resisting the contention that Leopardi is blind to the significance of social context, Williams argues:

> Leopardi was well aware that suffering is determined by social context in different places and at different times of history, that what caused one person harm did not cause harm to another or that individuals suffered differently from similar causes at different times of their lives. However relative the concept was, the capacity to suffer could still be the universal basis for moral worth. There are inescapable biological facts that produce common needs: the vulnerability and precariousness of existence remain constant, and given that human beings are human, and given that they exist the way they do, the capacity to feel pain and the desire not to suffer are shared by all.[83]

As Williams argues, for Leopardi, mutual compassion is all the good there is in life and it represents our worth or dignity. Highlighting the significance of the theme of solidarity traversing Leopardi's poem, Williams notes its centrality to scholarship examining the poem's social and political context, since 1948, arguing that his solidarity stanza serves as Leopardi's explanation of the concept of goodness in society. It shows, she argues, how, 'given the human predicament, human beings should stand in relation to one other', setting forth an alternative to the 'rank pride' he criticised throughout the *Zibaldone* and the *Operette*.[84] As Williams demonstrates, Leopardi's work reveals how the 'prerequisite of goodness' is our acceptance of the surety of our impending death, and that our strength or weakness of character is determined by how we relate to this fact:

> Life is a losing battle, we should accept defeat 'nobly', go along with a state of affairs that is certainly not to our advantage. Our acceptance of this state of affairs is the pre-requisite of goodness, the conception of goodness in *La ginestra* cannot be understood properly unless it is placed against this background.[85]

Highlighting the significance of the role of nobility in Leopardi's poem, she also maintains: 'In the last stanza of the poem the ginestra represents the right attitude to the human predicament, an attitude that gives personal nobility to the individual.'[86] Considering this reading in relation to the environmental crisis, it is important to emphasize a distinction that can be discerned between the analyses of Timpanaro and Williams, which have the potential to make a difference between two resulting courses of response to the poem. Firstly, we can accept that we will ultimately perish and choose, in response to being fuelled by fear and overwhelmed by this acknowledgement, not to act. Secondly, we might resolve to live in accordance with a conception of goodness and nobility while accepting our mortality. The latter of these, which, by virtue of various other excerpts from Leopardi's work that I have highlighted elsewhere, particularly in relation to his conception of 'works of genius' I believe is the most aligned with Leopardi's intent, is supported by Williams' interpretation of the last stanza. This also strikes me as having the most potential for being generative in informing our response to the overlapping crises we are confronted with today.

According to Negri, whose analysis aligns with Williams, Leopardi's final poem 'theorizes human community and the urgency of liberation', folding poetry into ethics to invent new figures of freedom.[87] Highlighting the extent to which Leopardi fulfilled his ambition of providing a diversion from a collapse into despair, Negri reflected in *Flower of the Desert* of the impact of contemplating Leopardi's work during a period in which he was engaged in a personal and political struggle. Here, Negri wrote:

> [T]his research helped me. In rereading Leopardi during the eighties, the years of the worst restoration after the crisis of 1968 and as we were plunging into the crisis of real socialism, this reading allowed me to reconstruct the stages of a philosophical and political discourse that proposed a project of transformation, beyond every illusion but with the capacity to imagine a new subjectivity and new heavens. I do not believe that this experience was mine alone or that it was a matter of individuals experiences. It is certainly singular, but by virtue of this singularity it is multiple. It involves not only Leopardi's experience, but refers to all periods of crisis in modernity: it concerns the Italian situation as well as the French, the European as well as the American. Leopardi's discourse is extremely potent [*puissant*].[88]

As Negri elucidates, the relevance of Leopardi's work extends beyond individuals, by proposing a project of transformation with the capacity to imagine a new subjectivity.

'A mere speck in the universe' and Leopardi's just society of citizens

As Giuseppe de Lorenzo argued in 'The Cosmic Conceptions of Leopardi', published in 1954, Leopardi took pleasure in proclaiming the concordance of his philosophy with that of the philosophers of antiquity, including that of Stoic thinkers, and even if they disagreed with one another.[89] Such harmony is particularly evident in the way Leopardi deals with the theme of consolation. In addition to expressing interest in the notion of consolation in his consideration of his mother's attempts to calm his younger brother, Leopardi also made concerted attempt to quell the anxiety that so frequently determines our response to our own mortality, which remains a problematic theme in Timpanaro's account of Leopardi's work. Seeking to reduce our suffering, Leopardi critically examines our fear, recognizing this as contributing to the distress we burden ourselves with. Throughout his philosophical thinking, he referred to the Stoic philosopher Seneca (*c*.4–65 CE), who played an important role in the consolatory tradition, which dating back to the fifth century BC, considered how to respond to the prominent role that trauma and loss had in the Ancient World when death usually came at an earlier age than in today's West.[90] In 1822, Leopardi praised Seneca's subtlety of style in the *Zibaldone*, considering the thinker whose work included the consolations written for Helvia, Marcia and Polybius [70].

As Amy Olberding has highlighted in her work on Seneca, the Stoic's insights in his letter on suicide and his work 'On Anger' allow the thinker to proffer 'a distinctively therapeutic version of Stoicism that takes as its principal charge the alleviation of anxiety about death'.[91] She contends that such anxiety, for Seneca, 'appears to conceive reconciliation to mortality a foundational cure before which many other maladies give way'.[92] Leopardi aligns himself with such positions in his work, where he takes up Seneca's strategies for dispelling grief as part of his endeavour to provide an alternative to the metaphysical optimism, which he criticised as a display of cowardice.

As I already mentioned previously, in his *Dialogues*, Seneca considered topics ranging from providence, the happy life, life's brevity, anger, leisure, tranquillity, gift-giving, forgiveness and more. In his work, Seneca decried our position in the cosmos, challenging the dominant anthropocentric views of his time by emphasizing humans' relatively tiny role in the scheme of the broader universe.[93] In *Natural Questions*, which Seneca wrote around AD 79, he minimizes, for example, the importance of Rome and her empire, relating them to the vastness of the cosmos. As he writes:

> The mind cannot despise colonnades, and ceilings gleaming with ivory, and topiary forests and rivers channelled into houses until it has toured the entire world and until, looking down from on high at the earth – tiny, predominantly covered by sea, and, even when it rises above it, mainly uncultivated, and either burnt or frozen – it has said to itself, 'This is that pinprick that is carved up among so many nations by sword and fire!'[94]

Surveying the world in an attempt to lift the mind above narrow human concerns, Seneca described the Earth as: 'a mere pinprick on which you sail, on which you wage war, on which you lay out your kingdoms, minute even when the ocean breaks on either side of them'.[95] This practice is taken up by Leopardi, who borrows Seneca's imagery depicting 'the earth and sea' as 'in truth no greater than a speck', in 'La ginestra', extending the theme he previously introduced elsewhere, in dialogues such as the 'Earth and Moon', and in his depiction of existence as 'only a spot' in his refutation of optimism in the *Zibaldone*.[96]

As Martha Nussbaum has examined in her work 'Kant and Stoic Cosmopolitanism', published in 1997, Kant too makes use of Seneca's imagery in his Second Critique, where he describes the loss of our vital force as giving our matter back to the planet, which in turn Kant describes as 'a mere speck in the universe'. Offering a consideration of how reflecting on our position within the context of the external universe undermines our 'importance as an animal creature', in *Critique of Practical Reason* (1788), Kant writes:

> The first view of a countless multitude of worlds annihilates, as it were, my importance as an animal creature, which after it has been for a short time provided with vital force (one knows not how) must give back to the planet (a mere speck in the universe) the matter from which it came.[97]

According to him, cosmopolitanism can be understood as a necessary step towards 'attaining a civil society which can administer justice universally', thereby resolving the 'greatest problem for the human species' by attending to the 'matrix within which all the original capacities of the human race may develop'.[98] For Kant, the more often and steadily one reflects on the 'countless multitude of worlds', the more we find our minds full of admiration and reverence, and find ourselves reminded that we are also ultimately fated, regardless of our earthly efforts, to return to the matter from which we came. Considering the influence of Stoic cosmopolitanism of Seneca, Aurelius and Cicero on Kant's thought, Nussbaum evaluates the relationship between such thinkers' ideas and Kant's 1795 work, *Perpetual Peace: A Philosophical Sketch*. Highlighting Kant's ambition to contain global aggression and promote universal respect for human dignity, Nussbaum describes how, for Kant:

> [this] will give us something far better to do with our time than to wait for the call of Being, or even to contemplate the horrors, many though there surely are to contemplate ... in short, if we want to give the world a paradigm from the ancient Greco-Roman worlds to inform its engagement with the political life, in a time of ethnic violence, genocidal war and widespread disregard for human dignity, it is this one that we should select.[99]

As Nussbaum notes, although Kant only discusses Stoic ideas in a brief and general way, and without precise textual detail, his ideas about cosmopolitan humanity show evidence of having been profoundly shaped by ancient Greek and Roman Stoicism, where the notion of the 'world-citizen' was first developed philosophically.[100] As was the case with Kant's work, Leopardi's thought also bears the markings of Stoic considerations although these are frequently more explicit. For Leopardi, this is evident in his insistence on the value of citizenship – which Paul Hamilton has examined in a chapter titled 'Leopardi and the Proper Conversation of a Citizen' published in 2013, where he argues that Leopardi's pessimism is '... generative of a sense of the community of truly authentic, because un-illusioned, citizens' – as well as in the importance he ascribes to the development of our moral capacity.[101]

According to Kant's categorical imperative, moral actions are necessary 'without reference to any purpose' and concern themselves solely with 'the form of action and the principle from which it follows'.[102] Just as Kant, who in his moral philosophy was able to recognize our material finitude and maintain his commitment to the moral worth of our actions, Leopardi also holds space in his later poetry not only for a truthful consideration of our standing in the universe, but also for insisting on the value of choosing to adhere to an ethical code.[103]

As well as being informed by the work of Seneca, as the translators of the *Zibaldone* have pointed out, Leopardi's relation to typical Stoic spiritual exercises is brought to light when considered in relation to Pierre Hadot's work, *Philosophy as a Way of Life*.[104] Considering in this work the ideas of the Roman emperor Aurelius, in his study, Hadot highlights the centrality to the Stoic's thought of the spiritual exercise known as the 'view from above', which Leopardi scatters references to throughout 'La ginestra'. In Book IX of his *Meditations*, where Aurelius set out his spiritual exercise, the philosopher issues a reminder to gain perspective on the problems and challenges we face in life.[105] This suggestion from Aurelius reads:

> 'Look from above' at the spectacle of myriad herds, myriad rites, and manifold journeying in storm and calm; diversities of creatures who are being born, coming together, passing away. Ponder, too, the life led by others long ago, the life that will be led after you, the life being led in uncivilized races; how many do not even know your name, how many will very soon forget it and many who praise you perhaps will very soon blame you; and that neither memorial nor fame nor anything else at all is worth a thought.[106]

For him, embracing our mortality and reflecting on our impermanence is the key to living with presence:

> The speed with which all of them vanish – the objects in the world, and the memory of them in time. And the real nature of the things our senses experience, especially those that entice us with pleasure or frighten us with pain or are loudly trumpeted by pride. To understand

those things – how stupid, contemptible, grimy, decaying, and dead they are – that's what our intellectual powers are for. And to understand what those people really amount to, whose opinions and voices constitute fame. And what dying is – and that if you look at it in the abstract and break down your imaginary ideas of it by logical analysis, you realize that it's nothing but a process of nature, which only children can be afraid of. (And not only a process of nature but a necessary one.)[107]

While it may seem strange to suggest that we can derive a call to action from Leopardi's use of Stoic imagery revealing the Earth to be a mere speck in the universe, it is worth noting that the intention of Aurelius in inviting such an exercise was to minimize our anxiety surrounding our woes and problems, which, in its most severe form can render us incapacitated by despair.[108] The thought of Aurelius encourages consideration for the broader picture of life, as a means for potentially alleviating a present pain.[109] Such exercises not only underpinned Leopardi's cosmic pessimism, but also shape the ethics he provides in 'La ginestra', where Leopardi describes 'this mere grain of sand called earth' amongst stars 'infinite in size and number'.[110] Taking up Aurelius' call to reflect on our cosmic significance, and his considering in *Meditations* that, 'if you want to talk about people, you need to look down on the earth from above', Leopardi asks in his poem: 'how do I think of you then, sons of men?' reminding us to consider our lives from such a universal perspective.[111]

Calming fear of the pain of death

The final example of the theme of consolation in Leopardi's work, which culminated in 'La ginestra' I turn to consider here, exemplifies how he brought ancient themes to bear on examples pertinent to his time, in relation to the ideas of thinkers including Frederik Ruysch (1638–1731), Bernard le Bovier de Fontenelle (1657–1757) and Comte de Buffon (1707–88). Leopardi's presentation of our relationship to death in 'La ginestra' returns to themes he had previously considered in the *Operette* in 'The Dialogue of Frederick Ruysch and His Mummies', written between 16 and 23 August 1824. Leopardi's work bears the imprint of his engagement with the thought of Fontenelle, in whose popular 1686 book *Conversations on the Plurality of Worlds* (*Entretiens sur la pluralité des mondes*), the writer made his central interlocutor a woman, allowing him to describe the new cosmology of the Copernican world view from a woman's perspective. Fontenelle had also been the secretary of the Royal Academy of Sciences, where the Dutch embalmer Frederik Ruysch, who Leopardi resolved to deploy as a character in his work, had briefly been a member. Although Fontenelle did not personally know Ruysch, his elegy to the figure in his history of the Royal Academy of Sciences was, alongside a study produced by Johann Friedrich Schreiber, one of the only two available sources from which nineteenth-century authors took their information on Ruysch.[112]

In Leopardi's dialogue, he uses the embalmer to think through his ideas relating to our mortality, which, as I will shortly show, also bore the markings of his engagement with the thought of Comte de Buffon. Opening in verse and adopting the viewpoint of the dead, Leopardi's work throws into question prevalent ways of relating to mortality found in Western cultures, paving the way for his examination of how we ought to relate to death in his mature vision. Portraying a dialogue between Ruysch, whose anatomy skills and revolutionary embalming techniques earned him the nickname the 'artist of death', Ruysch liaises with a group of corpses who came alive after midnight and disturbed him as he worked in his laboratory with their chorus. Having been permitted quarter of an hour to talk before returning to death, Ruysch resolved to make the most of his opportunity to learn from the experience of his subjects, asking what it is like to be dead.[113] The following conversation, in which Leopardi calms our fear surrounding death, ensued:

> RUYSCH: A thousand things to ask you spring to mind. But as time is short, and leaves no room for choice, let me know briefly what you felt in body and mind at the moment of death.

MUMMY: I didn't notice the moment of death itself.
THE OTHER MUMMIES: Nor did we.
RUYSCH: How could you not notice it?
MUMMY: Well, for example, just as you are never aware of the moment you fall asleep, however much you set your mind to it.
RUYSCH: But falling asleep is a natural thing.
MUMMY: And do you think that death is not natural? Show me a man, or an animal, or a plant, that does not die.[114]

Explaining to Ruysch that they felt no pain on the point of death, the Mummies refute the common assumption that death is exceedingly painful, describing it not as a feeling, but instead the very opposite. Relaying the general fear that 'the feeling of death is exceedingly painful', Ruysch describes to the Mummies: '... those who hold to the belief, all of them, or nearly all, agree with what I say; that is, that death is by its very nature, and beyond all comparison, a most intense pain.'[115] This conversation captures the attention that Leopardi paid to considerations regarding commonly held views surrounding death and highlights how the philosopher brought to bear the thought of Buffon, whose early considerations of what evolution means for the hierarchical position of humanity he was also informed by, on his consideration of death. For example, as we can see from Leopardi's first mention of Buffon, which appeared in the *Zibaldone*, he considered Buffon's natural history in relation to the potential pain one would feel during the 'separation of the soul from the body' Leopardi referred to in 'Frederick Ruysch and his Mummies'.[116] As Leopardi wrote four years prior on October 1820 of Buffon:

> In his *Histoire naturelle de l'homme*, Buffon challenges those who believe that the separation of the soul from the body must be very painful in itself. To his arguments add the following, which is perhaps the most convincing. If we choose to regard the soul as material, this would immediately rule out the question of separation, and death would be nothing other than the extinction of the vital force, which – whatever it consists of – is very rapidly extinguished. But if we consider it as something spiritual, is the soul perhaps a limb, which has

to be detached from the body, and therefore with great pain? Or is it not rather the case that, whatever the bonds between spirit and substance, they are certainly not physical, and the soul is not torn off like a limb but leaves naturally when it can no longer remain, in the same way that a flame goes out and leaves the matter that can no longer sustain it, and in this, to use an image, we neither see nor remotely suppose that any violence of pain is involved for the combustible material or the flame.

[Z282]

Leopardi's dialogue represents an example of his attempts to bring together Seneca's consolatory stance with the work of more recent thinkers, by relating to Buffon's refutation of the pain felt at the moment of death. Describing the moment of death in relation to Buffon in the *Zibaldone*, Leopardi reframes the traditional notion that the separation of the soul and the body should be seen as something violent, and suggests that it could instead be viewed as analogous to birth:

When it enters the body, it does so insensibly, and we are certainly unaware of it. Thus, its exit must also be without sensation, and quite different from our usual way of conceiving it. Just as people do not register or feel the beginning of their existence, so they do not feel or register its end, and there is no precise moment of consciousness or feeling involved in either the former or the latter.

[283]

These considerations show Leopardi's interest in recognizing our fear of death, and his sympathizing with the fear we often approach it with. In both the *Operette* and the *Zibaldone*, he considered an alternative to our usual way of conceiving death in a manner capable of offering a consolatory approach to our fear by suggesting that the moment of death may be 'easy, light and gentle', rather than, as Ruysch imagined it 'a most intense pain'.[117] Such an example is one of many that shows Leopardi's interest in recognizing the power of our fears to ignite our imagination, prompting us to fear the worst in a way that easily leads to us becoming consumed by it.

Crucially, as we have seen that several theorists have examined, the theme of our anxiety around death traverses Leopardi's poem.

Examining his work with these aspects of his thought to be found elsewhere in the *Zibaldone* and the *Operette* in mind helps to counter popular images of the unrelenting severity of Leopardi's thought, however, and serves to highlight a consolatory aspect of his philosophy that tends to be overlooked. This is especially poignant given that the difficulty we find in contending with our mortality traverses the ages. As Gillian Rose alluded to in her 1994 lecture on time and death, delivered at the University of Exeter's 'Against Time: Anachronism and the Human Sciences' conference, in which she advocated for the adoption of a courageous stance in the face of our mortality, Rose reflected on how: 'the inability to die has become the work of philosophy'. Unlike in the *Zibaldone*, in Leopardi's dialogue, it is the Mummies that give voice to the refutation of the commonly held idea concerning the intense feeling affiliated with death, when they respond to Ruysch in alignment with Buffon's viewpoint, questioning:

> [H]ow can it be that an intense feeling has anything to do with death? Or indeed, that death itself is by its very nature an intense feeling? When the ability to feel is not only scant and debilitated, but reduced to such a minimal thing that it languishes and is annihilated, do you think that a person is capable of strong feeling?[118]

Bringing such a stance to our biological frailty in 'La ginestra', as Negri has highlighted, Leopardi manages to intervene on the terrain he describes. This poem is the space in which Leopardi establishes his ethics, allowing him to ask, as Negri has argued:

> Is there an alternative, a way of rearticulating life and love and grasping their place and time? Does a hope of regaining the vigor of a natural and heroic childhood, of snatching the morals of life away from death, exist?[119]

The affirmative answer lies in Leopardi's insistence on developing and adhering to an ethical framework of courageous resistance even in the face of our known mortality and place in the universe. The recourse we can find in his work to the notions of the Greeks and the Romans demonstrates how he saw his writings as forming part of the process of *'recovering what has been lost'* through a renewal of the political and moral practices of ancient civilisations. The potential of such a project, for Leopardi, was its power to help us to emerge from the barbarous times that he believed we had yet to emerge from by virtue of the proportion of humanity whose suffering was rendered insignificant, thereby falsifying any claim to civilisation [**4289**]. The arguments of Bruno Latour, particularly in *We Have Never Been Modern* (1993), throw into question our assumptions about the consequences of the rise of science, urging us to rethink the definition and constitution of modernity, themes which overlap in important ways with Leopardi's insights, and open up new lines of enquiry.

Whilst Timpanaro has argued that to consider Stoic philosophy in relation to Leopardi's thought involves a departure from its impulses, I have sought to highlight that rather, the extent to which themes borrowed from ancient civilisation were pervasive throughout Leopardi's work reveals the strength of their significance to him. The themes appear as central to his project of social improvement and finding a way out of barbarous times, impacting on the shape of his work, and informing his response to his conviction that people too readily refuse to confront reality, preferring instead to seek comfort in illusions that will ultimately bring them harm.[120]

The political risk of acquiescing to nihilism

I hope to have made a convincing case that, despite the claims of some critics, the theme of consolation in fact plays an important role in Leopardi's late philosophical work. Considering Timpanaro's reading of Leopardi in the context of the overlapping crises we face today, I have tried to suggest that Timpanaro is too quick to overlook the generative potential that Leopardi appeared to discern of acknowledging the grief involved in facing the inescapably dolorous aspects of the human condition and responding to it with great care. As Leopardi appears to have understood, the temptation to assume that our actions have no power, or to concede to our despair too easily have the effect of turning away from our already diminishing chances of living full lives. In a time of astute environmental and political crisis like today, the risks associated with adopting such a position are difficult to overstate.

I turn to consider Leopardi's ethics in relation to the present political moment next, where I set out some examples of the mounting evidence to show the willingness of the world's largest climate polluters to preserve their profits, regardless of the costs to life, and governments' readiness to allow this in order to retain power. In light of such evidence, there has been an increase in calls for more direct action, from theorists like Andreas Malm in works like *How to Blow Up a Pipeline* (2021). Additionally, in *White Skin, Black Fuel: On the Danger of Fossil Fuel Capitalism* (2021), where the authors provide an account of the far right's role in the climate crisis, Malm and the Zetkin Collective examine some important possibilities to keep in mind, in a future where climate denialism is a less viable strategy, warning most notably, of the possibility of the use of 'climate nihilism' as a tool used by companies to retain their profits, with the danger of culminating in an 'aggressive affirmation'.[121] Keeping Timpanaro's analysis of the 'final formation' of Leopardi's thought in mind, alongside considerations of our place in the universe from a cosmic perspective, I strive to highlight the importance of guarding against the possibility of retreating into despair, given the risk that doing so would too easily allow an assent to the ongoing barbarism of those most responsible for expediting our planet's demise.

In the close of my examination of Leopardi's problematising works, I noted how Rousseau criticised Voltaire for neglecting to offer the consolation he found in the ideas of Pope and Leibniz. Although the content of Leopardi's work is deeply critical of the metaphysical optimism of Pope and Leibniz, as I have shown, 'La ginestra' bears the mark of their imprint, by heeding the importance, outlined by Rousseau to Voltaire, to attend to our apparent need for consolation, in order to ultimately support our ability to see things as they are. In the next section, I examine the limits of Leopardi's thought, which I argue is at its most problematic when Leopardi depicts a warlike relationship between people and nature.

The limits of Leopardi's thought

The following section looks at what I take to be, broadly, two of the most limiting aspects of Leopardi's final ethical position as it relates to environmental thinking and activism today. The first of these explores how his conclusion regarding our relationship with nature unwittingly helps perpetuate the frameworks of thought he was critical of in his critique of Christianity. My second appraisal examines the ease with which Leopardi overlooks the political opposition standing in the way of facilitating global and intergenerational ecological justice, which I have previously alluded to.

At 15th meeting of the Conference of the Parties to the UN Convention on Biological Diversity summit, known as COP15, which took place from 7 to 19 December 2022, the Danish economist, and Executive Director of the United Nations Environment (UNEA) Programme, Inger Andersen captured the state of our current relationship with nature, as she described: 'As far as biodiversity is concerned, we are at war with nature. We need to make peace with nature. Because nature is what sustains everything on Earth ... the science is unequivocal.'[122] Outlining what she describes as the current 'triple planetary crisis' in a speech prepared for delivery at the Opening Ceremony of the G20 Health Ministers' Meeting in late 2021, Andersen had previously asserted:

> The health impacts of the triple planetary crisis of climate change, nature and biodiversity loss, and pollution and waste are clear. Just as the linked threats of infectious diseases with pandemic potential, like COVID-19, are clear ...
>
> ... We are a species in peril, living on a planet in peril. But if we act urgently on the triple planetary crisis and pull the planet out of the emergency room, we can save lives and reduce the burden on healthcare systems.
>
> This means pandemic recovery measures that back green solutions for healthy and climate-resilient systems. This means decarbonization. This means backing solutions that work with nature.[123]

Andersen's remarks highlight the stakes of addressing our way of relating to nature today, helping to highlight the relevance of the most problematic feature of Leopardi's thought, namely, his conviction, which aligns with ideas we can find in Voltaire and later Freud, that we need to stand in opposition to nature in order to forge solidarity.

Violence and nature in the dominant progress story

Although Leopardi often expressed a sense of the way we violate nature, warning of the disastrous consequences if this was left unfettered, his philosophy increasingly came to rest on an opposition he subscribed to, which contributes to perpetuating a broken relationship between ourselves and nature. These problematic moments can be reconsidered, however, in light of the work of recent scholars attending to these ideas, whose work gives us the opportunity to reconstruct Leopardi's ethics in light of new evidence. For example, close analysis of Leopardi's writing reveals his interest in fostering the imagination and creating a radical new vision of the future. We see this in his recognition that we incline towards fear, which leads him to highlight that there is a space of hope that has been too easily abandoned in Western thought. Nonetheless, in his frequent adherence to the notion of a clearcut human/nature dichotomy, seen for example in the Icelander's claims that Nature is 'the declared enemy of men', Leopardi failed to see the negative impact – not only for people but also for the ecosystems we live within – of considering nature to be inimical.[124] In *Making Peace with the Earth* (2013), Shiva emphasises the significance of seeing ourselves within 'the ecological web of life', as she demonstrates the significance of shifting the paradigm today:

> The destructive Anthropocene need not be the only future, we can shift the paradigm. We can look at the destructive impact our species has had on the planet's biodiversity, ecosystems and climate systems and make that shift. An ecological shift entails not seeing ourselves as outside the ecological web of life, it means seeing ourselves as members of the earth family, with the responsibility of caring for other

species and life on earth in all its diversity. It creates the imperative to live, produce and consume within ecological limits and within our share of ecological space, without encroaching on the rights of other species and peoples.[125]

Shiva notes here a theme that I refer to later when I consider the influence of Leopardi's thinking about solidarity on Gilroy's thought, highlighting the importance of 'seeing ourselves as members of the earth family' with responsibility for life on earth in all its diversity. The broken way in which our relationship with nature is considered today, she argues, has enabled a position in which intellectual property rights have been claimed on life forms, creating a situation that she describes as an 'ethical, ecological, and economic perversion'. Demonstrating the damage caused by such perversions, she highlights the epidemic levels of farm sector suicides that have occurred in India over the past twenty years, when, between 1995 and 2018, 4 million farmers in the country, approximately forty-eight every day, took their lives in response to the debt inflicted upon them.[126] Alongside Shiva, Marie-Monique Robin also traces this tragic phenomenon back to the practices of the world's leading producer of Genetically Modified Organisms, Monsanto, who were acquired by Bayer in 2016, and who contributed to the severance of the tie between Indian farmers and the land they toil.[127] Considering the 'not-told story of India's seed', Shiva traces the violence of the 'green revolution' led by Monsanto in the place of the public sector, which purported to increase food production in Third World countries while obtaining patents for genetically modified seeds. She argues that the second green revolution had nothing to do with food security, and everything to do with increasing profits.[128]

Examining Monsanto's contribution to a 'war against the earth' doesn't lead Shiva to despair, however. Instead, she rejects the assumption of the neoliberal model of economic globalisation that there is no alternative. Insisting 'there are alternatives everywhere', Shiva affirms those that still allow us to envisage how we might establish the hope of making peace with the earth. As she highlights:

There are alternatives in indigenous cultures and local economies which people are defending with their lives on the line. Alternatives are emerging as a response to peak oil and climate change, and alternatives are emerging where people face economic closure.[129]

Her work helps to demonstrate the choice we face, of whether to continue blindly, destroying the planet as we go, or to adopt more creative ways of thinking and being, according to which economics, politics and culture all centre the Earth.[130] The former of these two choices aligns with the behaviours Leopardi indicated that he sought to address in outset of 'La ginestra', where he highlighted our love of 'darkness rather than light'. It would also correspond to Berdach's depiction of how, 'like upside-down sunflowers, we turn to the dark side rather than the light', considered by Freud. As Leopardi strives to convince us in his poem, though, we have the means within us to choose differently, and to cultivate the moral forces that would contribute to doing so. Both he and Shiva hold fast to the possibility of responding collectively to our challenges in a generative manner.

Demonstrating the need to bring the limits of the Earth to the core of our ways of life, the British social anthropologist Henrietta Moore has argued that the destruction of nature is the driving force of what she describes as the 'current dominant progress story', that is, the current way of relating to nature, which we need to change. According to Moore: '... this progress story is not inevitable. There are other ways and better stories. A new story of a more expansive prosperity delivered by redefining our relationship to the natural world is possible.' For Moore, similarly as for Shiva, while our collision course with nature feels inevitable, it isn't. Instead, it stems from the dominant vision of what prosperity is. As she argues, when 'a good life' is rooted in economic terms and measured with indicators such as income level, consumption level or employment status regardless of the impact on the world, prosperity can only ever be delivered through economic growth. Such economic progress stories, she argues, only acknowledge nature as an input to the economic machine, leading to a common misperception that the destruction of nature is a regrettable but necessary trade-off for a narrow view of progress. With these notions in mind, Moore argues that we need a new perspective on how we think about prosperity. She cites the Dasgupta Review on the Economics of Biodiversity (2021) to illustrate that we have drawn an unsustainable amount from nature, and must now learn, in order to survive as a species, to evolve in order to halt our destruction of the biodiversity we depend on.[131]

Patrick Vallance has recently made similar arguments in response to the latest report by Intergovernmental Science-Policy Platform on Biodiversity and Ecosystem Services (IPBES). Highlighting the ways in which the harmful activities of people, including habitat destruction, poor farming practices and pollution, have significantly altered ecosystems, he warns that biodiversity is declining at a faster rate than at any time in human history, with many species being driven past the point of recovery. This effect, he explains, reaches far beyond humans, touching upon among all living organisms, and affecting wider ecosystems. According to Vallance, we have overexploited the planet, that now our survival rests on establishing the political will and leadership required to address the challenges of carbon emissions and biodiversity loss.[132]

Shiva also highlights the potential ecological damage caused by the notion of limitless growth when she cites a question raised by Thomas Freidman in the wake of the economic crisis that began in 2008:

> Let's today step out of the normal boundaries of analysis of our economic crisis and ask a radical question –What if the crisis of 2008 represents something much more fundamental than a deep recession? What if it is telling us, that the whole growth model we created over the last fifty years is simply unsustainable, economically and ecologically, and that 2008 was when we hit the wall – when Mother Nature and the market both said 'no more'?[133]

We can read Leopardi's warnings in light of the arguments of these thinkers, and consider his ideas in light of Shiva's demonstration of how corporate globalisation has entrenched the violation Leopardi identified more than two hundred years ago:

> After two decades of corporate globalisation, we now have evidence of its ecological and social costs. A deregulated financial economy gave us the financial crisis: a deregulated food economy has given us a food crisis; a deregulated mining economy has turned every mineral-rich area into a war zone.
>
> The economic crisis that began in 2008, and still continues, forces us to raise questions about the contradiction between a model based on assumptions of limitless growth and a reality with ecological, social, political and economic limits.[134]

For Shiva, wealth fuels our war against nature. Furthering recent critiques of the warped nature of modern accounts of wealth, in *Oneness vs. the 1%* (2018), she builds upon from Oxfam's 2016 report 'An Economy for the 1%' that revealed that the world's richest 1 per cent own as much as the bottom 50 per cent of humanity. Examining the effects of this inequality for the Earth's ecological systems, she contends that the will to exclude embodied by the rise of the 1 per cent translates into an ecocidal and genocidal urge to exterminate:

> 1% is not just a number, it is a system, an economic system shaped by the rich and powerful, where unbridled greed and accumulation are seen as virtues to be rewarded by society, instead of aberrations which must be kept within limits through social and democratic processes. It is a model in which who produces, what is produced, or whether anything at all is in fact produced, are questions that disappear from the economic equation. They are replaced by tools of money-making, money making money, or what Aristotle called 'chrematistics'. It effects an economic apartheid between the haves and havenots, which translates into an ecological apartheid between the lives and live-nots, not just in the human family, but in the earth family. The rise of the 1% embodies a will to exclude, an urge to exterminate. Its inevitable consequences are ecocide and genocide.[135]

This compelling analysis demonstrates how the implications for the planet, society and democracy, of systemic inequality, which symbolises: 'a system of thought and an intellectual paradigm, based on a worldview of separation, extraction and extermination'.[136] By taking account of her demonstration of the need to acknowledge the importance of a harmonious relationship with nature and Moore's call for a reconsideration of the concept of prosperity, which accounts for environmental limits, we can begin to rework Leopardi's proposal to establish an ethics of solidarity. Although in his work, Leopardi raised questions about our assumptions of the limitless nature of the Earth's resources, a key problem with his thinking about nature was his failure to consider how a war against nature frequently in turn paves way for a war against people, particularly those who are opposed to limitless extraction. Today, corporate power and state power increasingly converge and emerge as militarized power. As Shiva has shown, our 'war against the earth' is increasingly used to impose unjust, undemocratic and unsustainable agendas on the Earth and its people.

For those defending their lands against those with vested interest in growth at all costs, this is particularly visible. Global Witness, who count killings of environmental defenders, have reported that a land and environmental defender was killed every two days in the past decade, with activists in Brazil, Colombia, Philippines and Mexico being particularly at risk of suffering violence at the hands of the police and military, who frequently benefit from impunity.[137] Another particularly recent example of the violence faced by those resisting environmental harm – in this case that caused by deforestation – is the police killing of Manuel 'Tortuguita' Terán, who was shot and killed in their efforts to protect the Weelaunee forest in Southeast Atlanta, resisting official's plans to decimate around 300 of 3,500 acres of woodland to make way for the construction of 'Cop City', a $90 million training facility. Progress towards the establishment of this facility within Atlanta's forest remains ongoing, in the face of ample evidence that the protection of forests may be one of our most important natural climate solutions by virtue of their capacity to behave as a 'carbon sink', by absorbing carbon from the atmosphere.[138]

By acknowledging that adopting nature as our enemy was neither as beneficial as Leopardi had imagined it to be, nor required, we can strengthen Leopardi's ethics. Rather than eschewing it entirely, we have a lot to gain from heeding his invitation to nurture greater care for neighbours and non-human others and from paying attention to his appreciation of the strength of our tendency to veer towards destruction. Simultaneously, to avoid falling prey to some of the weaknesses in his thought, we can also benefit from moving away from his insistence on treating nature as our shared enemy, which bears too great a risk of siding with who use violence against groups fighting to protect nature. While such a shift moves away from the letter of Leopardi's thought, in ways we will continue to see, it nonetheless strengthens the solidarity that features as an essential idea in his late philosophy.

Oppositional thinking

In her 1998 book *Fighting Words: Black Women and the Search for Justice*, Patricia Hill Collins provided a way of transcending group-specific politics, based upon Black feminist epistemology. Opening up the prospect of continuous change by taking the experience of Black women in the United States as her starting point, Collins' focus simultaneously extends beyond this social group, thereby expanding its sphere of influence by issuing a significant view of identity politics and oppression. Within her analysis, Collins illuminated the pervasiveness of what she calls 'binary oppositional thinking', a model of 'binary opposites', which she explains: 'constructs everything in one of two mutually exclusive categories (White/Black, man/woman, public/private …'. Capturing the violence inherent in such frameworks of thought, she elucidates: 'Presenting only two options fails to recognise how the two categories gain meaning only in relation to one another.' It ignores, as Collins describes: 'both the interconnectedness of knowledges and the accompanying difficulty of remaining oppositional in a context of multiplicity'.[139] Taking these insights into consideration in relation to Leopardi's late philosophy, we can begin to see how his portrayal of the categories of people and nature as mutually exclusive and necessarily oppositional not only overlooks our interconnectedness with nature, but also adheres to a broader, more pervasive logic. Such a logic – which White described in 'The Historical Roots of Our Ecologic Crisis' in terms of Christianity's establishment of a dualism of man and nature, according to which it was God's will for 'man' to exploit nature for his proper ends – assumes that categories ought to be thought of in binary terms, positing such thinking as higher in value than that which centres diversity, porosity and multiplicity.

Stuart Hall's 1992 essay 'The West and the Rest: Discourse and Power', in which he considers Peter Hulme's account of 'stereotypical dualism' also includes an examination of the construction of categories in this way. Referring to Hulme's 1986 book *Colonial Encounters*, Hall analyses how dualism comes into play in the way non-Western communities are often viewed by the West. His account of stereotyping, given here, captures the late depiction of nature we find in Leopardi's thought:

> A stereotype is a one-sided description which results from the collapsing of complex differences into a simple 'cardboard cut-out'. Different characteristics are run together or condensed into one. This exaggerated simplification is then attached to a subject or place. Its characteristics becomes the signs, the 'evidence,' by which the subject is known. They define its being, its *essence*. Hulme noted that,
>
> 'As always, the stereotype operates principally through a judicious combination of adjectives, which establish [certain] characteristics as [if they were] eternal verities ["truths"], immune from the irrelevancies of the historical moment: [e.g.] "ferocious", "warlike", "hostile", truculent and vindicative" – these are present as innate characteristics, irrespective of circumstances;
>
> ... [consequently, the Caribs] were locked as "cannibals" into a realm of "beingness" that lies beyond question. This stereotypical dualism has proved stubbornly immune to all kinds of contradictory evidence'.[140]

Leopardi's view of nature's 'cruel power' in 'La ginestra' falls into this trap, which, as Halls examines in relation to Hulme's thought, proves stubbornly immune to a range of contradictory evidence.[141] Expanding upon Hulme's notion of 'stereotypical dualism', Hall goes on to examine how such subjects may be split into two halves within such simplifications, to facilitate a hierarchical ordering:

> The world is first divided, symbolically, into good-bad, us-them, attractive-disgusting, civilized-uncivilized, the West-the Rest. All the other, many difference between and within these two halves are collapsed, simplified – i.e. stereotyped. By this strategy, the Rest becomes defined as everything that the West is not – its mirror image. It is represented as absolutely, essentially, different, *other*: the Other. This Other is then itself split into two 'camps': friendly-hostile, Arawak-Carib, innocent-depraved, noble-ignoble.[142]

Critics like Sebastiano Timpanaro and Perry Anderson have observed such a splitting, highlighting in their accounts of the shift in focus at different periods in Leopardi's thought how his consideration of nature is divided into two camps, most notably benign-malign, whilst Michael Caesar has referred to nature in Leopardi in terms of its 'elasticity'.[143]

Thomas Harrison examined the rarity of an 'ontologically rich' notion of nature in Leopardi's work in his 2019 article 'Towards a New Ecological Imagination: Post-Anthropocentric Leopardi', published in a special issue of the journal *Costellazioni* dedicated to Leopardi's thought. Examining the extent to which 'his thinking remains bound to the interests of human subjectivity', Harrison asks why Leopardi continues to endorse a set of human entitlements championed by the Enlightenment: 'Is that because Leopardi continues to endorse a set of human entitlements championed by the Enlightenment?' Even despite having been: 'a dogged foe of many anthropocentric commitments fostered by late-eighteenth and early-nineteenth century Europe'? Further questioning how: 'productive, balanced, and ecological' the notion of nature that Leopardi left us with can be considered to be, Harrison asks:

> What happens, however, if we extend – as indeed we must, to remain consistent with Leopardi's own thought – his critique of anthropocentrism to other dimensions of that thought, including his incriminations of natural existence and its discontents? Does

Leopardi's perspective on human being-in-the-world harbor sufficient resources to promote an ecological ethos?

He gives the response:

> The answer I believe is a qualified yes. Many of those resources are implicit in the faculty of the human imagination, on which Leopardi places great store, and which enables humans to discover ego-transcending values in nature. Other ecological resources lie in the ethics of fortitude, which Leopardi extols in classical civilization, mitigating the frustration of desire and teaching the acceptance of limits. As poet-thinker, Leopardi stood on the threshold of vanquishing anthropocentric ontology and its subjectivist ethos. His theoretical reflections contain the seeds for a decisive undoing of those tools and underpinnings of the subject which are reason, desire, and will, and for clearing the way for the sway of a Nature beyond good and evil.[144]

Harrison highlights fortitude and 'the faculty of the human imagination, on which Leopardi places great store', as examples of the ecological resources in the work of the 'poet-thinker'.[145] My own view aligns with Harrison's in the respects just considered, which inform the considerations that follow, in which I seek to return to the 'seeds for a decisive undoing' within Leopardi's work, to draw out the resources to promote an ecological ethos that remains harboured within his writings.

To return to the points raised by Collins, she cites the philosopher Kwame Anthony Appiah, who captures the scale of the conceptual challenge faced by anyone who tries to subject the Western tradition to critique, as Leopardi does throughout his work. As Appiah describes: 'The terms of resistance are already given to us, and our contestation is entrapped within the Western cultural conjuncture we affect to dispute.'[146] Leopardi – whose philosophical critique inspired Emanuele Severino depiction of him in *In viaggio con Leopardi* ('In Conversation with Leopardi') published in 2015, as a knight playing in a game of chess against Western civilisation – finds himself entrapped in precisely the way that Appiah depicts.[147] Earlier, I sought to suggest that

Leopardi's critique of anthropocentricism overlapped into a critique of the celebration of a culture of extractivism encouraged by philosophers like Bacon.

Leopardi built on this idea in 'Copernicus', where he suggested we are poorly prepared for a time when the Earth's resources run out. He questioned how we might power our streetlamps, ridiculing our separation from the world, and highlighting how it prevents us from recognising life's rebellion. However, ultimately, he was persuaded by Voltaire's reflections concerning 'nature's evil' following the Lisbon Earthquake of 1755 and concluded that nature should be seen as our shared enemy. Despite this drawback in his final position concerning our relation to nature, there is another area in Leopardi's thought that Appiah attends to, where Leopardi's position remains both exemplary and underexamined.

With regard to his reliance on the opposition between humanity and nature, in the final instance, Leopardi's ethics falls back on some of the same tropes of the same religious thought he was so disparaging of. However, despite this drawback of his work, in other aspects, his capacity to speak to contemporary concerns was exemplary. In an article titled 'Dialectics of Enlightenment', published in *The New York Review* in 2019, Appiah subjected Voltaire analysis of slavery to critique, questioning the place given to Voltaire in the history of Enlightenment thought. While noting Voltaire's staunch opposition to slavery and colonialism, Appiah draws attention to Voltaire's views concerning the inherent inferiority of Black people, who he deemed to belong to a different breed or species to white Europeans, highlighting the derogatory descriptions of Africans that appear in Voltaire's *Encyclopédie*.[148] Appiah's article prompted a response in the form of a letter titled 'Voltaire's Tears' from David Ball, who contested that readers would 'have had a more balanced view of Voltaire's attitude on race' had Appiah mentioned the scene in which a slave appears in Chapter 19 of *Candide*.

In his response to Ball's letter, Appiah attributed the importance of Voltaire's place in the history European moral attitudes to his hostility to cruelty. Crucially, he also argued – citing Bentham's relation to animals to support his claim – that Voltaire's position was an example of how one can be opposed to cruelty while still being racist: 'Jeremy Bentham's case for protecting animals from abuse was predicated on their ability to suffer as we do, not to reason as we can.' From these observations, he concluded: 'In the landscape of moral progress, empathy and respect turn out to be different edifices.'[149] While as Ball points out, Voltaire accords the slave in *Candide* empathy, as Appiah notes, Voltaire fails to accompany his empathy for Black people with respect.

In addition to his analysis of the barbarism on which modernity relied in the *Zibaldone*, Leopardi also considered the theme of racial slavery in the *Pensieri*, a collection of aphorisms and reflections, many of which were excavated from the *Zibaldone*, that he had begun to prepare for publication in 1832.[150] Noting the differing ways that Black people were considered in the sixteenth and the nineteenth centuries, and observing the appearance of racial slavery in both periods, Leopardi considered what this meant for the relationship between moral beliefs and actions:

> In the present century, black people are believed to be totally different from white in race and origin, yet totally equal to them with regard to human rights. In the sixteenth century, when blacks were thought to come from the same roots and to be of the same family as white, it was held, most of all by Spanish theologians, that with regard to rights blacks were by nature and Divine Will greatly inferior to us. In both centuries, blacks have been bought and sold and made to work in chains under the whip. Such is ethics; and such is the extent to which moral beliefs have anything to do with actions.[151]

I recall this passage a little later, when I consider the relationship between Leopardi's thought and Gilroy's account of his 'planetary humanism'. I include it here to suggest that, given the limits of Voltaire's work, we can find in Leopardi an alternative and underutilised source from within the history of Western philosophy. His work examines the ethical dearth of racial slavery with more critical depth, critically assessing the relationship between the Christian conviction of the basic equality of all human beings, and the continuation of the slave trade in his own century, throwing into question boasts of moral progress.

To briefly return to the theme of opposition that appears in Leopardi's philosophy, as we have seen, Leopardi's construction allows him to exonerate humanity because it 'makes nature guilty of everything'. Unfortunately, we do not have the means to see how Leopardi might have dealt with observations concerning the dangers of oppositionary thinking, or the alignment between his often-binary thought and the Christianity he subjected to critique. Appiah's assessment of the challenge of critiquing a system from within remains today and is captured in Adorno's proclamation from his assessment of ethics within a damaged life, in which he argued in *Minima Moralia*: 'Wrong life cannot be lived rightly.' This in turn prompted Adorno's examination in *Aesthetic Theory*, and elsewhere, of how autonomous art might intervene on such a terrain.[152] Although we will not find direct responses to the challenges set forth by Collins, Appiah and Hall in Leopardi's body of work, he did leave us with some grounds for conjecture, for example, in his notion of 'works of genius', as well as in his interest in plurality.

Plurality of worlds

Considering now the extent to which we might find the theme of multitude in a different sense in Leopardi's work, we can find a relationship between the way Leopardi considered animality and his philosophical consideration of the 'plurality of worlds'. To consider the significance of plurality for Leopardi, we must consider again the role of Copernicus in his thought, alongside that of Bernard Le Bovier de Fontenelle, who extended the work of Copernicus in relation to the 'plurality of worlds'. In 1819, Leopardi described in the *Zibaldone* the significance of Copernicus' new system in a passage that shares similarities with Kant's reflections in the *Critique of Practical Reason* on the consequences of 'a countless multitude of worlds'. Referring to the ability of the Copernican system's ability to completely change the idea of nature and humanity, Leopardi argued that this insight:

> ... shows man not to be a unique being, as the position, the motion, and the destiny of the earth are not unique, and opens up an immense

field of reflections, concerning the infinite number of creatures which according to all laws of analogy must inhabit the other globes analogous in all respects to our own.

[84]

This is a position that Leopardi explores in relation to animality in 'La ginestra', where he dwells on the lives of animals effected by the eruption of Mount Vesuvius, considering some of these creatures. He describes, for instance the 'ruined houses where the bat conceals its young', the blankets of hardened lava 'where the snake nests and coils under the sun', the lowing cattle in the 'happy farms and fields', and the 'familiar cave-like den' of the hare, reminding us throughout of all the nonhuman inhabitants destroyed by the 'implacable mountain'.[153] Leopardi also appears to extend his consideration of the consequences of the Copernican Revolution in relation to the insights of Fontenelle, whose *Conversations on the Plurality of Worlds*, was published in 1686. Extending Copernicanism, and the new complex universe described within it, Fontenelle's book expanded on the notion of the existence of a plurality of systems, existing alongside our own, made up of other systems of suns and planets, thereby weakening the notion of human life as being at the heart of the universe even further.[154]

Picking up on the significance of the role of 'the multitude' in Leopardi's work, Negri writes in the preface to *Flower of the Desert*:

> In *The Broom*, his last great poem, Leopardi clearly expresses the project of 'making the multitude', the conception of a resistance to domination in the form of a movement of recomposition of singularities. It is not merely a matter of folding poetry into ethics but of inventing new figures of freedom. Today that is our task.[155]

As Negri appears to refer to here, the focus on nonhuman lives in 'La ginestra' serves to recompose the singularities that Leopardi saw as weakened. He conceives this as a form of resistance to domination and an example of the inextricability of Leopardi's poetry and ethics within his work. Moreover, as Murphy has shown in *Antonio Negri: Modernity and the Multitude* (2011), the concept of the multitude is an important one in Negri's thought. Negri uses this to signify the working class in a manner that considers both class and politics, with reference to André Gorz's 1980 book *Farewell to the Working Class*. Writing of his own experience of rereading Leopardi, Negri clarifies the meaning of his reference to the 'recomposition of singularities' we find exemplified in Leopardi's last great poem, when he states:

> In rereading Leopardi during the eighties, the years of the worst restoration after the crisis of 1968 and as we were plunging into the crisis of real socialism, this reading allowed me to reconstruct the stages of a philosophical and political discourse that proposed a project of transformation, beyond every illusion but with the capacity to imagine a new subjectivity and new heavens. I do not believe that this experience was mine alone or that it was a matter of individual experience. It is certainly singular, but by virtue of this singularity it is multiple. It involves not only Leopardi's experience, but refers to all periods of crisis in modernity: it concerns the Italian situation as well as the French, the European as well as the American. Leopardi's discourse is extremely potent [*puissant*].[156]

For Negri, Leopardi's insights have a capacity to capture situations beyond that which they speak of, opening up necessary spaces in which to imagine a new subjectivity. We can see this when we read 'La ginestra', where, when Leopardi writes of the eruption of Mount Vesuvius in AD 79, his references to animality also apply to today's planetary crises, in which over three hundred species are lost to extinction every day.[157]

Before turning to review another weakness in Leopardi's thought, another theorist whose ideas concerning nature may be brought to bear on Leopardi's is Jack Halberstam, who examines the theme of wildness in *Queering Desire* (2020). Describing this as an unbounded space offering sources of opposition to the orderly impulses of modernity, Halberstam provides a resource to extend our thinking about the 'unending spaces', to which Leopardi dedicated his 1819 poem, 'L'Infinito'. Illuminating a radical queer practice, Halberstam's alternative history of sexuality – which transgresses Euro-American notions of the modern liberal subject – highlights the ways that nature prompts us to develop our thinking beyond the oppositionary categories. Attending to the lives and associations that are not lent the privilege of immediate recognition, Halberstam writes:

> The wild, when not figured as either a glorious unspoiled past or an exciting machinic future, when not a prefascist cleaving to war and masculinity nor a postliberal, postpolitical regime of anything goes, can, under certain circumstances, and on account of its now intuitive set of associations with the non-human, the animal, the queer, and the subordinated, be available for the exploration of subaltern and subterranean and particularly racialized forms of queer or perverse desire and embodiment ... But the an/archive of the wildness that lies beyond nature is, above all, a record of stolen life, Black life, Indigenous life, Brown life and death, lives lived well beyond the purview of recognition, respectability, and so on.[158]

Halberstam's invitation to consider the subordinated and the non-human represents the kind of different way of thinking that Leopardi anticipated that Copernicus' discoveries would open up. For Leopardi, one of the 'immense field of reflections' that the discoveries of Copernicus and Fontenelle revealed was an encouragement to apply the notion of the plurality of experiences to the non-human animals we share resources, habitats and significant environmental events with, as we see in 'La ginestra'. Leopardi's appreciation of our inclination towards anthropocentricism and his understanding that we are 'not to be a unique being' inform the considerations in his late poem of the non-human cost of the damage caused by Mount Vesuvius. This approach hints at moments in Leopardi's thought where he appreciated the value of thinking with plurality in mind, but he wasn't able to apply this to his conception of the relationship between humans and nature in his lifetime. Instead, through his final insistence upon two mutually exclusive categories, which he deemed it suitable to pit against one another, he succumbs to a framework of thought which treads on terrain that can too easily become misguided, discriminatory and prejudicial.

that we have so far neglected to take would actually have great benefits for the nation, for nature, for our children and grandchildren.'[164] What differentiates Hansen's analysis from those of Leopardi however are the scientific discoveries made since the philosopher-poet's lifetime. While Leopardi wrote in the early nineteenth century, Hansen was able to emphasize: 'we have all the ingredients we need to meet this challenge – except leadership willing to buck the special financial interests benefiting from business as usual.'[165] Writing to Prime Minister Fukuda to refute the arguments of those who maintain that the concept of 'phasing out all emissions from coal, and taking measures to ensure that unconventional fossil fuels are left in the ground or used only with zero-carbon emissions' would be too inconvenient, he proposes a challenge for people inclined towards such arguments.[166] According to this challenge, Hansen suggested that such individuals to spend a small amount of time composing a letter to be left for future generations to explain their choices:

> The letter should explain that the leaders realized their failure to take these actions would cause our descendants to inherit a planet with a warming ocean, disintegrating ice sheets, rising sea level, increasing climate extremes, and vanishing species, but it would have been too much trouble to make changes to our energy systems and to oppose the business interests who insisted on burning every last bit of fossil fuels. By composing this letter the leaders will at least achieve an accurate view of their place in history.
>
> My experiences in the U.K., Germany, and Japan are representative. My correspondence with other governments, notably Australia, and with several U.S. governors is available on my Web site. Most of the politicians advertised themselves as being 'green,' but what I learned was that, invariably, it amounted to greenwash, demonstrating token environmental support while kowtowing to fossil fuel special interests. To be generous, most of these leaders probably kidded themselves into believing that their modest green efforts were meaningful.[167]

Given that companies whose profits are threatened by the success of campaigns for environmental justice exploit division as a tactic to undermine opposition, this underlines the importance of taking note of the role of solidarity in Leopardi's philosophy. As so many authors and activists, including Shiva, Rich, Klein, Kolbert, Hansen and others, have shown, the success of attempts to maintain a status quo that secures profit growth depends on their ability to keep the public misinformed and weakened by a lack of unity. While Leopardi understood that solidarity and the offer of consolation could bolster our strength in our opposition to nature, we might also wish to consider redirecting the blame at the heart of his ethics once more. Perhaps, we might turn our focus away from nature, and more precisely towards those who actively hoard wealth for the benefit of a small minority, even when it runs the risk of hastening the extinction of vast numbers of species, including our own, and hindering the vitality of our planet.

By examining Leopardi's work through an ecological lens, Sofri's work helped to highlight the significance of Leopardi's recognition of the problem of failing to adjust to accommodate the finitude of dominant sources of energy. Today, as Timpanaro has also suggested, our problem is less a lack of resources, and more a surplus of opposition and an imbalance of power concerning finding sustainable ways of inhabiting our shared world. Given the increasing quantity of examples of companies willing to adopt increasingly unethical approaches to resist change in order to protect their profits, several of which I will touch on shortly, we can benefit from reflecting on Leopardi's examples of sources of consolation which can fortify us, and empower us to identify and fight unethical practices with more unity. Next, I briefly outline two recent examples to underline the significance of tackling political opposition when attending to the environmental crisis today.

Barriers to justice

Last year, in Washington DC, the Committee on Oversight and Reform made great strides in their efforts to reveal the disinformation and greenwashing campaigns of 'Big Oil'. Their tireless work brought to light a host of important documents that are significant in their capacity to demonstrate the industry's massive long-term investments in fossil fuel. In a memorandum dated 14 September 2022, which accompanied the release of a series of email exchanges, internal documents and tweets, the Committee issued their indictment of the fossil fuel industry arising from their investigation, stating:

> Fossil fuel companies have known since the late 1970s that their products contribute to climate change. From 1979 to 1983, fossil fuel companies and the American Petroleum Institute (API) participated in a task force that privately shared climate science research and discussed possible ways to reduce emissions. Despite knowing the truth about climate change, fossil fuel companies continued to contradict prevailing scientific knowledge and inject confusion into the public debate over climate change. During the 1990s, ExxonMobil, Chevron, BP, Shell, API, and the U.S. Chamber of Commerce joined the Global Climate Coalition, which vigorously fought potential climate change regulations and lobbied the U.S. government to derail international climate action to reduce carbon pollution emissions.[168]

Their campaign reveals the danger of waiting for companies like Shell and BP to halt the damage caused by their practices and implement the decisive changes needed to reduce emissions. According to representative remarks made public as a result of the Committee's work, Shell employees acknowledged that net zero emissions threatened their revenue, and consequently argued that focus on the responsibility for meeting shifting emissions targets should lie with society as a whole, so as to protect the company's ability to generate profit, regardless of the expense to our shared planet. They described emissions targets as 'a collective ambition for the world' in an effort to absolve themselves of the responsibility to act and urged their colleagues not to give the impression the company was willing to reduce carbon dioxide emissions to levels that do not make business sense. These documents highlight Big Oil's willingness to greenwash its record through deceptive advertising campaigns that borrow tactics from the tobacco industry. They reveal the use of delay tactics to allow them to collect revenue while continuing to be a primary cause of an ongoing climate catastrophe. As Rich argued at the outset of *Losing Earth*: 'Nearly everything we understand about global warming was understood in 1979.' By this time, the basic science could be conveyed relatively simply: 'the more carbon dioxide in the atmosphere, the warmer the planet. And every year, by burning coal, oil, and gas, human beings belched increasingly obscene quantities of carbon dioxide into the atmosphere.'[169] According to Chairwoman Maloney of the Committee, the approaches adopted by these companies were tantamount to '"gaslighting" the public', due to their claims to be part of the solution to climate change on one hand, while on the other, fighting to preserve business as usual.[170]

Another prominent example of a large company with a significant and detrimental environmental impact deceiving the public in order to protect revenue is the 'Volkswagen Scandal'. In 2013, graduate students working on a $70,000 grant at West Virginia University made a discovery that led to the revelation that 11 million Volkswagen cars had been fitted with an AI programme developed to recognize when they were in a test environment and manipulate the vehicles' behaviour and corresponding CO_2 measurements, giving the appearance they adhered to required standards to be permitted on the road, while polluting much more than allowed. The cars, when tested outside the conditions of the expected environment, came back with surprising results, leading to the discovery of the software. Given the opportunity to explain the reasons for the researchers' findings, Volkswagen lied in the hope of avoiding responsibility, until data was released in September 2015 that laid bare their unethical activity. Six executives from the company were charged with criminal offences in the aftermath of the revelations, and the Volkswagen was ordered to pay $4.3 billion in criminal and civil penalties.[171] These repercussions cannot undo the damage caused by the emissions of the cars it allowed to be on the road however, which researchers estimated caused fifty-nine premature deaths in the United States between 2008 and 2015, as a result of Volkswagen's violation of the Clean Air Act.[172]

Currently, it is too easy for the fossil fuel industry to exploit the tendency of humanity to veer towards darkness that Leopardi thought so carefully about. Through greater recognition of our need for consolation and more appreciation of the temptation to believe of environmental catastrophe 'that the evil in question could not be avoided', we make it much easier than we need to for those who seek to weaponize such tendencies as a means to protect their future profits. While Leopardi was exceptional in his ability to discern harmful patterns early on, today we have the assistance of evidence that was unavailable during his lifetime, which sadly confirms the validity of his warnings. We also have the benefit of clarity regarding the strength of opposition we face in terms of monetary and political forces seeking to preserve the deadly status quo.

Resignifying Leopardi today

In his work, Leopardi yearned for a society that did not rely on a neglect of the body and the senses in its efforts to educate the spirit. This aspect of his thought, in which he describes our severance from nature, which he depicts as like a 'tree cut off at the root' hints at the way Leopardi's deep appreciation of the loss of vitality in modern life points to a space we can attend. It suggests that our efforts could fruitfully be spent trying to bring into being a society which prioritizes spaces for the flourishing of the multitude of species with whom we share the Earth, in the place of a cynical commitment to growth at all costs. In her powerful memoir *In the Body of the World* (2016), Eve Ensler focused on attending to protecting, valuing and attending to the exile of the female body. Responding to the horrors of the rape and violence inflicted on women in the Congo where she worked, and subsequently to her diagnosis of uterine cancer, Ensler's work embodies that which we urgently need today. Such attention to the desperate need to respect to all women's bodies may help to provide an essential counter-narrative to centuries' worth of deeply engrained misogyny, which created fertile ground for the disregard of nature.

Illustrations of the ongoing significance of Leopardi's sense of a need to turn back on destructive endeavours to live cut off from nature are frequent in modern life. They are displayed in extreme form in suggestions of mining the moon, and in space tourism projects like Richard Branson's Virgin Galactic, Elon Musk's SpaceX and Jeff Bezos' Blue Origin, which evoke Leopardi's question in 'Copernicus' asking what we will do when faced with the exorbitant expense of dwindling resources, as well as Lucian's 'Trips to the Moon'. Echoing Leopardi's sense of a troubling imbalance in *Staying Alive: Women, Ecology, and Development* (1988), Shiva unpacks what she identifies as a 'maldevelopment in thought and action' rooted in patriarchal thinking, when she writes:

> In practice, this fragmented, reductionist, dualist perspective violates the integrity and harmony of man in nature, and the harmony between men and women. It ruptures the co-operative unity of masculine and feminine, and places man, shorn of the feminine principle, above nature and women, and separated from both.[173]

Reminding us of Mahatma Gandhi's statement, 'There is enough in the world for everyone's need, but not for some people's greed', Shiva demonstrates that the violation of the integrity of organic, interconnected and interdependent systems, comprising this maldevelopment 'sets in motion a process of exploitation, inequality, injustice and violence'.[174] Her arguments to show that neither the marginalisation of women nor ecological destruction is inevitable help bring Leopardi's response to our tendency towards self-destruction, and his refusal to conform in 'La ginestra' to bear on present conditions, opening up space in which to think outside of cynical and destructive value systems centred upon growth. Such generative considerations create the opportunity to envision new frameworks of value in society, according to which the flourishing not only of our whole species can take precedence, but in turn, through greater ecological harmony, can also serve to protect the multitude of species with which we share the planet.

Visionary thought, and keeping open the question of the future

As I highlighted earlier, for Negri, the nature of Leopardi's philosophical and political discourse was such that it helped him to resist. By being 'entirely open to time-to-come', Leopardi's work forged the space in which to 'glimpse a constitutive praxis of a new world' and invent an active disutopia. Offering a crucial reminder that, wherever pain and solitude become the real conditions of life, it is possible to open up a space of hope, as Negri's account helps to reveal, 'the poet is always animated by the hope of flight, a flight imagined as rupture of the present and invention of the future'.[175] The characterization of such a flight, for Negri, is construed as constructive: 'as determination of a future possibility, as project for a new culture'.[176] This aspect of Leopardi's work has been picked up by numerous theorists, who have noted the visionary nature of the opportunities opened up by Leopardi's thought, which allows room for the consideration of new, more beneficial, frameworks of value than those already existing.

In *Medicine and Ethics in Black Women's Speculative Fiction* (2015), Esther Jones brings this feature of Leopardi's philosophy into relation with more recent speculative fiction, particularly that written by Black women. As she writes, 'Leopardi's summary of dominant attitudes' towards Black people reveals that 'little has been done to change the overall attitudes of those in power'.[177] Jones goes on to examine case studies attesting to the lack of ethics involved in the treatment of Black people in medicine, where she includes the Tuskegee Syphilis Study conducted by the U.S. Public Health Service (USPHS) between 1932 and 1972 as a prime example of the ethically unjustified abuse of Black men for the purposes of medical research.[178] Examining how Black women, confronted with the double burden of both racism and misogyny, have created spaces to resist such oppression, she highlights the significance of imagining new strategies for survival via speculative fiction:

> Thus, it has been incumbent on black women to forge their own perceptions, their own sense of worth and value, to cultivate a

worldview and discourse in which survival is possible. Speculative fiction is one place where black women can be portrayed as self-actualized and strategies for survival are expressed. It is where radical forms of medical and social justice are imagined.[179]

As Jones argues, Black women speculative writers have utilized literature to theorise difference, thereby issuing a challenge to dominant misperceptions of Blackness and womanhood, 'while writing new prescriptions for how to relate humanely and ethically across differences'.[180] Jones' examination of Black women's creative use of literature to create space for new ways of thinking about the future, the imagination, dreams and vision is epitomized in the speculative fiction of Octavia Butler, who won both Hugo and Nebula Awards, including *Parable of the Sower* (1993), *Parable of the Talents* (1998) and *Fledgling* (2006). As the pleasure activist adrienne maree brown describes of Butler's work:

> [It] explores current social issues through the lens of sci-fi; is conscious of identity and intersecting identities; centers those who have been marginalized; is aware of power inequalities; is realistic and hard but hopeful; shows change from the bottom up rather than the top down; highlights that change is collective; and is not neutral – its purpose is social change and societal transformation.[181]

Butler, like Leopardi, was an astute observer of the human condition, who was talented in her ability to identify the undercurrent patterns latent in society and was similarly perplexed by our propensity towards self-destruction. One striking example of these aspects of her work can be found in *Parable of the Talents*, published in 1998, where, in her analysis of American society, and portraying a fictional dystopian leader, she describes Jarret's endeavour to 'Make America Great Again', prefiguring Trump's successful use of the slogan in his 2016 election campaign and an era mired by Trumpism.[182] Butler's work observed the centuries of survival and persistence encompassed in the Black struggle for justice, bringing these centre stage to highlight the cyclical nature of history, to issue prescient warnings and to provide powerful messages of hope. Her protagonist Lauren Oya Olamina, for example, cultivated the community 'Acorn', a symbol of new life, hope and possibility, arising out of her reflections on 'Earthseed', a religion according to which the principles 'God is Change. Shape God. The Destiny of Earthseed is to take root among the stars' are central.[183]

Butler's work, which, like Leopardi's, attended to post-apocalyptic scenes, and arose out of an appreciation of our need for affirmation, embodies the 'dreams and vision' of the philosopher-poet's visualization of the concerns of future generations.[184] As brown contends, Butler's 'visionary fiction' facilitates our intentions to bring new worlds into existence, for which we need to challenge the narratives that uphold current power dynamics and patterns.[185] As I suggested previously, Rebecca Solnit highlights the radical potential of writers' work, when she reminds us in *Hope in the Dark* of their importance for facilitating shifts in values by stating:

> Changes in ideas and values also result from work done by writers, scholars, public intellectuals, social activists, and participants in social media. It seems insignificant or periphery until very different outcomes emerge from transformed assumptions about who and what matters, who should be heard and believed, who has rights.[186]

The political potential of the peripheral view Solnit refers to here has also long since been a central topic of analysis within the feminism of Black theorists and writers like Toni Morrison and bell hooks, whose work highlighted the multitude of creative possibilities one could find at the fringe, wherein one's power could be found.

Having allowed a diversion to consider the comparisons which may be drawn between Leopardi's image of visions and the same theme today, I wish to also take a brief moment to reflect on the significance of the power of dreams for contemporary struggles for justice.[187] This is perhaps most powerfully illuminated in the famous image of Martin Luther King Jr., who, standing on the marble steps of the Lincoln Memorial in Washington DC on 28 August 1963, showed the power and importance of holding fast a dream of a better future as he demanded equal rights for Black people 100 years after Abraham Lincoln issued the Emancipation Proclamation to declare the freedom of all those held as slaves.[188] In his fight, King embodied Leopardi's depiction of adopting a courageous stance, as he led his community, advocating for the pain felt at the behest of injustice to be acknowledged as a normal and healthy response to ones' material conditions and seeking ways to channel such feelings into the creative outlet of effective non-violent direct action.[189]

Several years later, in 1967, King put forward the Vietnamese monk Thích Nhất Hạnh for the Nobel Peace Prize in 1967 in recognition of his grace and humility. Having turned away from reading Nietzsche's *Genealogy of Morals* and *Will to Power* in his efforts to assess what potential Christian love may have to effect social change, which left him feeling depressed, King's reaction to Nietzsche's work underlines the importance of recognizing the concern that was consistently at the forefront of Leopardi's mind to ensure that his own work avoided causing descents into paralysing despair.[190] Hạnh, to whom King turned as an alternative source of guidance, and in whose work themes of compassion and community are central, also attended to the question of how we should respond to the suffering inherent in being human with nobility. As he wrote in *The Art of Transforming Suffering* (2014), elucidating the importance of learning to attend to our suffering well, and the power that doing so gives us to enhance the solidarity of our communities:

> If we take care of the suffering inside us, we have more clarity, energy, and strength to help address the suffering violence, poverty and equity of our loved ones as well as the suffering in our community and the world. If, however, we are preoccupied with fear and despair in us, we can't help remove the suffering of others. There is an art to suffering well. If we know how to take care of our suffering, we not only suffer much, much less, we also create more happiness around us and in the world.[191]

The stance Hạnh suggests we adopt here is comparable to that set forth by Leopardi, whose admiration for the individual who 'shows he's great and strong in suffering' without adding to the problems of their neighbours, and who described the 'scented broom' as 'embellishing the lonely plain', brings home the importance, for Leopardi, of establishing ways to finding ways to respond appropriately to the fear and despair within us in a way that those around us experience as positive.[192]

Kindling hope for an optimistic will

With considerations of Leopardi's ethics of solidarity in mind, we can return to the reflections made by Gramsci in this regard in his *Prison Notebooks*, which Stuart Hall referred to when considering of his relevance for the study of race and ethnicity. In response to a question from Grahame Thompson regarding whether he had hope for the possibility that diversity and equality can come about, Hall commented:

> Optimism of the intellect, pessimism of the will. That it is increasingly difficult if undeniable, and also that the difficulties now operate on such a large scale; you know, when one talks about global forces, it seems almost they occupy the full stage, as it were, of one's awareness ... I think we are always, always working on the mess.[193]

Leopardi's thought helps us attend to the difficulties we face on a planetary scale by showing us how, by adopting the stance embodied by those ancient statues in Rome, that Staël depicts in *Corinne* as works of geniuses, we can bring together our *patience with perseverance, as* Leopardi's exemplary farmer does in 'La ginestra'.[194]

To see how such a perseverance of will can be applied to efforts to convince politicians to take decisive action on climate change, we can consider arguments found in the work *The Future We Choose: Surviving the Climate Crisis*, by Christiana Figueres and Tom Rivett-Carnac. Here, the authors examine what they describe as a position of stubborn optimism, developing their approach to optimism with recourse to the work of the positive psychology. In particular, they draw on the ideas of Martin Seligman, which attends to a gap in scientific literature of the last half century by examining how we can learn to flourish, imbue our lives with meaning, and build strength and virtue.[195] Describing what could be gained from such optimism, they write:

> Optimism is about actively proving, through every decision and every action, that we are capable of designing a better future.
>
> From the darkness of an Alabama jail, Martin Luther King, Jr., kept calling for the realization of a deeply held dream, no matter how bleak its prospects. Many others have done the same throughout history: John F. Kennedy refusing to accept that nuclear war was inevitable. Gandhi marching to the ocean to collect forbidden salt.
>
> In all these cases, key people believed that a better world was possible, and they were willing to fight for it. They didn't ignore difficult evidence or present things in a way that wasn't true. Instead they faced reality with a fierce belief that change could happen, however impossible it might have seemed at the moment.[196]

Leopardi's thought can help us recognize and sustain the moral forces within us to empower ourselves. In *The Principle of Hope*, originally published in 1954, Ernst Bloch argued that nurturing the imagination can help us resist the exploitation of escapism:

> Everybody's life is pervaded by daydreams: one part of this is just stale, even enervating escapism, even booty for swindlers, but another part is provocative, is not content just to accept the bad which exists, does not accept renunciation. This other part has hoping at its core, and is teachable. It can be extricated from the unregulated daydream and from its sly misuse, can be activated undimmed. Nobody has ever lived without daydreams, but it is a question of knowing them deeper and deeper and in this way keeping them trained unerringly, usefully, on what is right. Let the daydreams grow even fuller, since this means they are enriching themselves around the sober glance; not in the sense of clogging, but of becoming clear.[197]

This assessment of the daydreams that purvey everyday life aligns with Leopardi's refusal to accept that the certainty of our finitude must necessarily lead to despair. Bloch's depiction that hope is something that is teachable can also be found in Leopardi's thought. Immediately after his reflection concerning the way his mother consoled his younger brother, for example, Leopardi considered our propensity to imagine the worst in a reflection on how readily we kindle fear and how infrequently we create room for hope, writing:

> If you have a sworn enemy in a certain city, and you see that there is a storm overhead, does the hope pass through your mind that he might be killed? So why then are you frightened if that storm passes over you, when the probability that it will kill is so small that you can't even find a basis for the thing that needs so small a base in order to rise up in us, namely hope? The same can be said for a hundred other dangers. If they were to bring a probability of good, it would seem ridiculous not to place any hope in them, and yet these dangers produce fear in us. So it is. Though it is easy to kindle hope, and without any cause, it is even easier to kindle fear. But it seems to me that this reflection helps a lot to temper it. Fear is, therefore, richer in illusions than hope is.
>
> [66]

Solnit's work is exemplary in describing and cultivating a habit of pushing back against this tendency. Heeding the need for collective transformation to be 'rooted in rage but pointed towards vision and dreams', as the co-founder of the Black Lives Matter movement Patrisse Cullors has argued, Solnit describes how grief and hope can coexist in *Hope in the Dark*, where she writes:

> The tremendous human rights achievements – not only in gaining rights but in redefining race, gender, sexuality, embodiment, spirituality, and the idea of the good life – of the past century have flowered during a time of unprecedented ecological destruction and the rise of innovative new means of exploitation. And the rise of new forms of resistance, including resistance enabled by an elegant understanding of that ecology and new ways of people to communicate and organize, and new exhilarating alliance across distance and difference.[198]

To nurture the ability to foster such achievements, Solnit examines the importance of belief in the value of concrete action. She notes how the past century's human rights achievements were facilitated by a refusal of the arguments of optimists 'who think it will all be fine without our involvement' and pessimists who take the opposite position. Demonstrating the potential value of acknowledging uncertainty, and rejecting reasons not to act, she calls for an embrace of the 'unknown and the unknowable', which is the space in which Solnit defines hope:

> Hope locates itself in the premises that we don't know what will happen and that in the spaciousness of uncertainty is room to act. When you recognise uncertainty, you recognise that you may be able to influence the outcomes – you alone or you in concert with a few dozen or several million others.[199]

By uniting Leopardi's reflection that we lean more readily towards fear than hope with Solnit's argument for seizing the space of uncertainty as precisely the political arena in which we have the opportunity act, we can begin to formulate a philosophy for the environmental crisis that is firmly rooted in Leopardi's philosophical thought. His assessment of our predisposition is particularly important in the context of adopting responsible ways to face the environmental crisis. It helps to guide us away from the temptation of inaction, instead encouraging us to recognize the value of committing to something even without having any assurance as to where it may lead. By shifting our focus away from a tendency to be complacent and towards committing ourselves to seizing the opportunities that remain available to us, as Leopardi's exemplary Broom does, we can minimize the damage we are causing to communities already suffering on the frontline of the climate crisis, and to future generations, who we can express our love to by changing the way we live our lives today.

By looking at Solnit's work, which deals with the tendency to misplace our hope in the way Leopardi identified, we can find ways to counteract this. For example, Solnit calls upon Bloch's *The Principle of Hope* work to examine the relationship between false hope and easy despair, where he claimed: 'Fraudulent hope is one of the greatest malefactors, even enervators, of the human race, concrete hope is its most dedicated benefactor.'[200] While Leopardi is widely recognized for his critique of what Bloch used the term 'fraudulent hope' to describe, it may also be productive to consider the ways that Bloch believed we have the capacity to disrupt such movements, which he described in his account of the work it takes to learn 'concrete' hope:

> Its work does not renounce, it is in love with success rather than failure. Hope, superior to fear, is neither passive like the latter, nor locked into nothingness. The emotion of hope goes out of itself, makes people broad instead of confining them, cannot know nearly enough of what it is that makes them inwardly aimed, of what may be allied to them outwardly. The work of this emotion requires people who throw themselves actively into what is becoming, to which they themselves belong.[201]

Attending to the work of hope that Bloch would later describe, Leopardi provided examples of nobility in order to help depict an alternative to fraudulent hope, which would avoid its pitfalls. In doing this, he established fertile ground for a true hope that would benefit the human race to be considered.

Planetary humanism

Although I have examined how a significant weakness in Leopardi's thought is his inability to appreciate how violence against nature leads to violence against those who seek to protect it, one of his strengths was his recognition of the extent to which the toleration of racism at the heart of Enlightenment thought requires a fundamental re-examination of its value. By virtue of this recognition, well in advance of the theorists of the Frankfurt School, Leopardi delivered a fundamental critique of the Enlightenment, with an awareness of the significance of slavery at its core. Even today, his analysis goes much further than many Euro-American postmodern theorists, who continue to give too little weight to the significance of slavery for what Jürgen Habermas called the Enlightenment Project, as Gilroy points out in his work. In *The Black Atlantic: Modernity and Double Consciousness* (1993), for example, Gilroy notes that the history of slavery still frequently fails to be considered as 'a part of the ethical and intellectual heritage of the West as a whole', in the way it ought to be.[202] As he observes:

> There is little attention given to the possibility that much of what is identified as postmodern may have been foreshadowed, or prefigured, in the lineaments of modernity itself. Defenders and critics of modernity seem to be equally unconcerned that the history and expressive culture of the African diaspora, the practice of racial slavery, or the narratives of European imperial conquest may require all simple periodisations of the modern and the postmodern to be drastically rethought.[203]

For him, Leopardi, whose work includes a critique of this prefiguration, represents an exception to this trend. Writing in 'Where every breeze speaks of courage and liberty' (2018), he claims:

> During earlier stages of the romantic repudiation of enlightenment, the Mediterranean world fostered the bleak, cosmic preoccupation of the philosopher poet Giacomo Leopardi. They lent themselves to the construction of a ruthless change of scale in which the trivial antics of human beings were reduced to a negative, fluctuating or marginal presence in the recursive, tragic complexity of life. Among many "romantic" European voices, Leopardi's is notable – though hardly alone – because his idiosyncratic philosophical outlook demanded that he develop an interest in the ethics of slavery ancient and modern. This is explicitly revealed in his aphoristic Pensieri. Racial slavery is one fleeting instance of the perfidy of human beings and the wholesale failure of their trifling ethical systems over which Leopardi's cosmic pessimism about our species is erected.[204]

Gilroy refers to Leopardi's passage in the *Pensieri* that I introduced earlier as an example provided by the poet to highlight the 'perfidy of human beings', which we saw was a prominent theme especially within his 1824 dialogues.

In *Against Race: Imagining Political Culture beyond the Color Line* (2001), highlighting the complexity of identity-based politics within an overdeveloped world, Gilroy warns that 'shortcuts to solidarity' add to the attractiveness of authoritarian solutions to routine experiences of oppression, repression and abuse.[205] For Gilroy, essentialist approaches have an inherent political weakness to them in that, in the period after emancipation, they reveal the inherent instability of their own characterizations, which 'relied upon the effects of racial hierarchy to supply the binding agent'.[206] More recently, Olúfẹ́mi Táíwò has taken up this exploration of identity politics from a similar perspective, in *Elite Capture: How the Powerful Took Over Identity Politics (And Everything Else)* (2022), where he examines the multifarious ways elites co-opt radical critiques of racial capitalism to serve their own ends.

Seeking an alternative to such shortcuts, Gilroy turns to Leopardi's work as a resource in the development of his 'planetary humanism', allowing him to dare to imagine future solidarities based on the shared condition of our species as a whole, in its cosmic fragility.[207] In this regard, the influence of Leopardi on Gilroy's thought, which appears to be underpinned by the call for 'universal solidarity' Anderson described in *Spectrum* that Leopardi provides is particularly apparent.[208] Similarly as for Williams, for whom the moral framework of Leopardi's work rests upon the universal principle of suffering, for Gilroy also, the sense of fragility Leopardi leaves us with in this explicity cosmic sense appears to be the foundation of the ethics and politics that Gilroy seeks to construct. Explaining the 'postmodern planetary consciousness' he invokes in his 2003 article '"Where Ignorant Armies Clash by Night": Homogeneous Community and the Planetary Aspect', Gilroy writes:

> It too relies on a re-imagining of the world that is as extensive and profound as any of the revolutionary changes in the perception and representation of space and matter that preceded it. This time, the world becomes not a limitless globe, but a small and finite place, one planet among others with strictly limited resources that are allocated unequally. This is not the globalised mindset of the fortunate unrestricted traveller or some unexpected fruit of insulated post-scarcity and indifferent overdevelopment.[209]

Specifying our position as one planet among others, on a small and finite globe, he continues:

> It is a critical orientation and an oppositional mood triggered by comprehension of the simple fact that environmental and medical crises do not stop at national boundaries and by a feeling that the sustainability of our species is itself in question.[210]

Gilroy invokes the campaigns Shiva writes of to resist the corporate control of 'the substance of life itself, especially in the form of seeds' to highlight the contemporary significance of Leopardi's critique of the instrumentalization and degradation of life. Giving an example of the 'cosmopolitan solidarity from below', he envisions what such a practice would look like in action, describing 'the worldwide battles to secure free access to the water of which are own bodies are largely composed', while highlighting the extent to which corporate ownership seeks to take ownership of every aspect of life.[211]

In a conversation with Sindre Bangstad in 2018 on the 25th anniversary of the publication of *The Black Atlantic*, Gilroy highlights that Frantz Fanon, who like Aimé Césaire, he describes as 'planetary humanist', had the mentality of a doctor, who was always wanting to heal: 'every argument about violence, every single comment on violence is framed or qualified by an argument about healing'.[212] Following in the footsteps of the francophone Césaire, Gilroy wanted to take up the project he set out in his 1959 article 'L'homme de culture et ses responsabilités', where he argued: 'We must make a humanism made to the measure of the world'.[213] It is for such a project that Leopardi's work, as we saw from reviewing dialogues like 'Hercules and Atlas', 'Earth and the Moon', and 'Copernicus', attended to such an endeavour. Indeed, Gilroy's thought recalls Leopardi's wish to create a philosophy which 'by its nature it aims to cure', and he describes to Bangstad how he recalls the work of Leopardi, when he tries to find hope [4428]. He remarks: 'If you've read my work as carefully as it sounds like you have, you will know that I am a distant follower in the footsteps of Giacomo Leopardi. I am a cosmic pessimist: 'what is this acid spot in time that goes by the name of life?'[214] By bringing Leopardi's role in the theoretical lineage of planetary humanism to the fore, Gilroy highlights the contemporary significance of his insistence on the smallness of our planet in the larger scheme of the universe. Considering his appreciation of Leopardi's potential to reinvigorate a sturdier concept of solidarity upon which we can build effective means of resistance, I propose returning once again to the work of Shiva, who articulates the ambition of an alternative vision to the 'money machine', which we can strive to create, when she reminds us of the possibilities we are presented with to resist:

> We can seed another future, deepen our democracies, reclaim our commons, regenerate the earth as living members of a One Earth Family, rich in our diversity and freedom, one in our unity and interconnectedness. It is a healthier future. It is one we must fight for. It is one we must claim.
>
> We stand at a precipice of extinction. Will we allow our humanity as living, conscious, intelligent, autonomous beings to be extinguished by a greed machine that does not know limits and is unable to put a break on its colonisation and destruction? Or will we stop the machine and defend our humanity, freedom, and autonomy to protect life on earth?[215]

Such dreams and visions are perhaps what Leopardi had in mind not only when he examined fictional dialogues from the past but also the real future conversations he imagined. In his late poetry, he provided the tools and examples with which to empower us to make such visions a reality, by igniting within us and enthusiasm that could lead to meaningful action, which remind us of our power to decide our future, not as means to refute material circumstances, but as a stark reminder of the possibility of real hope. In his work, he compels us to feel the opportunity we have to shift the paradigm by confronting our fears with as much nobility, grace and strength, as we can collectively summon.

The entrenched prejudice of historical anthropocentrism

A significant strength of Leopardi's work that contributes to its value as a prescient resource today was his appreciation of how deeply engrained anthropocentricism is in the human psyche and in our culture. The attention he gives to ancient thinkers who dealt with our inclination to assume our centrality demonstrates how far back in literary history we can find concern being expressed with our willingness to position ourselves at the heart of the universe. Today, there remains a recognizable need for greater respect for the natural world, outside of considering the benefits of a healthy planet for human health. The increasingly significant cross-disciplinary One Health approach, for example, which has its roots in the work of Wildlife Conservation Society (WCS), refers to the health of human civilisation and the state of the natural systems on which it depends, while nonetheless often inadvertently perpetuating anthropocentric framing. The philosopher Peter Singer, for example, in whose seminal text *Animal Liberation* in 1973 he criticised the 'bare-faced – and morally indefensible – preference for members of our own species', has highlighted this in recent discussions. Contributing to the article 'A Bolder One Health: Expanding the Moral Circle to Optimize Health for All', published in 2021, he and his co-authors argued that, despite the great strides that One Health initiatives have made, there remains substantial work to do to address the entrenched prejudice of anthropocentricism:

> The One Health philosophy has simultaneously been ground-breaking and too conventional. On the one hand, it offers a radical program of reimagining human and nonhuman co-vulnerability and its effects on health. On the other hand, it has not yet embraced the progress made in philosophy and science that has exposed historical anthropocentrism as an entrenched prejudice. While it is important to pursue specific and small-scale research activities and programs, deeply appreciating the bigger moral and strategic picture as part of One Health's central philosophy is urgent and vital.[216]

Returning to Leopardi's work, with its deep appreciation of the long history of critiquing our insistence on honing in solely on the human picture can help to begin to address such present tendencies. Considering his dialogues can be used to support the development of One Health, which Singer and his colleagues argue 'should be more imaginative and adventurous in its core philosophy and ultimately in its recommendations and activities'.[217] As I showed in my introduction to Leopardi's work from 1824, 'An Imp and a Gnome', the philosopher subjected our problematic tendency to centre ourselves in all our considerations regarding the universe to critique, when he wrote: '... [humans had] not only persuaded themselves that the things of the world had no purpose other than to serve them, but reckoned that everything else put together, compared with the human race, was a mere trifle'.[218] To help One Health reach its full potential, revisiting such arguments, and incorporating their insights into today's practices could prove pivotal.

Daniela Bini has elucidated the significance of this aspect of Leopardi's work in *A Fragrance from the Desert: Poetry and Philosophy in Giacomo Leopardi*. Here, she highlighted how Leopardi regularly took heed of the concerns of the ancients, taking issue with 'the theme of human presumption' whilst insisting that 'man's most dangerous error has been his anthropocentric fallacy'.[219] It is evident that we continue to find it difficult to break away from seeking to find utility in everything, especially other beings and nature. This reveals how deeply entrenched the anthropocentrism of the Western mindset is, and the extent to which this continues to be thoughtlessly perpetuated today. Reaching back into history, and engaging with Leopardi, and those he was inspired by can help the One Health philosophy overcome its shortcomings and embrace important progress from philosophy. His *Operette* is filled with examples of the myriad ways we may slip up and fall back into entrenched prejudice. Another instance can be found in 'Copernicus', where the Moon is driven to exclaim 'Still harping on men!' in response to the Earth.

As Brian Moore argued in his study *Ecological Literature and the Critique of Anthropocentrism* (2017), despite anthropocentricism being considered to be a contemporary term, there is evidence of both anthropocentric thought and anti-anthropocentricism in the work of the ancients, which is commonly overlooked:

> [T]he assumption that modern works are more questioning about anthropocentrism than ones written before the birth of modern science is not completely safe. ... the genesis of the rejection of anthropocentrism would appear to be a post-Darwinian reaction, but it also has some connections to the aesthetic of the Sublime that arose in the eighteenth century, and then, a little before that, it appears to be a result of the Enlightenment, yet certain aspects of it appear before the rise of modern science, and more than a few seeds of the idea stretch back well into early American Indian animism, ancient Greek and Roman philosophy, and Eastern religions.[220]

Characterizations of anthropocentrism as a uniquely modern phenomena fail to consider the strengths of marginalised indigenous knowledge, as well as how opposition to such thought reaches back to ancient Greek and Roman philosophy, where it can be found 'rooted in the beginnings of the Western intellectual tradition'.[221] As Moore notes, while a general trend towards anthropocentricism can also be discerned in the thought of the ancient Greeks and Romans, there are a number of notable examples of challenges to such thinking, particularly in the thought of Lucian, Seneca, Democritus, Empedocles, Lucretius and others.[222]

Establishing important precedents that challenge and overturn anthropocentric points of view, considering these thinkers today reminds us that critiques of anthropocentrism have already developed substantially over the course of over 800 years, from the Presocratics to late antiquity.[223] As Moore argues, considering the limited means for measuring and observing the universe, the observations of many ancient and medieval writers were exceptionally astute. For many, this led them to reject the notion that the earth is unique, and in turn consider how our planet is tiny 'almost irrelevant in the cosmos' in their own thought.²²⁴ Indeed, Copernicus had examined this, as he wrote to Pope Paul III, describing how he had returned to these ideas in an endeavour to make sense of his own discoveries:

> I undertook the task of rereading the works of all the philosophers which I could obtain to learn whether anyone had ever proposed other motions of the universe's spheres than those expounded by the teachers of astronomy in the schools. And in fact first I found in Cicero that Hicetas supposed the earth to move. Later I also discovered in Plutarch that certain others were of this opinion. I have decided to set his words down here, so that they may be available to everybody:
>
> 'Some think that the earth remains at rest. But Philolaus the Pythagorean believes that, like the sun and moon, it revolves around the fire in an oblique circle. Heraclides of Pontus and Ecphantus the Pythagorean make the earth move, not in a progressive motion, but like a wheel in a rotation from west to east about its own center.'²²⁵

In more recent years, the idea of returning to the ancients with a view to examining what insights can be drawn from their thoughts to apply to environmental thinking today has been increasingly taken up. One related example of this is the study *Italy and the Ecological Imagination: Ecocritical Theories and Practices* (2022), in which contributors have looked to historical records that have shaped our environmental imagination to explore non-anthropocentric modes of thinking and interacting with the non-human world.

Bringing together the insights of those who highlight the need for One Health to heed the rich philosophical history of questioning anthropocentrism with Leopardi's tendency to reach back to the resources provided by the ancient satirists, we can extend Leopardi's appreciation of the necessity of compassion, we can return again to Shiva's work. Quoting from Einstein, at the outset of *Making Peace with the Earth* to help to demonstrate the need for us to widen our circle of compassion, she writes:

> A human being is a part of the whole called by us the Universe, a part limited in space and time. He experiences himself, his thoughts

and feelings, as something separated from the rest, a kind of optical delusion of his consciousness. This delusion is a kind of prison for us, restricting us to our personal desires and to affection for a few persons nearest to us. Our task must be to free ourselves from this prison by widening our circle of compassion to embrace all living creatures and the whole of nature in its beauty.[226]

By extending the compassion that Leopardi provides to people to encompass the broader range of being he intimates considering in 'La ginestra', we can reach a greater appreciation of the way in which we delude ourselves to imagine we are separate from the ecosystems we are destroying with our extractivist, short-sighted and thoughtless ways of being. By taking more seriously the notion that he was influenced by the Stoics' interest in philosophy as a way of life, in addition, we can also reach a greater appreciation of the ways in which the poet sought to remedy the problems he is known to depict.

Conclusion

In 'La ginestra' Leopardi made us sensitive to 'the nothingness of things', while providing enough consolation, to help opening up and revive our hearts to the possibility of reaching our full potential as humans, neighbours and citizens. Heeding Aurelius' call to remember our place in the universe, Leopardi combines the way of conceiving death he drew from Seneca with his consideration of Copernicus and Fontenelle, whose ideas he also makes use of. Reflecting on the plurality of worlds on the flanks of Vesuvius, he also reminds us of the way our home is shared with a multitude of other species, highlighted in 'La ginestra' with recourse to snakes, cows, bats, hares, ants and the exemplary flower of the wilderness.

Perhaps the most significant limitation we find in his late philosophical work is the way his thought contributes to the ongoing war against nature, which itself contributes to the environmental crisis. Despite this major weakness, I have nonetheless sought to show that his work remains both a valuable and an underutilised resource for us today. By highlighting the importance of solidarity, demonstrating the extent to which the need to centralise the human story can be traced back to the ancients, who offered their own critiques of this, and in showing sensitivity to the need to question whether we can truly consider a civilisation which rests upon the subordination of a significant portion of the human race to be worthy of its name, his work offers critical insights on central topics of discussion today. His ability to show images of a character imbued with courage and nobility, and his efforts to cultivate in us the encouragement to foster this within ourselves, means his work offers us firstly a non-human and then a human role model of compassion, with which he prompts us to find our own internal strength to make the fundamental necessary changes in our minds and actions. In these ways, in his late philosophical lyric poetry, Leopardi begins to forge an ethics which gives us a means of resisting futility while staking our claim to a meaningful life in which we might hope to flourish, that arises out of his equally impressive critique of Enlightenment thought.

Conclusion: Planetary solidarity

Today, we have the opportunity to draw on and make use of Leopardi's methods and prescient insights. We can extend his work, which emphasises the significance of solidarity, by taking heed of his warnings of the risks of being overwhelmed by senseless pride, and of the value of protecting a space in which to dream, in order to apply them to a new vision, which brings all people and species into the fold of a solidarity that works with nature and the one planet we collectively share.

Leopardi was a forerunner to many of central figures whose work was shaped by engagement with his ideas, who I have discussed to varying degrees throughout this study. His work was exemplary in its capacity to tie together ideas dealt with by writers traversing the centuries preceding him. Through diagnosing and attending to themes such as the value of human worth, nobility, grace, compassion, solidarity, strength, misplaced pride, anthropocentrism, our position in the cosmos and our mortality, the research he undertook throughout his life ultimately led him to the conclusions he delicately weaved throughout 'La ginestra', written in the face of his own mortality while staying in Villa delle Ginestre. In this philosophical poem, as Pamela Williams has argued, Leopardi delivers his final verdict concerning our relation to nature, developed in light of the ongoing debates concerning the Lisbon Earthquake, which he transposed on to 'the terrifying mountain, Vesuvius the destroyer', of which he had a view as he wrote.[1]

'La ginestra' underlines our power to choose noble lives, in spite of the material challenges to this issued by our time, reminding us of our tendency to rescind a hope that would be reasonable to foster and evoke an enthusiasm that stands to empower us as we seek to collectively protect the chances for life of present and future, human and non-human generations. His study of the history of classical scholarship from Antiquity exposed him to a long-established tradition that has been classified as 'consolatory'. He self-consciously built upon this tradition, as well as that of using dialogues to practise philosophy, which he found in authors ranging from Seneca, Lucian to Alexander Pope, whose considerations of death, satire, dialogues and philosophical poems informed the development of his own work. His own contribution to the philosophical ideas he found in Pope, Leibniz and Voltaire came in the form of his late poetry, which examined the issues he had previously tackled in his own dialogues and reflected on continuously in his notebooks and letters of correspondence.

Using Leopardi to attend to the environmental crisis

Challenging the claims of those who have argued that Leopardi's pessimism 'could not be put to any kind of Gaian service', I have considered how, although we have many persuasive reasons to reject the conclusions Leopardi arrived at regarding our relationship with nature today, we would risk losing too much if we allowed this to discount the value of his philosophy for ecological thinking. Insights from theorists ranging from Vandana Shiva, Patricia Hill Collins, Kwame Anthony Appiah, and many others have prompted recognition of the problems involved in the opposition between humans and nature that Leopardi ultimately came to rest upon. Examining the work of such thinkers helps to show that by establishing solidarity on a foundation built upon an opposition between people and nature Leopardi ultimately risks undermining the same solidarity he appears to envision, as well as how the oppositional thinking underpinning his ethics was rooted in the Christian tradition he otherwise criticised so vigilantly.[2]

By refusing to discount the potential of Leopardi's writing for our present planetary crisis, I have sought to hold fast to an opportunity we otherwise risk losing, which involves underscoring Leopardi's understanding of the significance of our need for consolation. I have argued that we can apply Leopardi's insight some of the most pressing challenges we face today, in the context of the environmental crisis, particularly the need to work together effectively and collectively to hold the fossil fuel industry to account. I have also demonstrated how, for Leopardi, ultimately our moral forces are within us, in order to show how his work serves as a rich resource to support our endeavours to maintain the optimistic will and 'patience allied with perseverance', for which Gramsci advocated.

While the work of Robert Solomon and others has shown that the affirmative nature of Nietzsche's philosophy has too readily been overlooked, I have suggested that a similar tendency is often at play in the reception of the work of Leopardi, whose influence on Nietzsche also remains underappreciated. This limited focus on the diagnostic aspect of Leopardi's thought appears to be particularly discernible in scholarship currently available for English readers, with a few notable exceptions, which I have sought to build upon. Despite the validity of criticisms of Leopardi's late thought, these limitations, I have argued, do not fully discount the contemporary value of his work, which comes together in his late philosophical poem 'La ginestra', nor does it cancel out the rich potential of his work for helping us as we consider we might best respond to the environmental crisis.

Hope and vision: Seeds for sustained strength

In 'La ginestra', Leopardi foreshadows the question Rachel Berdach posed in her novel *The Emperor, the Sages and Death* (1938): 'why we, like upside-down sunflowers, turn to the dark side rather than the light?', which informed Freud's philosophy of grief. In his own response to the similar judgement Leopardi found in the Gospel of John: 'men love darkness rather than light', which he places at the outset of 'La ginestra' to situate the meditation of the question that follows, he signals a different approach to his ongoing commitment to encourage us to see ourselves as we are. In a departure from his earlier, perhaps more well-known diagnostic work, where he utilized humour and satire, his late lyric poetry allows him to offer the embodiment of an approach characterized by consolation.

The prominence of Leopardi's consideration of the state of 'extreme dejection, disenchantment, nothingness, boredom, and discouragement about life' is notable in his poem, as critics like Timpanaro and Anderson have emphasised. However, as we have seen with recourse to the readings of thinkers, including Williams, Negri and Murphy, this work also represents a moment in his oeuvre when his efforts to make us sensitive to the 'nothingness of things' simultaneously allow him to counteract the 'indifference and insensibility' he believes such a recognition 'must naturally inspire'. Through his responsive efforts to open and 'revive the heart', Leopardi's late philosophical poem serves the function he depicted in his consideration of 'works of genius', which he believed must 'always bring consolation'. Today, the significance of Leopardi's philosophy of consolation is its ability to serve as a resource to remind us of the political importance of attending to our anxiety – which the environmental crisis inspires in us – with empathetic awareness, to support our endeavour to meet such challenges with the strength they demand.

Bearing in mind the strength of the resistance to change that Leopardi evaluates in his consideration of the consequences of the Copernican Revolution, an inability to manage the confrontation with extreme dejection and disenchantment, which we are increasingly faced with, makes fear of such a confrontation particularly easy to weaponise. As we have seen in relation to the warnings of contemporary environmental thinkers like Malm, who echoes Leopardi's insights, for those seeking to preserve the status quo, such responses provide a useful means through which to inspire indifference. The connections Leopardi drew between the thought of Epictetus and his consideration of the distress felt by his little brother when his stick was thrown out of the window, Leopardi elucidates this sensitivity he felt to the possibility that certain forms of consolation, such as the comforting notion 'that the particular good could not be obtained, or that the evil in question could not be avoided', can serve to pacify us. With this feature of Leopardi's thought in mind, we can use the example of his awareness of the significance of empathy to recognize our own inclination to be overwhelmed and begin to seek to overcome this in ways that are less detrimental to the prospect of defining and bringing into being our visions of a just society. In doing so, we might find ourselves bolstered by a newfound attendance to hope, and begin to turn, like a sunflower, or a noble soul, towards the light.

Afterword

Over two centuries have passed since Leopardi warned us to turn back our 'unrestrained violation of nature'. Since then, we have accelerated our violation of nature, and bear witness to its damaging consequences almost daily. Leopardi's writings, particularly his later and more compassionate works, have the potential to provide crucial motivation in choosing to respond differently to those whom he derided in his own age for turning their backs 'on the light that made it clear'. Inspired by Hall's call for narratives of historical reconstruction which allow us to reinterpret the future, I have sought to reinscribe, relocate and resignify Leopardi's thought to support the development of an ethics of survival amidst the environmental crisis. A close examination of some of Leopardi's most central ideas, I have argued, may inspire a newfound enthusiasm at the prospect of living by hope rather than fear, and cultivate our strength to resolve to act in the interest of a solidarity that extends beyond humans, to the rest of the living world.

The adoption of a stance of tranquil strength – like that embodied by both the 'gentle broom', and the anxious farmer bending to his vines – may allow our hopes that the world can return to a state of prior vitality the chance they need to actualise. Moreover, while it may perhaps go against Leopardi's own philosophy, the cultivation of a more empathetic relation with nature could also mark a generative extension of it, bringing the world into a healthier state. Referring back to his image of the Earth as a plaything for Hercules and Atlas in the *Operette*, relating more sensitively towards might benefit the world, helping to 'pump it up a bit', like the days when it 'bounced back and leapt around like a roebuck'.[1] Today, we have the benefit of a wealth of thinkers who have considered the question of how we can turn our fear into hope in great depth. An exemplary writer among these is Solnit, who reminds us: 'the real goal is to amplify the power and reach of existing alternatives'.[2] We might bring Solnit's invitation into dialogue with Leopardi's observation that it is easy to kindle fear, which is 'richer in illusions than hope'. In doing so, we can begin to reveal the multitude of ways we might resist those who stoke the flames of fear with a resolve to redirect our attention to the alternatives that exist everywhere.

As Shiva has argued, and Leopardi inferred in his reflection of hope as a muscle, such alternatives abound once we begin to look for them. They include the crucial efforts of the Committee on Oversight and Reform in Washington DC, whose work contributes to revealing fossil fuel companies' disinformation and greenwashing campaigns and holding them accountable for the damage they seek to continue causing. Closer to home is the heartening example of two local activists, Hilary Powell and Daniel Edelstyn, the filmmakers behind the 2021 feature documentary 'Bank Job'. Seizing upon the phrase: 'Every building a power station' from Ann Pettifor's book *The Case for the Green New Deal* (2019), Powell and Edelstyn successfully organised the installation of solar panels on every house in their street in Walthamstow in East London with the funds they raised from living on their roof, bringing energy democracy to life. These examples add to those sought out and amplified by writers like Solnit and Shiva, who point out the sustained efforts taking place in indigenous cultures and local economies, which people are defending with their lives. The ongoing work of such activists and writers amplifies the latent benefits waiting to be reaped from effective collective action and reminds us of the power that can be seized if we nourish the hope that we otherwise might allow to be wrested from us.

Notes

Introduction

1. Vandana Shiva, *Making Peace with the Earth* (London: Pluto Press, 2013), 9.
2. Patrick Vallance, 'We've overexploited the planet, now we need to change if we're to survive', 8 July 2022. Available online: https://www.gov.uk/government/speeches/weve-overexploited-the-planet-now-we-need-to-change-if-were-to-survive (accessed 23 February 2023).
3. Shiva, *Making Peace with the Earth*, 9.
4. Khalil, H., Ecke, F., Evander, M. et al. Declining ecosystem health and the dilution effect. *Scientific Reports*, 6, 31314 (2016): 1.
5. Matthew Arnold, *Poetry of Byron* (London: Macmillan, 1881), xxiii.
6. Giacomo Leopardi, trans. Patrick Creagh, *Operette Morali* (New York: Columbia University Press, 1983), 9–10.
7. Erik Pietro Sganzerla and Michele Augusto Riva, 'The Disease of the Italian Poet Giacomo Leopardi (1798–1837): A Case of Juvenile Ankylosing Spondylitis in the 19th Century', *Journal of Clinical Rheumatology* 23, no. 4 (June 2017): 223–5.
8. Shiva, *Making Peace with the Earth*, 5.
9. James Hansen, *Storms of My Grandchildren: The Truth about the Coming Climate Catastrophe and Our Last Chance to Save Humanity* (United Kingdom: Bloomsbury Publishing, 2011), 205.
10. Joel C. Gill and Bruce D. Malamud, 'Anthropogenic Processes, Natural Hazards, and Interactions in a Multi-hazard Framework', *Earth-Science Reviews* 166 (2017): 246–69, 247.
11. Nathaniel Rich, *Losing Earth: The Decade We Could Have Stopped Climate Change* (United Kingdom: Pan Macmillan, 2019), 195.
12. Vandana Shiva, Kartikey Shiva, *Oneness Vs. the 1%: Shattering Illusions, Seeding Freedom* (United Kingdom: Chelsea Green Publishing, 2020), 40.
13. Ibid., 7.
14. Stuart Hall and Paul Du Gay, eds., *Questions of Cultural Identity: SAGE Publications* (United Kingdom: Sage, 1996), 59.

15 Pierre Hadot, *Philosophy as a Way of Life: Spiritual Exercises from Socrates to Foucault* (United Kingdom: Wiley, 1995), 245.
16 Arthur Schopenhauer, 'Gespräche, hrsg. von A.' Hübscher, Stuttgart–Bad Cannstatt (1971): 220.
17 A. M. Capodivacca, 'Nietzsche's *Zukunftsphilologie*: Leopardi, Philology, History', *California Italian Studies* 2, no. 1 (2011). http://dx.doi.org/10.5070/C321009024 Retrieved from https://escholarship.org/uc/item/2528k6vm. 7; Antonio Negri, *Flower of the Desert: Giacomo Leopardi's Poetic Ontology* (New York: State University of New York Press, 2015), xiv.
18 Perry Anderson, *Spectrum: From Right to Left in the World of Ideas* (United Kingdom: Verso, 2005), 193.
19 Ibid.
20 Donna Haraway, *Staying with the Trouble: Making Kin in the Chthulucene* (United Kingdom: Duke University Press, 2016), 56.
21 Ibid., 3.
22 Negri, *Flower of the Desert*, xvi. Branches of broom plants had medicinal use since the early Middle Ages, and were mentioned in the earliest printed herbals, including the *Hortus Sanitatis* (1491) and the *Grete Herball* (1516). Grieve, *A Modern Herbal*. 124. On a flower essence website, (Flower Essence Services, 'Scotch Broom For Meeting The Challenges Of Our Times', the Broom, referred to as Scotch Broom as it is known in much of the Pacific Northwest, is described as 'an antidote to pessimism and despair' with respect to our relation to world events: 'Scotch Broom essence has also been used for people facing natural and man-made disasters, such as wars, earthquakes, floods and economic crises. The effect has nothing to do with denial of the challenges we are facing. Rather, the healing message of Scotch Broom is to take such challenges as opportunities and calls to action, to find the ways that we can draw upon our inner strength and conviction to make a difference in the world.' http://www.fesflowers.com/scotch-broom-meeting-challenges-our-times2/ (accessed 4 February 2022).
23 Mark Neocleous, 'Negri in Prison', *Radical Philosophy* 092, Nov/Dec 1998.
24 Negri, *Flower of the Desert*, xi.
25 Ibid., xi.
26 Ibid., 2.
27 Ibid., 301.

28 Leopardi, *Operette*, 98.
29 Britannica, T. Editors of Encyclopedia. 'Lisbon earthquake of 1755'. Encyclopedia Britannica, 25 October 2022. https://www.britannica.com/event/Lisbon-earthquake-of-1755.
30 Antonio Negri, *Subversive Spinoza:(UN) Contemporary Variations: Antonio Negri* (United Kingdom: Manchester University Press, 2004), 72.
31 Peter Lecouras, 'Leopardi's Reception in England: 1837 to 1927', *Italica* 86, no. 2 (2009): 313–27, 312.
32 Giacomo Leopardi, *Canti: Poems: A Bilingual Edition* (United States: Farrar, Straus and Giroux, 2010), 285.
33 Paul Gilroy, *Against Race: Imagining Political Culture beyond the Color Line* (Cambridge: Belknap Press of Harvard University Press, 2000), 356.
34 Rebecca Solnit, *Hope in the Dark: Untold Histories, Wild Possibilities* (United Kingdom: Canongate Books, 2016), xiv.

Chapter 1

1 John Pryor, 'Review of Merchant Culture in Fourteenth-Century Venice: The Zibaldone da Canal', *Parergon* 12, (1994): 134–6.
2 Leopardi, *Operette*, 14.
3 Negri, *Flower of the Desert*, xiv. & Nicholas Rennie, *Speculating on the Moment*, (Germany: Wallstein, 2005), 226.
4 Leopardi, *Canti*, xiii.
5 Leopardi, *Operette*, 14.
6 Rennie, *Speculating on the Moment*, 226.
7 Negri, *Flower of the Desert*, xiv.
8 Prue Shaw, *The Letters of Giacomo Leopardi 1817–1837*, (United Kingdom: Taylor & Francis, 2017), 107.
9 Timothy Murphy, 'Flower of the Desert: Poetics as Ontology from Leopardi to Negri', *Genre* 44, no. 1 (1 March 2011): 75–91: 80–2.
10 Negri, *Flower of the Desert*, 122.
11 Ibid., 118–19.
12 Ibid., 121.
13 Ibid., 119.
14 Ibid., 118–19.

15 After his death, Leopardi's sister, Paolina, and Ranieri prevented Leopardi's remains from being thrown into a mass grave in accordance with the strict hygiene rules required at the time, arranging instead to have him clandestinely buried in the crypt of San Vitale Church in Fuorigrotta.
16 P.J. Imperato, G.H. Imperato and A.C. Imperato, 'The Second World Cholera Pandemic (1826–1849) in the Kingdom of the Two Sicilies with Special Reference to the Towns of San Prisco and Forio d'Ischia', *Journal of Community Health* 40, no. 6 (December 2015): 1224–86.
17 John Basore, trans. *Seneca: Moral Essays*, vol. 1 (Harvard: Loeb Classical Library, 1928), 5.
18 Michael Caesar, 'Leopardi's Operette Morali and the Resources of the Dialogue', *Italian Studies* 43, no. 1 (1988): 21–40: 26.
19 Alessandro De Angelis, *Galileo Galilei's 'Two New Sciences': For Modern Readers*. (Switzerland: Springer Nature, 2021). xii.
20 Giovanni Carsaniga, *Giacomo Leopardi: The Unheeded Voice* (Edinburgh: Edinburgh University Press, 1977), 28–9.
21 Ibid., 29.
22 Ibid., 31.
23 Ibid., 28–9.
24 Plato, trans. Lee Henry Desmond Pritchard, and M.S. Lane, *The Republic*, (London: Penguin, 2007), 349.
25 Aleksandra Koman, 'With Rhymes about the Human Fate. Philosophy in the Poetry of Giacomo Leopardi', *Acta Universitatis Lodziensis. Folia Litteraria Polonica* 59, no. 4 (2020): 101–14: 101.
26 Ibid.
27 Ibid.
28 Lowry Nelson, *Poetic Configurations: Essays in Literary History and Criticism* (United States: Pennsylvania State University Press, 2010), 241.
29 Negri, *Flower of the Desert*, 258.
30 Ibid., 258.
31 Italo Calvino, *Six Memos for the Next Millennium* (United Kingdom: Penguin Books Limited, 2009), 12 & 24.
32 Tobias Dahlkvist, *Nietzsche and the Philosophy of Pessimism: A Study of Nietzsche's Relation to the Pessimistic Tradition: Schopenhauer, Hartmann, Leopardi*, (Uppsala: Uppsala University, 2007), 102.

33 Negri, *Flower of the Desert*, xxiv.
34 Ibid.
35 David Herman, The Sontag Essay, *Prospect Magazine*, https://www.prospectmagazine.co.uk/magazine/thesontagessay, 20 February 2005.
36 Negri, *Flower of the Desert*, 291.
37 Rennie, *Speculating on the Moment*, 226.
38 Leopardi, *Zibaldone*, 5275.
39 Leopardi, *Operette*, 83.
40 Ibid., 83.
41 Jones, *Essay on Man*, xvii.
42 Ibid., cii.
43 Leopardi, *Zibaldone*, 2164.
44 Jones, *Essay on Man*, xvii.
45 Leopardi, *Operette*, 10.
46 Leopardi, *Canti*, 106.
47 Stuart Hall, 'Old and New Identities, Old and New Ethnicities', in *Culture, Globalisation, and the World-System: Contemporary Conditions for the Representation of Identity*, (United States: University of Minnesota Press, 1997), 48–9.
48 Ibid., 20.
49 Gilroy, *Postcolonial Melancholia*, 74.
50 Gilroy, '"Where Every Breeze Speaks of Courage and Liberty": Offshore Humanism and Marine Xenology, or, Racism and the Problem of Critique at Sea Level: The 2015 Antipode RGS-IBG Lecture', *Antipode* 50, no. 1 (2018): 7.
51 Eleonora Montuschi, 'Order of Man, Order of Nature: Francis Bacon's Idea of a "Dominion" over Nature', *The Governance of Nature Workshop*, LSE, 27 (2010): 28.
52 Peter Harrison, 'Subduing the Earth: Genesis 1, Early Modern Science, and the Exploitation of Nature', *The Journal of Religion* 79 (1999): 86–109.
53 Klein, *On Fire*, 59.
54 Carolyn Merchant, 'The Scientific Revolution and The Death of Nature', *Isis* 97, no. 3 (2006): 513–33, 513. & Merchant, Carolyn. 'The Death of Nature: Women, Ecology, and the Scientific Revolution', (1980), 168–72.
55 Benjamin Farrington, 'The Philosophy of Francis Bacon', *Science and Society* 30, no. 1 (1966): 36.

56 Conner Clifford, *A People's History of Science: Miners, Midwives, and Low Mechanicks* (United Kingdom: Hachette, 2009), 403–4.
57 Kathryn Yusoff, *A Billion Black Anthropocenes or None* (Minnesota: University of Minnesota Press, 2018), 2.
58 Lynn White Jr, 'The Historical Roots of Our Ecological Crisis', *Science* 155: 1967,1203–07.
59 Friedrich Nietzsche, *The Gay Science* (United Kingdom: Cambridge University Press, 2001), 119–20.
60 Emanuele Severino, *In viaggio con Leopardi: la partita sul destino dell'uomo* (Italy: Rizzoli, 2015), 10–11.
61 Daniela Bini. 'Giacomo Leopardi's Ultrafilosofia', *Italica* 74, no. 1 (1997): 52–66, 53.
62 Timpanaro, *On Materialism*. (London: London Review of Books, 1975), 118.
63 Ibid., 118.
64 Esposito, *Living Thought*, 122.
65 John Gray, *The Soul of the Marionette: A Short Inquiry into Human Freedom* (Harvard: Macmillan, 2015), 31.
66 Esposito, *Living Thought*, 22.
67 Theodor Adorno and Max Horkheimer, *Dialectic of Enlightenment* (United Kingdom: Verso, 1997), 9. & Esposito, *Living Thought*. 119.
68 Roberto Esposito, *Living Thought*, 126.
69 Gray, *The Soul of the Marionette*, 33.
70 Ibid., 27–30.
71 Martin Gorsky, Bernard Harris, Patricia Marsh and Ida Milne, 'The 1918/19 Influenza Pandemic & COVID-19 in Ireland and the UK', *Historical Social Research*, 33, no. 1 (2021): 93–226.
72 Rose, 'To Die One's Own Death', *London Review of Books*.
73 Ibid.
74 Sigmund Freud, *The Future of an Illusion* (London: Penguin, 2008), 22.
75 Ibid.
76 Leopardi, *Canti*, 287.
77 Rose, 'To Die One's Own Death', *London Review of Books*, 19 November 2020. Available online: https://www.lrb.co.uk/the-paper/v42/n22/jacqueline-rose/to-die-one-s-own-death (accessed 23 February 2023).
78 Mike Davis, *The Monster Enters: COVID-19, Avian Flu and the Plagues of Capitalism* (United Kingdom: Verso Books, 2022), 12.

79 Rose, 'To Die One's Own Death'.
80 Ibid.
81 Jacqueline Rose, *Why War? Psychoanalysis, Politics and the Return to Melanie Klein*, (Cambridge: John Wiley & Sons, 1993), 95.
82 Sigmund Freud, *The Standard Edition of the Complete Psychological Works of Sigmund Freud*, vol. 19 1923–1925 (London: Hogarth Press, 1961), 45.
83 Rose, 'To Die One's Own Death'.
84 See, for instance: 'Race and Its Disavowal', in Stuart Hall, *Familiar Stranger: A Life between Two Islands* (United Kingdom: Penguin Books Limited, 2017) & Catherine Hall, and Daniel Pick, 'Thinking about Denial', *History Workshop Journal* 84 (2017), https://doi.org/10.1093/hwj/dbx040.
85 Leopardi, *Operette*, 190–1.
86 Ibid., 61.
87 Ibid., 177.
88 Negri, *Flower of the Desert*, 71.
89 Sheridan Blau, 'Pope's "Chain of Being" and the Modern Ecological Vision', *CEA Critic* 33, no. 2 (1971): 20–2, 20.
90 Charles Darwin, *The Origin of Species: 150th Anniversary Edition* (United States: Penguin Publishing Group, 2003), 17.
91 S. Sandford (2018). 'Kant, Race, and Natural History', *Philosophy & Social Criticism* 44, no. 9: 950–77.
Staffan Müller-Wille and Hans-Jörg Rheinberger also address the theme of race in Linnaeus' work, highlighting how his system extended a caste system put in place in fifteenth-century Spain and Portugal, to put forward a universal scheme of racial classification. See: Müller-Wille, Staffan and Hans-Jörg Rheinberger. 'Heredity – The Production of an Epistemic Space.' (2004), 21.
92 Lee Alan Dugatkin, 'Buffon, Jefferson and the Theory of New World Degeneracy', *Evolution: Education and Outreach* 12 (2019), 15.
For more on Jefferson's zibaldone, see: Douglas Wilson, ed. *Jefferson's Literary Commonplace Book* (United States: Princeton University Press, 1989).
93 Lee Alan Dugatkin, *Mr. Jefferson and the Giant Moose: Natural History in Early America* (Chicago: University of Chicago Press, 2009), xi & 81.
94 Leopardi, *Operette*, 47.
95 Ibid.

96 Ibid., 48.
97 Ibid., 46–7.
98 Ibid., 47–8.
99 Max Weber, trans. H.H. Gerth, and C.W. Mills, *From Max Weber: Essays in Sociology* (United Kingdom: Oxford University, 1946), 51 & 155.
100 Leopardi, *Operette*, 51–2.
101 Ibid.
102 Walter Benjamin, *The Arcades Project* (United Kingdom: Harvard University Press, 2002), 894.
103 Ibid., 63.
104 Megan Lambert, *The Lowest Cost at Any Price: The Impact of Fast Fashion on the Global Fashion Industry* (Lake Forest: Lake Forest College, 2014), 98.
105 Leopardi, *Operette*, 52.
106 Leopardi acknowledged in **[Z1631]** that such a view was not unique to his times, observing how Homer frequently called him own times degenerate by contrast with the physical strength of Trojan times.
107 Emanuela Cervato, Mark Epstein and Giulia Santi, eds. *Mapping Leopardi: Poetic and Philosophical Intersections* (Cambridge: Cambridge Scholars Publishing, 2019), 199.
108 Esposito, *Living Thought*, 120.
109 Ibid.
110 Ibid.
111 Ibid., 119.
112 Ibid.
113 Ibid., 121.

Bruno's response to Copernicus' heliocentric hypothesis was to set himself the task of restoring an authentic ancient philosophy by elaborating upon what could be discerned in surviving Egyptian and Pythagorean records with the help of insights preserved in Greek philosophy. Knox, Dilwyn, 'Giordano Bruno', *The Stanford Encyclopedia of Philosophy* (Summer 2019 Edition), Edward N. Zalta (ed.), URL = https://plato.stanford.edu/archives/sum2019/entries/bruno/.

Bruno's philosophy was also shaped by his engagement with Copernican astronomy. For a full account of this, see: Ernan McMullin, 'Bruno and Copernicus', *Isis* 78, no. 1 (1987): 55–74.
114 Esposito, *Living Thought*, 121.

115 Ibid., 122.
116 Ibid.
117 Leopardi, *Operette*, 99.
118 Negri described these gnomes ruling over the forests and meadows as a representation and denunciation of both anthropocentrism and teleology: Negri, *Flower of the Desert*, 124.
119 Leopardi, *Operette*, 58.
  This seems to be a reference to the seventeenth century French text *Le comte de Gabalis, ou entretiens sur les sciences secrètes*, (*The Count of Cabala, Or Dialogs on the Secret Sciences*) by Henri de Montfaucon de Villars.
120 Leopardi, *Operette*, 59.
121 Negri, *Flower of the Desert*, 124.
122 In her work, *The Ahuman Manifesto: Activism for the End of the Anthropocene* (2020), 13, Patricia MacCormack argues that humanity's absence will see the revival of non-human life. Taking this observation to its ultimate conclusion, MacCormack advocates for 'the deceleration of human life through cessation of reproduction' as a means of 'forsaking our human privilege' as a radical means with which to 'affirm the world'.
123 Leopardi, *Operette*, 59.
124 Ibid., 70.
125 Lucinda Dirven, 'The Author of "De Dea Syria" and His Cultural Heritage', *Numen* 44, no. 2 (1997): 153–79.
126 Wendy Gay Pearson, 'Speculative Fiction and Queer Theory', in *Oxford Research Encyclopedia of Communication* (United States: Johns Hopkins University, 2022).
127 Lucian, trans Paul Turner, *Satirical Sketches* (United States: Indiana University Press, 1990), 113.
128 Leopardi, *Operette*, 72.
129 Esposito, *Living Thought*, 121.
130 Di Rosa, *Mapping Leopardi*, 411.
131 Ibid., 412.
132 Leopardi, *Canti*, 12.
133 Di Rosa, *Mapping Leopardi*, 353.
134 Adriana Cavarero, *Horrorism: Naming Contemporary Violence* (United States: Columbia University Press, 2009), 15.
135 Leopardi, *Operette*, 102.

136 Leopardi, *Zibaldone*, xlviii.
137 Aurelius, trans. Gregory Hays. *The Meditations of Marcus Aurelius* (Canada: Random House Inc, 2002), xxviii.
138 Ibid.
139 Leopardi, *Operette*, 59–61.
140 Ibid., 176.
   In relation to this dialogue, Di Rosa argues that: 'Deleuze and Guattari's perception of "becoming-matter," recalls Leopardi's stratonismo (Strato's philosophy), specifically the presence of forces of production and reproduction, as well as the idea of a matter that incessantly engenders new materialities'. 424.
141 Leopardi, *Operette*, 104.
142 Ibid., 99.
143 Ibid.
144 Ibid.
145 Ibid., 100.
146 Aurelius, *Meditations*, lxxv.
147 Ibid., 101.
148 Ibid., xliii, 24, 35.
149 Tavis Smiley, and Cornel West, *The Rich and the Rest of Us* (United States: Hay House, 2012), 11.
150 Leopardi, *Canti*, 172.
151 Sebastiano Timpanaro, *The Freudian Slip: Psychoanalysis and Textual Criticism* (London: Verso Books, 2011), 201.
152 Timpanaro, *The Freudian Slip*, 212.
153 Ibid., 193.
154 Leopardi, *Operette*, 260.
155 Leopardi also considers in this work how, whenever one finds faults or vices in others, these same capabilities and defects can similarly be found in ourselves, softening our heart when we get irritated by them. See: *Operette*, 179–82.
156 Ibid., 180–1.
157 Ibid.
158 Ibid., 101.
159 Ibid., 101, 103.
160 Freud, *The Future of an Illusion*, 27.

161 Timpanaro, *The Freudian Slip*, 115.
162 Ibid., 201.
163 Sebastiano Timpanaro, 'The Pessimistic Materialism of Giacomo Leopardi', *New Left Review* 116, no. 29–50 (1979): 31.
164 Leopardi, *Operette*, 245.
165 Aleksandr Ėtkind, *Nature's Evil: A Cultural History of Natural Resources* (London: Polity Press, 2021), 7.
166 Russell Dynes, 'The Dialogue between Voltaire and Rousseau on the Lisbon Earthquake: The Emergence of a Social Science View', *Disaster Research Center* (1999): 3.
167 Voltaire, and William F. Fleming. "The Lisbon Earthquake", *New England Review* 26, no. 3 (1990–2005): 183–93: 183.
168 Voltaire. *Philosophical Dictionary* (United States: Dover Publications, 2010), 228.
169 Piperno, *Mapping Leopardi*, 102.
170 'Sillographers' and 'In Praise of Birds' are other examples of the genre.
171 Magnús T. Gudmundsson, Rikke Pedersen, Kristín Vogfjörd, Bergthöra Thorbjarnardóttir, Steinunn Jakobsdóttir and Matthew J. Roberts, 'Eruptions of Eyjafjallajökull volcano, Iceland', Eos Archives (2010): 190.
172 Voltaire, *Philosophical Dictionary*, 230.
173 Leopardi, *Operette*, 103.
174 Ibid.
175 Christophe Litwin, 'Rousseau and Leibniz: Genealogy vs. theodicy', in *The Rousseauian Mind*, edited by Eve Grace and Christopher Kelly. (United Kingdom: Taylor & Francis, 2019), 82.
176 Voltaire. trans. K. Carabine, and James Fowler, *Candide and Other Works*. (Hertfordshire: Wordsworth Editions Limited, 2014), 78.
177 Ibid., 116.
178 Ibid.
179 Timpanaro, 'Between Nature and Society: Introductions to On Materialism', *Verso*, 18 August 2017. Available online: https://www.versobooks.com/blogs/3363-between-nature-and-society-introductions-to-on-materialism (accessed 23 Feb 2023).
180 Perry Anderson, *Considerations on Western Marxism* (London: Verso Books, 2016), 92.
181 Jones, *Essay on Man*, xvi, xxvi.

182 Jones, *Essay on Man*, ciii.
183 Susan L. Cutter (2021). 'The Changing Nature of Hazard and Disaster Risk', *Anthropocene, Annals of the American Association of Geographers* 111, no. 3: 819–27.
184 For a comparison of pessimism in Rousseau and Leopardi, see: Joshua Foa Dienstag. *Pessimism: Philosophy, Ethic, Spirit* (Ukraine: Princeton University Press, 2006).
185 Litwin, *The Rousseauian Mind*, 78.
186 Thomas Kuhn, *The Copernican Revolution* (United Kingdom: University of Chicago Press, 2012), 1.
In an assessment written for the Roman Inquisition in 1616, which related to Galileo's trial for heresy based on his support of heliocentrism, Copernicus' propositions in *On the Revolutions* were described as: 'foolish and absurd in philosophy, and formally heretical since it explicitly contradicts in many places the sense of Holy Scripture, according to the literal meaning of the words and according to the common interpretation and understanding of the Holy Fathers and the doctors of theology.' Maurice A. Finocchiaro, ed. *The Galileo Affair: A Documentary History*. (United Kingdom: University of California Press, 1989), 146.
187 Nicholas Copernicus and Jerzy Dobrzycki, *On the Revolutions*, vol. 2 (United Kingdom: Palgrave Macmillan UK, 2016), 3.
188 Ibid., 3.
189 Giovanni Bignami, 'A Complete History of Astronomy', *Nature* 417, no. 6890 (2002): 692.
190 Leopardi, *Operette*, 245.
191 Dobrzycki, *On the Revolutions*, 3.
192 Gilroy, *Postcolonial Melancholia*, 74.
193 Leopardi, *Operette*, 60–1.
194 Alessandro De Angelis, *Galileo Galilei's 'Two New Sciences': For Modern Readers*. (Switzerland: Springer Nature, 2021), xii.
195 Leopardi, *Operette*, 190.
196 Ibid., 195.
197 Ibid., 189.
198 Ibid., 197.
199 Ibid., 60–1.
200 Ibid., 197.

201 Rennie, *Speculating on the Moment*, 138.
202 Cervato, *Mapping Leopardi*, 409.
203 Dennis Looney 'Leopardi's "Il Copernico" and Paradigm Shifts in Art', *Annali d'Italianistica* 23 (2005): 133–46: 133.
204 William J. Ripple, Christopher Wolf, Thomas M. Newsome, Mauro Galetti, Mohammed Alamgir, Eileen Crist, Mahmoud I. Mahmoud and William F. Laurance, '15,364 Scientist Signatories from 184 Countries, World Scientists' Warning to Humanity: A Second Notice', *BioScience* 67, no. 12, (December 2017): 1026–8.
205 Leopardi, *Operette*, 190.
206 Science Museum Group, 'A Peep at the Gas Lights in Pall Mall'. 1980–362. Science Museum Group Collection Online. Accessed 13 January 2023. https://collection.sciencemuseumgroup.org.uk/objects/co66455/a-peep-at-the-gas-lights-in-pall-mall-print.
207 Molena, Francis, 'Remarkable Weather of 1911: The Effect of the Combustion of Coal on the Climate – What Scientists Predict for the Future' in *Popular Mechanics* (March 1912), 341.
208 Examining current societal trends with regard to avoiding further injustice towards Indigenous communities, scholars have warned that relational tipping points might already have been crossed, showing the urgency we need to address such issues with, in order to avoid causing further damage. See: Kyle Whyte, 'Too Late for Indigenous Climate Justice: Ecological and Relational Tipping Points', *Wiley Interdisciplinary Reviews: Climate Change* 11, no. 1 (2020): e603.
209 Christiana Figueres and Tom Rivett-Carnac, *The Future We Choose: The Stubborn Optimist's Guide to the Climate Crisis* (London: Vintage, 2021), 100.
210 Leopardi, *Operette*, 197.
211 Figueres and Rivett-Carnac, *The Future We Choose*, 100.
212 Expanding on Leopardi's recognition of the way we resist narratives that threaten our ability to have positive images of ourselves, the *Zibaldone* is littered with observations that highlight that this is a trend with a long history. One example of this can be seen as Leopardi considers the similarities between the stories told in different Italian towns, of which he wrote:

> 'I myself have heard various stories told in Italian towns, very distant from one another, various claims about the origins of

proverbs, various celebrated ridiculous events, etc., said to have happened expressly to one person in one town; and it was the same in every city, always exactly the same story with just a different name; and I had already heard many of the stories since my childhood told in my own home town and by my parents, with the names of people from the town or region. And some of them I have also found in ancient Italian storytellers, with other names, and the stories are now told as if they happened just a little while ago, to people know to the narrators, or known to someone from whom they heard them [4224]'. This also reappears in Leopardi's examination of Ovid's sources, of which Leopardi commented: 'And how many tales or stories from mythical or heroic times are found repeated with different names and places in various writers, not just Greek and Latin but also Greek along!' [4372].

According to the psychologist William Hirstein, the phenomenon of seemingly healthy people continually making false claims that they believe to be true is an example of what he describes as 'confabulation'. As he writes: 'Confabulators seem to believe their claims, and the consensus among those who study them is that they are not deliberately lying, even though they have an obvious motive to do so on most occasion, to appear normal and healthy.' This has generated new literature according to which psychologists have sought to understand the motivation and emotions underpinning peoples' tendency to expound theories they cannot believe. William Hirstein, ed. *Confabulation: Views from Neuroscience, Psychiatry, Psychology and Philosophy* (Oxford: Oxford University Press, USA, 2009), 1.

Chapter 2

1 Leopardi, *Canti*, 287.
2 Calvino, *Six Memos*, 46.
3 Rennie, *Speculating on the Moment*, vol. 8. (Germany: Wallstein Verlag, 2005), 131.
4 Galassi, *Canti*, xiii.
5 Ibid.

6   Leopardi, *Operette*, 98.
7   Margaret Grieve, *A Modern Herbal*, vol. 2. Courier Corporation, 2013, 125. & Plant, John S., and R. E. Plant. 'Understanding the Royal Name Plantagenet. How DNA Helps', *Guild of One Name Studies* (2010): 14.
8   Murphy, 'Flower of the Desert: Poetics as Ontology from Leopardi to Negri', 2011, 76.
9   Ibid., 80–1.
10 Bini, *A Fragrance from The Desert*, 93.
11 Robert Solomon, 'A More Severe Morality: Nietzsche's Affirmative Ethics' in *Nietzsche as Affirmative Thinker*, (Germany: Springer Netherlands, 2012), 71.
12 Ibid., 76.
13 Ibid., 80.
14 Ibid., 87.
15 Robert Solomon, *Living with Nietzsche: What the Great 'Immoralist' Has to Teach Us* (United Kingdom: Oxford University Press, 2006), 116.
16 For an in-depth discussion of Rennie's examination of the relationship between the work of Leopardi and Nietzsche, see: Keith Ansell-Pearson, 'Review of Speculating on the Moment: The Poetics of Time and Recurrence in Goethe, Leopardi, and Nietzsche by Nicholas Rennie', *Journal of Nietzsche Studies*, 35/36, no. 1 (2008): 198–200.
17 Angela Matilde Capodivacca, 'Nietzsche's Zukunftsphilologie: Leopardi, Philology, History', *California Italian Studies* 2, no. 1 (2011).
18 Nietzsche, *Gay Science*, 92.
19 Capodivacca, 'Nietzsche's Zukunftsphilologie'.
20 Ibid.
21 Friedrich Nietzsche, 'On Truth and Lies in a Nonmoral Sense', Truth: Engagements across Philosophical Traditions (2005): 14–25, 14.
22 Leopardi, *Operette*, 61.
23 Ibid., 59.
24 Perry Anderson, *Spectrum: From Right to Left in the World of Ideas* (United Kingdom: Verso, 2005), 195.
25 Leopardi, *Canti*, 297.
26 Leopardi, *Operette*, 245.
27 Carsaniga, *Giacomo Leopardi*, 70.
28 Leopardi, *Canti*, 291.
29 Ibid., 457.

30 Pamela Williams. 'Leopardi's Philosophy of Consolation in "La ginestra"', *The Modern Language Review* 93, no. 4 (1998): 986.
31 In doing so, Leopardi adopts the approach he expressed via Eleander, who remarked: 'I wish in my writings not so much to carp at our species, as to deplore fate.' Leopardi, *Operette*, 184.
32 Williams, 'Leopardi's Philosophy of Consolation in 'La ginestra', 986.
33 Bini, A Fragrance from the Desert, 63.
34 Robert C Solomon, *Living with Nietzsche: What the Great 'Immoralist' Has to Teach Us* (United Kingdom: Oxford University Press, 2003), 23.
35 Leopardi, *Canti*, 293.
36 Kathleen Marie Higgins, *Comic Relief: Nietzsche's Gay Science* (Greece: Oxford University Press, 2000), 102: 109.
37 Emilio Di Vito, 'Materialistic and Poetic Humanism in G. Leopardi', in *Life the Human Quest for an Ideal: 25th Anniversary Publication Book II* (Germany: Springer, 1996), 224.
38 Leopardi, Canti, 293.
39 Ibid.
40 Timpanaro, *On Materialism*, 65.
41 Ibid., 11.
42 Ibid., 67.
43 Leopardi, *Canti*, 307.
44 Ibid., 297.
45 Ibid., 307.
46 Ibid., 303.
47 Ibid., 295.
48 Ibid., 307.
49 Timpanaro, *On Materialism*, 20.
50 Ibid., 67.
51 Anderson, *Spectrum*, 193.
52 Timpanaro, *On Materialism*, 67.
53 Ibid., 66. This heroic calm, studied by Leopardi, is considered by Staël in *Corinne*, where she compares the grief depicted by an ancient sculpture to the subject of the cold and oppressive social conditions of her time, writing: 'In some instances, an ancient sculptor only produced one statue during his life – it was his whole history. – He perfected it every day: if he loved, if he was beloved, if he received from nature or the fine arts any

new impression, he adorned the features of his hero with his memories and affections: he could thus express to outward eyes all the sentiments of his soul. The grief of our modern times, in the midst of our cold and oppressive social conditions, contains all that is most noble in man; and in our days, he who has not suffered, can never have thought or felt. But there was in antiquity, something more noble than grief – an heroic calm – the sense of conscious strength, which was cherished by free and liberal institutions'. Leopardi also takes up and used Staël's description of our age as 'cold by nature, or even lukewarm'. See, for example: *Operette*, 183.

54 Images that would become central to existentialist thought can also be found in Leopardi's work. For example, on 9 August 1821, he wrote in the *Zibaldone*: 'The majority of men in the last analysis have no desire or yearning to live except for the sake of living. The real object of life is life, and laboring with great effort to drag a heavy, empty cart up and down the same road' **[1476]**. This Sisyphean theme would later be taken up again by the absurdist, Albert Camus, in his philosophical examination of suicide in the *Myth of Sisyphus*. On the topic of suicide, Leopardi wrote in **[1798]**: 'Suicide is counter to nature. But do we live according to nature? Have we not totally abandoned it to follow reason?'

55 Anderson, *Spectrum*, 193.

56 For an account of the Stoic ideal of attaining freedom from passion, see: Sedley, David. Passions. Stoicism, 1998, doi:10.4324/9780415249126-A112-1. Routledge Encyclopedia of Philosophy, Taylor and Francis, https://www.rep.routledge.com/articles/thematic/stoicism/v-1/sections/passions

57 Negri, *Flower of the Desert*, 117.

58 Dario Del Puppo, 'Nourishment and Nature in Leopardi', *Italica* 93, no. 4 (2016): 693–704. http://www.jstor.org/stable/44504613. 693–5. During his time of exile in Torre del Greco, Leopardi benefited from a private chef, Pasquale Ignarra. In letters he wrote to his sister, he spoke of the well-being he found in the good food he enjoyed as a result, and of his visits to the food outlets on the Neapolitan streets, where he enjoyed macaroni, in addition to quenching his love for sorbets.

59 Iris Murdoch in her novel *The Nice and the Good*, where she describes happiness in relation to her protagonist Willy Kost as: 'a matter of one's most ordinary everyday mode of consciousness being busy and lively

and unconcerned with self'. See: Iris Murdoch, *The Nice and the Good* (United Kingdom: Penguin Books, 1971), 179.
60 Esposito, *Living Thought*, 122.
61 For an analysis of 'genius' in *Corinne*, see: Gayle Levy, 'A Genius for the Modern Era: Germaine de Staël's "Corinne"', *Nineteenth-Century French Studies* 30, no. 3/4 (2002): 242–53. http://www.jstor.org/stable/23537773.
62 M. Martina Piperno, *Temporalities and Fractures in Post-Napoleonic Italy: Leopardi and Vico's Legacy* (Warwick: University of Warwick, 2016), 117.
63 Stuart Hall and Paul Du Gay, eds. *Questions of Cultural Identity* (United Kingdom: SAGE Publications, 1996), 59.
64 For an examination of the prominence of the use of fables as a vehicle for social and political in Italy in the eighteenth century, see: Kenneth McKenzie, 'Italian Fables of the Eighteenth Century', *Italica* 12, no. 2 (1935): 39–44. https://doi.org/10.2307/476382.
65 Leopardi, *Canti*, 289.
66 Voltaire and William F. Fleming, 'The Lisbon Earthquake', *New England Review (1990–)* 26, no. 3 (2005): 183–93. http://www.jstor.org/stable/40245285. 183.
67 Leopardi, *Operette*, 184.
68 Leopardi, *Canti*, 303.
69 Ibid., 305.
70 For an examination of the role of dialogues in Bruno's work, including in relation to Torquato Tasso, who appeared in dialogue with his Guardian Spirit in Leopardi's *Operette*, see: 'Bruno's Cabala and Italian Dialogue Form', in *The Cabala of Pegasus* (New Haven: Yale University Press, 2008), xxxviii–l. https://doi.org/10.12987/9780300127911-003 & Eugenio Canone and Leen Spruit, 'Rhetoric and Philosophical Discourse in Giordano Bruno's Italian Dialogues', *Poetics Today* 28, no. 3 (2007): 363–91.
71 Leopardi, *Operette*, 251.
72 Hadot, *Philosophy as a Way of Life*, 27.
73 Ibid.
74 Leopardi, *Operette*, 106.
75 Roberta Cauchi-Santoro has also argued in *Beyond the Suffering of Being: Desire in Giacomo Leopardi and Samuel Beckett* (2016), that compassion is a central theme in Leopardi's oeuvre, which throws into question nihilist readings of the author.

76 Williams, 'Leopardi's Philosophy of Consolation in 'La ginestra''. https://doi.org/10.2307/3736271. 987.
77 Leopardi, *Canti*, 297.
78 Williams, 'Leopardi's Philosophy of Consolation in 'La ginestra'', 989.
79 Ibid.
80 Ibid.
81 Ibid., 990.
82 Ibid.
83 Ibid.
84 Ibid., 985–7.
85 Ibid., 989.
86 Ibid., 987.
87 Antonio Negri, *Subversive Spinoza:(UN) Contemporary Variations: Antonio Negri*, (United Kingdom: Manchester University Press, 2004). Note 23. 77 & Negri, *Flower of the Desert*, xxi.
88 Negri, *Flower of the Desert*, xxi.
89 Giuseppe de Lorenzo, 'The Cosmic Conceptions of Leopardi'', *East and West* 5, no. 3 (1954): 198–204, 199.
   In his article, Lorenzo also defended Leopardi's work from Benedetto Croce's criticism that the degree to which his thought was so intrinsic to his poetry detracted from it.
90 Marcus Wilson, 'Seneca the Consoler? A New Reading of His Consolatory Writings', in *Greek and Roman Consolations: Eight Studies of a Tradition and Its Afterlife*, edited by Han Baltussen. (United Kingdom: Classical Press of Wales, 2012), 93–121, 94.
   As Douglas Walton has examined in *Appeal to Pity: Argumentum Ad Misericordiam*, however, Seneca's analysis of the implications of pity as an ethical concept, in works such as *On Mercy*, are comparable to yet more negative than those found in the work of Aristotle. Douglas Walton, *Appeal to Pity: Argumentum Ad Misericordiam* (United States: State University of New York Press, 2016), 51.
91 Amy Olberding, '"A Little Throat Cutting in the Meantime": Seneca's Violent Imagery', *Philosophy and Literature* 32, no. 1 (2008): 130–44, 130.
92 Ibid., 131.
93 Harry M. Hine 'Rome, the Cosmos, and the Emperor in Seneca's "Natural Questions"'. *The Journal of Roman Studies* 96 (2006): 42–72. http://www.

jstor.org/stable/20430488. 50 & Matthew Roller, 'The Dialogue in Seneca's Dialogues (and Other Moral Essays)', *The Cambridge Companion to Seneca* (2015): 54–67, 54.

94   Lucius Annaeus Seneca, *Natural Questions*, trans. Harry M. Hine (United Kingdom: University of Chicago Press, 2014), 137.
95   Moore, *Ecological Literature and the Critique of Anthropocentrism*, 55.
96   Leopardi, *Canti*, 300.
97   Immanuel Kant, *Critique of Pure Reason* (United Kingdom: Palgrave Macmillan, 2007), 161–2.
98   Howard Caygill, *A Kant Dictionary* (United Kingdom: Wiley, 1995), 137.
99   Martha C. Nussbaum, 'Kant and Stoic Cosmopolitanism', *Journal of Political Philosophy* 5, no. 1 (1997): 1–25, 4.
100 Ibid.
101 Hamilton, Paul, 'Leopardi and the Proper Conversation of a Citizen', *Realpoetik: European Romanticism and Literary Politics* (Oxford, 2013; online edn, Oxford Academic, 23 Jan. 2014), https://doi.org/10.1093/acprof:oso/9780199686179.003.0009, (accessed 1 July 2023).
102 Caygill, *A Kant Dictionary*, 100.
103 Richard Koffler explicitly places Leopardi and Kant side by side in his study Richard Koffler, 'Kant, Leopardi, and Gorgon Truth', *The Journal of Aesthetics and Art Criticism* 30, no. 1 (1971): 27–33. https://doi.org/10.2307/429570.
104 Leopardi, *Zibaldone*, 2164.
105 Marcus Aurelius. Meditations. Modern Library, 2003, 276. This was examined by Pierre Hadot in Philosophy as a *Way of Life: Spiritual Exercises from Socrates to Foucault* (1995).
106 Marcus Aurelius Antoninus, trans. Arthur Spenser Loat Farguharson, *The Meditations of Marcus Aurelius Antoninus* (United Kingdom: Oxford University Press, 1998), 86.
107 Aurelius, *Meditations*, 20.
108 For an exploration of the notion that understanding anthropocenic conceptions of scale can help strengthen philosophical and social engagement with the role of humans in the Anthropocene, see: Gabriele Dürbeck, and Philip Hüpkes, eds. *Narratives of Scale in the Anthropocene: Imagining Human Responsibility in an Age of Scalar Complexity* (United Kingdom: Taylor & Francis, 2021).

109 Donald Robertson, *The Philosophy of Cognitive – Behavioural Therapy (CBT): Stoic Philosophy as Rational and Cognitive Psychotherapy* (London: Routledge, 2018), 250.
110 Ginestra lines 179 and 192.
111 Leopardi, *Canti*, lines 298–300 & Aurelius, *Meditations*, 92.
112 Luuc Kooijmans, *Death Defied: The Anatomy Lessons of Frederik Ruysch* (Harvard: Brill, 2010), xv and 435.
113 Leopardi, *Operette*, 134.
114 Ibid., 134–5.
115 Ibid., 135.
116 Ibid., 136.
117 Ibid., 135.
118 Leopardi, *Operette*, 135.
119 Negri, *Flower of the Desert*, 123.
120 In her work in *Cruel Optimism* (2011), Laurent Berlant referred to the detrimental effects caused by our attachment to an obstacle hindering our capacity to flourish when she wrote: 'A relation of cruel optimism exists when something you desire is actually an obstacle to your flourishing. It might involve food, or a kind of love; it might be a fantasy of the good life, or a political project. It might rest on something simpler too, like a new habit that promises to induce in you're an improved way of being. These kinds of optimistic relation are not inherently cruel. They become cruel only when the object that draws your attachment actively impedes the aim that brought you to it initially.' Lauren Berlant, *Cruel Optimism* (United States: Duke University Press, 2011), 1.
121 Andreas Malm, *White Skin, Black Fuel: On the Danger of Fossil Fascism* (London: Verso Books, 2021), 491–2.
122 Inger Andersen (2022), 'We Are at War with Nature': UN Environment Chief Warns of Biodiversity Apocalypse', *Guardian*, 6 December. Available online: https://www.theguardian.com/environment/2022/dec/06/cop-15-un-chief-biodiversity-apocalypse (accessed 23 February 2023).
123 Andersen (2021), 'The Triple Planetary Crisis and Public Health', *UNEP*, 5 September. Available online: https://www.unep.org/news-and-stories/speech/triple-planetary-crisis-and-public-health (accessed 23 February 2023).
124 Leopardi, *Operette*, 102.

125 Shiva, *Making Peace with the Earth*, 9.
126 Nanda Kishore Kannuri and Sushrut Jadhav, 'Cultivating Distress: Cotton, Caste and Farmer Suicides in India', *Anthropology & Medicine* 28, no. 4 (December 2021) : 558–75.
More recently Bayer has sought to introduce genetically modified crops in Nigeria in a move concerning which the molecular biologist Ifeanyi Casmir stated in an interview on 8 November 2018: 'Our traditional seeds are superior to what is being handed down to us, we are gradually with our eyes open, entering into slavery …'. See: Charmaine Pereira, '"Walking into Slavery with Our Eyes Open"– the Space for Resisting Genetically Modified Crops in Nigeria', *Feminist Africa* 2, no. 1 (2021): 99–125, 100.
127 Robin has given a comprehensive account of the attack underway on the production and distribution of food, which is increasingly controlled by multinational corporations in her 2008 film *The World According to Monsanto*, which was also released as a book, while more recently, Taggart Siegel and Jon Betz's 2016 documentary, 'SEED: The Untold Story', extends the exploration of the relationship between seeds and intellectual property, featuring Shiva and the anthropologist and primatologist Jane Goodall.
128 Robin Marie-Monique, *The World According to Monsanto: Pollution, Corruption, and the Control of Our Food Supply* (United States: New Press, 2014), 307–10.
129 Shiva, *Making Peace with the Earth*, 8.
130 Ibid., 7.
131 Henrietta Moore, (2020), 'Towards a New Progress Story Which Redefines Our Relationship to Nature', 13 July. Available online: https://www.henriettalmoore.com/post/towards-a-new-progress-story-which-redefines-our-relationship-to-nature (accessed 23 February 2023).
132 Vallance, 'We've Overexploited the Planet, Now We Need to Change if We're to Survive'.
133 Shiva, Making Peace with the Earth, 6.
134 Ibid., 5–6.
135 Vandana Shiva, and Kartikey Shiva, *Oneness Vs. the 1%: Shattering Illusions, Seeding Freedom* (United Kingdom: Chelsea Green Publishing, 2020), 30.

136 Ibid., 16.
137 Press Release (2022), 'A Deadly Decade for Land and Environmental Activists – with a Killing Every Two Days', *Global Witness*, 29 September. Available online: https://www.globalwitness.org/en/press-releases/deadly-decade-land-and-environmental-activists-killing-every-two-days/ (accessed 23 February 2023).
138 V.H.A. Heinrich, R. Dalagnol, H.L.G. Cassol et al. 'Large Carbon Sink Potential of Secondary Forests in the Brazilian Amazon to Mitigate Climate Change', *Nat Commun* 12, no. 1785 (2021). https://doi.org/10.1038/s41467-021-22050-1
139 Patricia Hill Collins, *Fighting Words: Black Women and the Search for Justice* (United Kingdom: University of Minnesota Press, 1998), 87.
140 Stuart Hall, and Bram Gieben, *The Formations of Modernity: Understanding Modern Societies an Introduction* (United Kingdom: Wiley, 1992), vol. 2.
141 Binoy Kampmark points out its occurrence in relation to the depiction of nature following extreme weather events in: 'Media war metaphors mistake Mother Nature as the real enemy', published in *Independent Australia* in Jan 2023, where he highlights that a recent proliferation of reports has sensationalized 'Anthropomorphised Mother Nature' as the enemy. He argues that such reports have the effect of preventing us from taking accountability for our role fuelling the environmental crisis.
142 Hall and Gieben. 'The West and the Rest', 216.
143 Anderson, *Considerations on Western Marxism*, 208; Timpanaro, *The Freudian Slip*, 193; and Leopardi, *Zibaldone*, 75.
144 Thomas Harrison, 'Towards a New Ecological Imagination: Post-Anthropocentric Leopard', *Costellazioni* 4, no. 10 (2019): 126.
145 Ibid., 126–7.
146 Collins, *Fighting Words*, 87.
147 See also: Luigi Capitano, 'Aristotle, Leopardi, Severino: The Endless Game of Nothingness', *Eternity & Contradiction Journal of Fundamental Ontology* 3, no. 5 (2021): 75–96.
148 Kwame Anthony Appiah (2019), 'Dialectics of Enlightenment', *The New York Review*, 9 May. Available online: https://www.nybooks.com/

articles/2019/05/09/irrationality-dialectics-enlightenment/ (accessed 23 February 2023).
149 David Ball (2019), 'Voltaire's Tears', *The New York Review*, 6 June. Available online: https://www.nybooks.com/articles/2019/06/06/voltaires-tears/ (accessed 23 February 2023).
150 Giacomo Leopardi, *Pensieri: A Bilingual Edition*, trans. W.S. Di Piero (United States: Louisiana State University Press, 1981), 17.
151 Ibid., 111.
152 Theodor Adorno, *Minima Moralia: Reflections from Damaged Life* (United Kingdom: Verso Books, 2005), 39.
153 Leopardi, *Canti*, 299.
154 Lucía Ayala, *The Making of Copernicus,* ed. Wolfgang Neuber, Claus Zittel and Thomas Rahn (Leiden: Brill, 2014), 213.
155 Negri, *Flower of the Desert*, xxi.
156 Ibid.
157 Shiva, *Making Peace with the Earth*, 9.
158 Jack Halberstam, *Wild Things: The Disorder of Desire* (United Kingdom: Duke University Press, 2020), 25.
159 Sebastiano Timpanaro, 'Il «Leopardi Verde»', *Belfagor* 42, no. 6 (1987): 613–37, 616.
160 Leopardi, *Canti*, 106.
161 Anderson, *Spectrum*, 208.
162 Timpanaro, 'Il «Leopardi Verde »', 621–2.
163 Damian Carrington (2023), '"No Miracles Needed": Prof Mark Jacobson on how wind, sun and water can power the World', *Guardian*. 23 January. Available online: https://www.theguardian.com/environment/2023/jan/23/no-miracles-needed-prof-mark-jacobson-on-how-wind-sun-and-water-can-power-the-world (accessed 23 February 2023).
164 James Hansen, *Storms of My Grandchildren: The Truth about the Coming Climate Catastrophe and Our Last Chance to Save Humanity* (United Kingdom: Bloomsbury Publishing, 2011), 306.
165 Ibid.
166 Ibid., 308.
167 Ibid.
168 Press Release (2022), 'Ahead of Hearing, Committee Releases Memo Showing Fossil Fuel Industry Is Misleading the Public About

Commitment to Reduce Emissions', 14 September. Available online: https://oversightdemocrats.house.gov/news/press-releases/ahead-of-hearing-committee-releases-memo-showing-fossil-fuel-industry-is (accessed 23 February 2023).

169 Nathaniel Rich, *Losing Earth: The Decade We Could Have Stopped Climate Change* (United Kingdom: Pan Macmillan, 2019): 3–4.

170 Selected investigation documents: https://oversight.house.gov/sites/democrats.oversight.house.gov/files/2022/FossilFuelDocumentsForRelease.pdf

171 Jack Ewing, *Faster, Higher, Farther: The Inside Story of the Volkswagen scandal* (United Kingdom: Random House, 2017), 11.

172 Steven R.H. Barrett, Raymond L. Speth, Sebastian D. Eastham, Irene C. Dedoussi, Akshay Ashok, Robert Malina and David W. Keith. 'Impact of the Volkswagen Emissions Control Defeat Device on US Public Health', *Environmental Research Letters* 10, no. 11 (2015): 114005.

173 Shiva, *Staying Alive: Women, Ecology, and Survival in India*, vol. 84 (New Delhi: Kali for Women, 1988), 5.

174 Ibid., 5.

175 Negri, *Flower of the Desert*, 21.

176 Ibid., 22.

177 Esther Jones, *Medicine and Ethics in Black Women's Speculative Fiction* (United States: Palgrave Macmillan, 2016), 6.

178 According to Allan Brandt's synopsis:

> In 1932 the U.S. Public Health Service (USPHS) initiated an experiment in Macon County, Alabama, to determine the natural course of untreated, latent syphilis in black males. The test comprised 400 syphilitic men, as well as 200 uninfected men who served as controls. The first published report of the study appeared in 1936 with subsequent papers issued every four to six years, through the 1960s. When penicillin became widely available by the early 1950s as the preferred treatment for syphilis, the men did not receive therapy. In fact, on several occasions the USPHS actually sought to prevent treatment. Moreover, a committee at the federally operated Center for Disease Control decided in 1969 that the study should be continued. Only in 1972, when accounts of the study first appeared in the national press, did the Department of Health, Education and

Welfare halt the experiment. At that time seventy-four of the test subjects were still alive; at least twenty-eight, but perhaps more than 100, had died directly from advanced syphilitic lesions. In August 1972, HEW appointed an investigatory panel which issued a report the following year. The panel found the study to have been 'ethically unjustified', and argued that penicillin should have been provided to the men. https://dash.harvard.edu/bitstream/handle/1/3372911/Brandt_Racism.pdf?sequence=1&isAllowed=y

See: Allan M. Brandt, 'Racism and Research: The Case of the Tuskegee Syphilis Study', *The Hastings Center Report* 8, no. 6 (1978): 21.

179 Jones, *Medicine and Ethics in Black Women's Speculative Fiction*, 6.
180 Ibid.
181 adrienne maree brown, *Octavia's Brood: Science Fiction Stories from Social Justice Movements* (United Kingdom: AK Press, 2015), 10.
182 Octavia E. Butler, *Parable of the Talents: A Novel*, vol. 2 (United States: Seven Stories Press, 1998), 33.
183 Butler, *Parable of the Sower* (United States: Open Road Media, 2012), 3.
184 For a study of Butler's approach to religion, see: Kimberly T. Ruffin, 'Parable of a 21st Century Religion: Octavia Butler's Afrofuturistic Bridge between Science and Religion', *Obsidian III* 6, no. 7 (2005): 87–104. http://www.jstor.org/stable/44511664. The handwritten affirmative notes in which Butler motivated herself to bring about her vision of her future are held as part of the Octavia E. Butler Collection at the Huntington Library in California.
185 Brown, *Octavia's Brood*, 279.
186 Solnit, *Hope in the Dark*, xiii.
187 For an assessment of the relationship between Nietzsche's concept of 'eternal recurrence' and the recurrent theme of vision in Leopardi's work, see: Nicholas Rennie, *Speculating on the Moment*, vol. 8 (Germany: Wallstein, 2005).
188 Stephen B Oates, *Let the Trumpet Sound: A Life of Martin Luther King, Jr* (United States: Canongate Books, 1998), 258.
189 Martha Nussbaum, *Anger and Forgiveness: Resentment, Generosity, Justice* (United Kingdom: Oxford University Press, 2016), 221.
190 Oates, *Let the Trumpet Sound*, 31. As King stated in his speech delivered in Atlanta on 16 August 1967:

> Power, properly understood, is the ability to achieve purpose. It is the strength required to bring about social, political or economic changes. In this sense power is not only desirable but necessary in order to implement the demands of love and justice. One of the greatest problems of history is that the concepts of love and power are usually contrasted as polar opposites. Love is identified with a resignation of power and power with a denial of love. It was this misinterpretation that caused Nietzsche, the philosopher of the 'will to power', to reject the Christian concept of love. It was this same misinterpretation which induced Christian theologians to reject Nietzsche's philosophy of the 'will to power' in the name of the Christian idea of love. What is needed is a realization that power without love is reckless and abusive and that love without power is sentimental and anemic. Power at its best is love implementing the demands of justice. Justice at its best is love correcting everything that stands against love.

Martin Luther King Jr., *Where Do We Go from Here: Chaos or Community?* (United States: Beacon Press, 2010), 37.
191 Thích Nhất Hạnh, *No Mud, No Lotus: The Art of Transforming Suffering* (London: Parallax Press, 2014), 18.
192 Leopardi, *Canti*, 287.
193 Hall, *Race and Difference*, 426.
194 Gramsci, *Quaderni del carcere*, II (Turin: Giulio Einaudi 1974), 1187.
195 Seligman, *Authentic Happiness*, xi.
196 Christiana Figueres and Tom Rivett-Carnac, *The Future We Choose: Surviving the Climate Crisis,* 100.
197 https://www.marxists.org/archive/bloch/hope/introduction.htm
198 Solnit, *Hope in the Dark,* xii.
199 Ibid.
200 Ibid., 19.
201 Ernst Bloch, 'The Principle of Hope'. Available online: https://www.marxists.org/archive/bloch/hope/introduction.htm (accessed 23 February 2023).
202 Gilroy, *The Black Atlantic*, 42, 49.
203 Ibid., 43.
204 Gilroy, 'Where Every Breeze Speaks of Courage and Liberty', 7.
205 Gilroy, *Against Race,* 38.

206 Ibid.
207 Writing of this form of humanism in relation to the music of B.B. King and highlighting Gilroy's sense of the need to consider the connection between human life and the inhumanities of racism addressed in Gilroy, Paul, *After Empire: Melancholia or Convivial Culture?* (United Kingdom: Routledge, 2004), Les Back observes:

> The experience of B.B. King chimes with Paul Gilroy's argument for the usefulness of the idea of 'planetarity' to convey a different sense of human experience (Gilroy, 2004: xi). This quality of experience involves both movement and contingency. For Gilroy, the art and lives of musicians – from Curtis Mayfield to Bob Marley – offer clues about ways to think about the link between human life and inhumanities of racism. His sense of planetary humanism aims to link the two and develop an ethics and politics 'capable of comprehending the universality of our elemental vulnerability to the wrong we visit upon each other' (Gilroy, 2004: 4).

See: Back, L. (2015). How Blue Can You Get? B.B. King, 'Planetary Humanism and the Blues Behind Bars', Theory, Culture & Society 32, no. 7–8 (2015): 274–85. doi:10.1177/0263276415605579.281.
208 Anderson, *Spectrum*, 193.
209 P. Gilroy, 'Where Ignorant Armies Clash by Night', *International Journal of Cultural Studies* 6, no. 3 (2003). doi:10.1177/13678779030063002. 272.
210 Ibid.
211 Ibid., 272, 275.
212 Paul Gilroy, Tony Sandset, Sindre Bangstad and Gard Ringen Høibjerg, 'A Diagnosis of Contemporary Forms of Racism, Race and Nationalism: A Conversation with Professor Paul Gilroy', *Cultural Studies* 33, no. 2 (2019): 180.
213 Ibid.
214 Ibid., 184.
215 Shiva, Oneness and the 1%, 242.
216 S. Coghlan, B.J. Coghlan, A. Capon *et al*. 'A Bolder One Health: Expanding the Moral Circle to Optimize Health for All', *One Health Outlook* 3, no. 21 (2021). https://doi.org/10.1186/s42522-021-00053-8
217 Ibid.

218 Leopardi, *Operette*, 61.
219 Bini, *A Fragrance from the Desert*, 74.
220 Bryan L. Moore, *Ecological Literature, and the Critique of Anthropocentrism* (Germany: Springer, 2017), viii.
221 Ibid., 47.
222 Ibid.
223 Ibid.
224 Ibid., 48.
225 Copernicus, *On Revolutions*, 4–5.
226 Shiva, *Oneness and the 1%*, 1.

Conclusion

1 Leopardi, *Canti*, 2–3.
2 It hasn't been possible to examine the potential ecological potential of Leopardi's interest in the 'plurality of worlds' in more detail than I have provided here. However, one potential point of departure for such a project is Dipesh Chakrabarty's work *One Planet, Many Worlds: The Climate Parallax* (2022), where Chakrabarty examines the separation between 'natural' and 'human' histories, to ask: Does having different worlds make it difficult for humans to deal with a planet that is one?

Afterword

1 Leopardi, *Operette*, 49.
2 Solnit, *Hope in the Dark*, xv.

Bibliography

Works by Leopardi

The Canti, translated and annotated by Jonathan Galassi (New York: Farrar, Straus, and Giroux, 2010).
The Letters of Giacomo Leopardi 1817–1837, selected and translated by Prue Shaw (Leeds: Northern Universities Press, 1998).
The Moral Essays (Operette morali), translated by Patrick Creagh (New York: Columbia University Press, 1983).
Pensieri, translated by W.S. Di Piero (Baton Rouge: Louisiana State, 1981).
Zibaldone, edited by Michael Caesar and Franco D'Intino (New York: Farrar Straus Giroux, 2013) and abbreviated as Caesar/D'Intino. References to the *Zibaldone* include the page numbers to Leopardi's original manuscript.

***

Adorno, Theodor. *Minima Moralia: Reflections from Damaged Life*. United Kingdom: Verso Books, 2005.
Adorno, Theodor and Max Horkheimer. *Dialectic of Enlightenment*. United Kingdom: Verso Books, 1997.
Alan Dugatkin, Lee. *Mr. Jefferson and the Giant Moose: Natural History in Early America*. Chicago: University of Chicago Press, 2009.
Anderson, Perry. *Spectrum: From Right to Left in the World of Ideas*. United Kingdom: Verso, 2005.
Anderson, Perry. *Considerations on Western Marxism*. London: Verso Books, 2016.
Ansell-Pearson, Keith. 'Review of Speculating on the Moment: The Poetics of Time and Recurrence in Goethe, Leopardi, and Nietzsche by Nicholas Rennie'. *Journal of Nietzsche Studies*, 35/36, no. 1 (2008): 198–200.
Arnold, Matthew. *Poetry of Byron*. London: Macmillan, 1881.
Aurelius, Marcus. *The Meditations of Marcus Aurelius*, translated by Gregory Hays. Canada: Random House Inc, 2002.
Ayala, Lucia. 'Cosmology after Copernicus: Decentralisation of the Sun and the Plurality of Worlds in French Engravings'. In *The Making of Copernicus*, edited by Wolfgang Neuber, Claus Zittel and Thomas Rahn. Leiden: Brill, 2014.

Back, Les. 'How Blue Can You Get? BB King, Planetary Humanism and the Blues behind Bars'. *Theory, Culture & Society* 32, nos. 7–8 (2015): 274–85.

Barrett, Steven R.H., Raymond L. Speth, Sebastian D. Eastham, Irene C. Dedoussi, Akshay Ashok, Robert Malina and David W. Keith. 'Impact of the Volkswagen Emissions Control Defeat Device on US Public Health'. *Environmental Research Letters*, 10, no. 11 (2015): 1–10.

Benjamin, Walter. *The Arcades Project*. United Kingdom: Harvard University Press, 2002.

Berlant, Lauren. *Cruel Optimism*. United States: Duke University Press, 2011.

Bignami, Giovanni. 'A Complete History of Astronomy'. *Nature*, 417, (2002): 692. https://www.nature.com/search?q=astronomy%20history%20Giovanni&journal=nature&order=relevance.

Bini, Daniela. 'Giacomo Leopardi's Ultrafilosofia'. *Italica* 74, no. 1 (1997): 52–66.

Bini, Daniela. *A Fragrance from the Desert: Poetry and Philosophy in Giacomo Leopardi*. United States: University of Texas, 1983.

Blau, Sheridan. 'Pope's "Chain of Being" and the Modern Ecological Vision'. *CEA Critic* 33, no. 2 (1971): 20–2.

Bloch, Ernst. *The Principle of Hope*. United Kingdom: MIT Press, 1995.

Brandt, Allan M. 'Racism and Research: The Case of the Tuskegee Syphilis Study'. *The Hastings Center Report*, 8, no. 6 (1978): 21–9.

Bruno, Giordano. *The Cabala of Pegasus*. New Haven: Yale University Press, 2008.

Butler, Octavia E. *Parable of the Talents: A Novel*, vol. 2. United States: Seven Stories Press, 1998.

Butler, Octavia E. *Parable of the Sower*. United States: Open Road Media, 2012.

Caesar, Michael. 'Leopardi's Operette Morali and the Resources of the Dialogue'. *Italian Studies* 43, no. 1 (1988): 21–40.

Calvino, Italo. *Six Memos for the Next Millennium*. London: Penguin Books Limited, 2009.

Canone, Eugenio and Leen Spruit. 'Rhetoric and Philosophical Discourse in Giordano Bruno's Italian Dialogues'. *Poetics Today* 28, no. 3 (2007): 363–91.

Capitano, Luigi. 'Aristotle, Leopardi, Severino: The Endless Game of Nothingness'. *Eternity & Contradiction Journal of Fundamental Ontology*, 3, no. 5 (2021): 75–96. https://ojs.pensamultimedia.it/index.php/eandc/article/view/5133.

Capodivacca, Angela Matilde. 'Nietzsche's Zukunftsphilologie: Leopardi, Philology, History'. *California Italian Studies* 2, no. 1 (2011): 7.

Carsaniga, Giovanni. *Giacomo Leopardi: The Unheeded Voice*. Edinburgh: Edinburgh University Press, 1977.

Cauchi-Santoro, Roberta. *Beyond the Suffering of Being: Desire in Giacomo Leopardi and Samuel Beckett*. Italy: Firenze University Press, 2016.

Cavarero, Adriana. *Horrorism: Naming Contemporary Violence*. United States: Columbia University Press, 2009.

Caygill, Howard. *A Kant Dictionary*. United Kingdom: Wiley, 1995.

Cervato, Emanuela, Mark Epstein and Giulia Santi, eds. *Mapping Leopardi: Poetic and Philosophical Intersections*. Cambridge: Cambridge Scholars Publishing, 2019.

Clifford, Conner. *A People's History of Science: Miners, Midwives, and Low Mechanicks*. United Kingdom: Hachette, 2009.

Coghlan, S., B.J. Coghlan, A. Capon, et al. 'A Bolder One Health: Expanding the Moral Circle to Optimize Health for All'. *One Health Outlook* 3, no. 21 (2021): 1–4.

Copernicus, Nicholas. *On the Revolutions*, edited by Jerzy Dobrzycki. Vol. 2. United Kingdom: Springer, 2016.

Cutter, Susan L. 'The Changing Nature of Hazard and Disaster Risk'. *Anthropocene, Annals of the American Association of Geographers* 111 (2021): 819–27.

Tobias Dahlkvist, *Nietzsche and the Philosophy of Pessimism: A Study of Nietzsche's Relation to the Pessimistic Tradition: Schopenhauer, Hartmann, Leopardi*, (Uppsala: Uppsala University, 2007), 102.

Darwin, Charles. *The Origin of Species: 150th Anniversary Edition*. United States: Penguin Publishing Group, 2003.

Davis, Mike. *The Monster Enters: COVID-19, Avian Flu and the Plagues of Capitalism*. United Kingdom: Verso Books, 2022.

De Angelis, Alessandro. *Galileo Galilei's 'Two New Sciences': for Modern Readers*. Switzerland: Springer International Publishing, 2022.

De Lorenzo, Giuseppe. 'The Cosmic Conceptions of Leopardi'. *East and West* 5, no. 3 (1954): 198–204.

Del Puppo, Dario. 'Nourishment and Nature in Leopardi'. *Italica* 93, no. 4 (2016): 693–704.

Dienstag, Joshua Foa. *Pessimism: Philosophy, Ethic, Spirit*. United Kingdom: Princeton University Press, 2006.

Dirven, Lucinda. 'The Author of "De Dea Syria" and His Cultural Heritage'. *Numen* 44, no. 2 (1997): 153–79.

Di Vito, Emilio. 'Materialistic and Poetic Humanism in G. Leopardi'. In *Life the Human Quest for an Ideal: 25th Anniversary Publication Book II*. Germany: Springer, 1996.

Dynes, Russell R. 'The Dialogue between Voltaire and Rousseau on the Lisbon Earthquake: The Emergence of a Social Science View'. *International Journal of Mass Emergencies & Disasters* 18, no. 1 (2000): 97–115.

Esposito, Roberto. *Living Thought: The Origins and Actuality of Italian Philosophy*. United States: Stanford University Press, 2012.

Ėtkind, Aleksandr. *Nature's Evil: A Cultural History of Natural Resources*. London: Polity Press, 2021.

Ewing, Jack. *Faster, Higher, Farther: The Inside Story of the Volkswagen Scandal*. United Kingdom: Random House, 2017.

Farrington, Benjamin. 'The Philosophy of Francis Bacon'. *Science and Society*, 30, no. 1 (1966): 36.

Figueres, Christiana and Tom Rivett-Carnac. *The Future We Choose: The Stubborn Optimist's Guide to the Climate Crisis*. London: Vintage, 2021.

Finocchiaro, Maurice A. *The Galileo Affair: A Documentary History*. United Kingdom: University of California Press, 1989.

Fleming, William, F. 'The Lisbon Earthquake'. *New England Review* 26, no. 3 (2005): 183–93.

Freud, Sigmund. *The Standard Edition of the Complete Psychological Works of Sigmund Freud*, vol. 19 1923–1925. London: Hogarth Press, 1961.

Freud, Sigmund. *The Future of an Illusion*. London: Penguin, 2008.

Gill, Joel C., and Bruce D. Malamud. 'Anthropogenic Processes, Natural Hazards, and Interactions in a Multi-hazard Framework'. *Earth-Science Reviews* 166 (2017): 246–69.

Gilroy, Paul. *Against Race: Imagining Political Culture beyond the Color Line*. Cambridge: Belknap Press of Harvard University Press, 2000.

Gilroy, Paul. '"Where Ignorant Armies Clash by Night" Homogeneous Community and the Planetary Aspect'. *International Journal of Cultural Studies* 6, no. 3 (2003): 261–76.

Gilroy, Paul. *Postcolonial Melancholia*. United States: Columbia University Press, 2005.

Gilroy, Paul. '"Where Every Breeze Speaks of Courage and Liberty": Offshore Humanism and Marine Xenology, or, Racism and the Problem of Critique at Sea Level: The 2015 Antipode RGS-IBG Lecture'. *Antipode* 50, no. 1 (2018): 3–22.

Gorsky, Martin, Bernard Harris, Patricia Marsh and Ida Milne. 'The 1918/19 Influenza Pandemic & COVID-19 in Ireland and the UK'. *Historical Social Research*, 33, no. 1 (2021): 93–226.

Gramsci, Antonio. 'Quaderni del carcere'. *Trans/Form/Ação* 2 (1975): 198–202.

Gray, John. *The Soul of the Marionette: A Short Inquiry into Human Freedom*. Harvard: Macmillan, 2015.

Grieve, Margaret. *A Modern Herbal*, vol. 2. United States: Courier Corporation, 2013.

Gudmundsson, Magnús T., Rikke Pedersen, Kristín Vogfjörd, Bergthöra Thorbjarnardóttir, Steinunn Jakobsdóttir, and Matthew J. Roberts. 'Eruptions of Eyjafjallajökull volcano, Iceland' (2010): 190–1.

Hadot, Pierre. *Philosophy as a Way of Life: Spiritual Exercises from Socrates to Foucault*. United Kingdom: Wiley, 1995.

Halberstam, Jack. *Wild Things: The Disorder of Desire*. United Kingdom: Duke University Press, 2020.

Hall, Catherine, and Daniel Pick. 'Thinking about Denial'. *History Workshop Journal* 84 (2017): 1–23.

Hall, Stuart, and Bram Gieben. 'The West and the Rest: Discourse and Power' *Race and Racialization, 2E: Essential Readings* (1992): 215.

Hall, Stuart, and Paul Du Gay. *Questions of Cultural Identity: SAGE Publications*. London: Sage, 1996.

Hall, Stuart, and Paul Du Gay. 'Old and New Identities, Old and New Ethnicities' in Culture, Globalization, and the World-System: Contemporary Conditions for the Representation of Identity'. In *Culture, Globalization, and the World-System: Contemporary Conditions for the Representation of Identity*, edited by Anthony D. King, 41–68, 48–9. United States: University of Minnesota Press, 1997.

Hall, Stuart and Paul Du Gay. *Familiar Stranger: A Life between Two Islands*. United Kingdom: Penguin Books Limited, 2017.

Hamilton, Paul. 'Leopardi and the Proper Conversation of a Citizen'. In *Realpoetik: European Romanticism and Literary Politics*. Oxford: Oxford University Press, 2013.

Hanh, Thích Nhất Hạnh. *No Mud, No Lotus: The Art of Transforming Suffering*. London: Parallax Press, 2014.

Hansen, James. *Storms of My Grandchildren: The Truth about the Coming Climate Catastrophe and Our Last Chance to Save Humanity*. United Kingdom: Bloomsbury Publishing, 2011.

Haraway, Donna J. *Staying with the Trouble: Making Kin in the Chthulucene*. United Kingdom: Duke University Press, 2016.

Harrison, Peter. 'Subduing the Earth: Genesis 1, Early Modern Science, and the Exploitation of Nature'. *The Journal of Religion*, no. 79 (1999): 86–109.

Harrison, Thomas. 'Towards a New Ecological Imagination: Post-Anthropocentric Leopard'. *Costellazioni* 4, no. 10 (2019): 126.

Heinrich, V.H.A., Dalagnol, R., Cassol, H.L.G., et al. 'Large Carbon Sink Potential of Secondary Forests in the Brazilian Amazon to Mitigate Climate Change'. *Nature Communications*, 12, no. 1785 (2021): 1–11.

Higgins, Kathleen Marie. *Comic Relief: Nietzsche's Gay Science*. United Kingdom: Oxford University Press, 2000.

Hill Collins, Patricia. *Fighting Words: Black Women and the Search for Justice*. United Kingdom: University of Minnesota Press, 1998.

Hine, Harry M. 'Rome, the Cosmos, and the Emperor in Seneca's "Natural Questions"'. *The Journal of Roman Studies* 96 (2006): 42–72.

Imperato, Pascal James, Gavin H. Imperato and Austin C. Imperato. 'The Second World Cholera Pandemic (1826–1849) in the Kingdom of the Two Sicilies with Special Reference to the Towns of San Prisco and Forio d'Ischia'. *Journal of Community Health*, 40, no. 6 (2015): 1224–86.

Jones, Esther. *Medicine and Ethics in Black Women's Speculative Fiction*. United States: Palgrave Macmillan, 2016.

Kannuri, Nanda Kishore and Sushrut Jadhav. 'Cultivating Distress: Cotton, Caste and Farmer Suicides in India'. *Anthropology & Medicine* 28, no. 4 (2021): 558–75.

Kant, Immanuel. *Critique of Pure Reason,* translated by Gary Banham, Howard Caygill, and Norman Kemp Smith. London: Palgrave, 2007.

Khalil, Hussein, Frauke Ecke, Magnus Evander, Magnus Magnusson and Birger Hörnfeldt. 'Declining Ecosystem Health and the Dilution Effect'. *Scientific Reports*, 6, no. 6 (2016): 31314.

Klein, Naomi. *On Fire: The (Burning) Case for a Green New Deal*. United States: Simon & Schuster, 2019.

Koffler, Richard. 'Kant, Leopardi, and Gorgon Truth'. *Journal of Aesthetics and Art Criticism*, 30, no. 1 (1971): 27–33.

Koman, Aleksandra. 'With Rhymes about the Human Fate. Philosophy in the Poetry of Giacomo Leopardi'. *Acta Universitatis Lodziensis. Folia Litteraria Polonica* 59, no. 4 (2020): 101–14.

Kuhn, Thomas. *The Copernican Revolution*. United Kingdom: University of Chicago Press, 2012.

Lambert, Megan. *The Lowest Cost at Any Price: The Impact of Fast Fashion on the Global Fashion Industry*. Lake Forest: Lake Forest College, 2014.

Lecouras, Peter. 'Leopardi's Reception in England: 1837 to 1927'. *Italica* 86, no. 2 (2009): 313–27.

Levy, Gayle. 'A Genius for the Modern Era: Madame de Staël's Corinne'. *Nineteenth-Century French Studies* 30, no. 3/4 (2002): 242–53.

Litwin, Christophe. 'Rousseau and Leibniz: Genealogy vs. Theodicy'. In *The Rousseauian Mind*, edited by Christopher Kelly and Eve Grace. United Kingdom: Taylor & Francis, 2019.

Looney, Dennis. 'Leopardi's "Il Copernico" and Paradigm Shifts in Art'. *Annali d'Italianistica* 23 (2005): 133–46, 133.

Lucian. *Satirical Sketches*, translated by Paul Turner. United States: Indiana University Press, 1990.

Luther King Jr. Martin. *Where Do We Go from Here: Chaos or Community?* United States: Beacon Press, 2010.

Malm, Andreas, and The Zetkin Collective. *White Skin, Black Fuel: On the Danger of Fossil Fascism*. United Kingdom: Verso Books, 2021.

Maree Brown, adrienne. *Octavia's Brood: Science Fiction Stories from Social Justice Movements*. United Kingdom: AK Press, 2015.

Marie-Monique, Robin. *The World According to Monsanto: Pollution, Corruption, and the Control of Our Food Supply*. United States: New Press, 2014.

McMullin, Ernan. 'Bruno and Copernicus'. *Isis* 78, no. 1 (1987): 55–74.

Merchant, Carolyn. *The Death of Nature: Women, Ecology, and the Scientific Revolution*. San Francisco: Harper & Row, 1980.

Merchant, Carolyn. 'The Scientific Revolution and The Death of Nature'. *Isis* 97, no. 3 (2006): 513–33.

Molena, Francis. 'Remarkable Weather of 1911: The Effect of the Combustion of Coal on the Climate – What Scientists Predict for the Future' in *Popular Mechanics*, March 1912: 341.

Montuschi, Eleonora. 'Order of Man, Order of Nature: Francis Bacon's Idea of a "Dominion" Over Nature'. *The Governance of Nature Workshop*, LSE, 1, no. 27 (2010): 28.

Moore, Bryan L. *Ecological Literature and the Critique of Anthropocentrism*. United Kingdom: Springer, 2017.

Murphy, Timothy. 'Flower of the Desert: Poetics as Ontology from Leopardi to Negri'. *Genre* 44, no. 1 (2011): 75–91.

Negri, Antonio. *Subversive Spinoza:(UN) Contemporary Variations: Antonio Negri*. United Kingdom: Manchester University Press, 2004.

Negri, Antonio. *Flower of the Desert: Giacomo Leopardi's Poetic Ontology*. United States: State University of New York Press, 2015.

Nelson, Lowry. *Poetic Configurations: Essays in Literary History and Criticism*. United States: Pennsylvania State University Press, 2010.

Neocleous, Mark. 'Negri in Prison'. *Radical Philosophy* 92 (1998): 54–4.

Nietzsche, Friedrich. *The Gay Science*. United Kingdom: Cambridge University Press, 2001.

Nietzsche, Friedrich. 'On Truth and Lies in A Nonmoral Sense'. Truth: Engagements across Philosophical Traditions (2005): 14–25, 14.

Nussbaum, Martha C. 'Kant and Stoic Cosmopolitanism'. *Journal of Political Philosophy* 5, no. 1 (1997): 1–25.

Nussbaum, Martha C. *Anger and Forgiveness: Resentment, Generosity, Justice*. United Kingdom: Oxford University Press, 2016.

Oates, Stephen B. *Let the Trumpet Sound: A Life of Martin Luther King, Jr*. United States: Canongate Books, 1998.

Olberding, Amy. "A Little Throat Cutting in the Meantime': Seneca's Violent Imagery'. *Philosophy and Literature* 32, no. 1 (2008): 130–44.

Pearson, Wendy Gay. 'Speculative Fiction and Queer Theory'. In *Oxford Research Encyclopedia of Communication*. United Kingdom: Oxford University Press, 2022.

Pereira, Charmaine. '"Walking into Slavery with Our Eyes Open"– the Space for Resisting Genetically Modified Crops in Nigeria'. *Feminist Africa* 2, no. 1 (2021): 99–125.

Piperno, Martina. 'Temporalities and Fractures in Post-Napoleonic Italy: Leopardi and Vico's Legacy'. PhD diss., University of Warwick, 2016.

Plant, John S., and R.E. Plant. 'Understanding the Royal Name Plantagenet. How DNA Helps'. *Guild of One Name Studies* (2010).

Plato. *The Republic*, translated by Lee Henry Desmond Pritchard and M.S. Lane. London: Penguin, 2007.

Pope, Alexander. *An Essay on Man*, edited by Tom Jones. Princeton: Princeton University Press, 2016.

Pryor, John. 'Review of Merchant Culture in Fourteenth-Century Venice: The Zibaldone da Canal'. *Parergon* 12 (1994): 134–6.

Rennie, Nicholas. *Speculating on the Moment*. Germany: Wallstein, 2005.

Rich, Nathaniel. *Losing Earth: The Decade We Could Have Stopped Climate Change*. United Kingdom: Pan Macmillan, 2020.

Ripple, William J., Christopher Wolf, Thomas M. Newsome, Mauro Galetti, Mohammed Alamgir, Eileen Crist, Mahmoud I. Mahmoud and William F. Laurance. '15,364 Scientist Signatories from 184 Countries, World Scientists' Warning to Humanity: A Second Notice'. *BioScience*, 67, no. 12 (2017): 1026-8.

Robertson, Donald. *The Philosophy of Cognitive – Behavioural Therapy (CBT): Stoic Philosophy as Rational and Cognitive Psychotherapy*. London: Routledge, 2018.

Roller, Matthew. 'The Dialogue in Seneca's Dialogues (and Other Moral Essays)'. *The Cambridge Companion to Seneca* (2015): 54-67.

Rose, Jacqueline. *Why War? Psychoanalysis, Politics and the Return to Melanie Klein*. Cambridge: Wiley, 1993.

Ruffin, Kimberly T. 'Parable of a 21st Century Religion: Octavia Butler's Afrofuturistic Bridge between Science and Religion'. *Obsidian III*, no. 6/7 (2005): 87-104.

Sandford, Stella. 'Kant, Race, and Natural History'. *Philosophy & Social Criticism* 44, no. 9 (2018): 950-77.

Seligman, Martin E.P. *Authentic Happiness*. Australia: Random House Australia, 2011.

Seneca, Lucius Annaeus. *Seneca: Moral Essays*, translated by John Basore. Harvard: Loeb Classical Library, 1928.

Seneca, Lucius Annaeus. *Natural Questions*, translated by Harry M. Hine. United Kingdom: University of Chicago Press, 2014.

Severino, Emanuele. *In viaggio con Leopardi: la partita sul destino dell'uomo*. Italy: Rizzoli, 2015.

Sganzerla, Erik Pietro, and Michele Augusto Riva. 'The Disease of the Italian Poet Giacomo Leopardi (1798-1837): A Case of Juvenile Ankylosing Spondylitis in the 19th Century'. *Journal of Clinical Rheumatology* 23, no. 4 (2017): 223-5.

Shaw, Prue. *The Letters of Giacomo Leopardi 1817-1837*. London: Taylor & Francis, 2017.

Shiva, Vandana. *Staying Alive: Women, Ecology, and Survival in India*. New Delhi: Kali for Women, 1988.

Shiva, Vandana. *Making Peace with the Earth*. London: Pluto Press, 2013.

Shiva, Vandana, and Kartikey Shiva. *Oneness Vs. the 1%: Shattering Illusions, Seeding Freedom*. London: Chelsea Green Publishing, 2020.

Smiley, Tavis and Cornel West. *The Rich and the Rest of Us*. United States: Hay House, 2012.

Solnit, Rebecca. *Hope in the Dark: Untold Histories, Wild Possibilities*. London: Canongate Books, 2016.

Solomon, Robert C. *Living with Nietzsche: What the Great 'Immoralist' Has to Teach Us*. United Kingdom: Oxford University Press, 2003.

Timpanaro, Sebastiano. *On Materialism*. London: London Review of Books, 1975.

Timpanaro, Sebastiano. 'The Pessimistic Materialism of Giacomo Leopardi'. *New Left Review* 116 (1979): 29–50.

Timpanaro, Sebastiano. 'Il «Leopardi Verde»'. *Belfagor*, no. 6 (1987): 613–37.

Timpanaro, Sebastiano. *The Freudian Slip: Psychoanalysis and Textual Criticism*. London: Verso Books, 2011.

Voltaire. *Candide and Other Works*, translated by Carabine, K., and James Fowler. Hertfordshire: Wordsworth Editions Limited, 2014.

Voltaire. *Voltaire's Philosophical Dictionary*. Project Gutenberg Literary Archive Foundation, 2006.

Walton, Douglas. *Appeal to Pity: Argumentum Ad Misericordiam*. United States: State University of New York Press, 2016.

Weber, Max. *From Max Weber: Essays in Sociology,* translated by H.H. Gerth and C.W. Mills. United Kingdom: Oxford University, 1946.

White Jr, Lynn. 'The Historical Roots of Our Ecological Crisis'. *Science*, 155, no. 3767 (1967): 1203–7.

Williams, Pamela. 'Leopardi's Philosophy of Consolation in "La ginestra"'. *The Modern Language Review* 93, no. 4 (1998): 985–96.

Wilson, Marcus. 'Seneca the Consoler? A New Reading of His Consolatory Writings'. In *Greek and Roman Consolations: Eight Studies of a Tradition and Its Afterlife*, edited by Han Baltussen, 93–121. Classical Press of Wales, 2013.

Yovel, Yirmiyahu. *Nietzsche as Affirmative Thinker: Papers Presented at the Fifth Jerusalem Philosophical Encounter*, April 1983. Germany: Springer Netherlands, 2012.

Yusoff, Kathryn. *A Billion Black Anthropocenes or None*. Minnesota: University of Minnesota Press, 2018.

Index

Adorno, Theodor 14, 35, 48, 112, 157
Aesopian fables 29, 120–1
affirmation
    as aggressive 143
    and destruction 52
    in Leopardi's philosophy 100, 141
    as a need 171
    in Nietzsche's ethics 16, 104, 191
    and vision 221
Alcorn, John 129
ancients
    art, *see also* works of genius 10, 119
    borrowing from 2, 41
    concerns of 183
    critiques of 187
    as exemplary 28
    and health 62
    living well 104
    and moderns 28, 46, 62
    paganism 45
    politics 108
    practices 8–9, 45, 104, 107–8, 118, 120, 142
    as a resource 120
    returning to 185
    revitalising 118
    satire 27
    strengths of 116
    thinkers 18, 23, 35
    vitality of 64
    works of 26, 35, 49, 184
Andersen, Inger 144–5
Anderson, Perry 74, 82, 105, 107, 114, 115, 117, 153, 161–2, 179, 192
anger 113, 133
anthropocentrism 42, 74, 185, 189
    ancients 9, 18, 184
    culture 91
    in contemporary thought 12, 183
    as an impulse 15, 160, 182
    Leopardi's critique of 17, 21, 34, 46, 49, 64, 66, 68, 118, 153–5
    and Christianity 45, 55
    tendencies 85
    and illusions 130
    views 133
anthropogenic climate change 93
ants 186, 122
anxiety 113, 133, 137, 140, 192
aphorisms 26, 156
Appiah, Kwame Anthony 154, 155–7, 190
Aurelius, Marcus 4, 9, 38, 69, 72, 104, 110, 126, 128, 135–7, 186
Autonomia Operaia 14
awe 134–5

Bacon, Francis 42–4, 46, 68, 155
Ball, David 155
barbarism 23, 27
    as civilisation's opposite 37
    as 'corrupted civilisation' 82
    inherent in modernity 39, 156
    as ongoing 143
    persistence of 96
    of racism 33, 40
    reliance on 40
battle 102, 180
    with friends 129
    against inhabitants, *see also* war
    against people 76
    life as 131
    against nature 115
    regular 77
Benjamin, Walter 10–1, 35, 61
Bentham, Jeremy 155–56
Berdach, Rachel 50–1, 147, 191

Big Oil 43, 164–5
binary thought 151–2, 157
Binni, Walter 16, 25
biodiversity 1, 84, 94, 144–5, 148
blindness 4, 129
Bologna 77, 108
Book of Genesis 42
boundaries 30, 32, 148, 180
brother 26, 105, 126, 133, 175, 192
Bruno, Giordano 64, 126, 203, 213

Caesar, Michael 22, 28, 153
calm 126, 133, 137–8
    depthless 39
    heroic 116, 211–12
    storm and 135
    strength 125
Candide 37, 81–2, 108, 155–6
Canti 20, 23–4, 96, 99, 101–2
Capitoline Hill 126
carbon dioxide 2, 6, 94, 148, 150, 158, 162–3, 165–6
Carsaniga, Giovanni 18, 29, 109
Cavarero, Adriana 68
Cervato, Emanuela 18, 30, 62
Césaire, Aimé 180
chess 47, 154
Christianity 82, 144, 152, 157
    and anthropocentricism 55
    burden of guilt 45–6
    decline of 9
    as destructive of life 48–9
    and extractivism 42
    history of 46
Cicero, Marcus Tullius 135, 185
citizenship 2, 20, 128, 132, 135, 186
    and duties 69
    just society of 108
    role of 62
    themes of 20
civilisation *see also* barbarism 4, 53, 142, 154, 182, 187
    ancient 8–9, 120
    as revival 107

coal 5, 94, 163, 166, 208, 231
collective forgetting 54, 96
colonialism 45, 152, 155
Committee on Oversight and Reform 164–6, 195
commonality 111, 129
community 4, 179
    citizenship 135
    and distrust 71–2
    and hope 171–2
    global 179
    liberation 16, 19, 132, 172
companions 62, 73
compassion 34, 75, 122, 172, 189, 194
    circle of 185–7
    intraspecies 64
    mutual 131
Conference of the Parties to the UN Convention on Biological Diversity, *see* COP 15 144
consolation 2, 10, 16, 77, 91
    consolation philosophiae 118
    in Rousseau's thought 83–5, 97, 128, 143
    Seneca's influence 9, 104
    false 111
    as fortifying 164
    work of 122, 124
consumption 61, 147
COP 15, see Conference of the Parties to the UN Convention on Biological Diversity 144
Copernican Revolution 56, 67, 85, 87–9, 95–6, 138, 158, 192
'Copernicus' 57, 66–7, 89–92, 95, 100, 107, 126, 155, 161, 168, 180, 183
Copernicus, Nicolaus 95, 107, 126, 203, 207
    consideration of 185–6
    discoveries 160–1
    new system 157

On the Revolutions of the Heavenly Bodies 85–8
  thought of 29
corporate interests *see also* multinational corporations 1, 43, 79, 149–50, 180
  barriers 94
  climate change denial 6–7
cosmic pessimism 3, 66, 99, 109, 137, 143
  situating 38, 42, 57, 178
Cosmopolitanism 134–5, 180
cosmos 66, 115–6, 120, 133–4
  our place within 120, 113, 184, 189
  vastness of 134
Costellazioni 17, 153
courage 2, 187
  and liberty 42, 178
  moral 26
  of truth 47
  resistance 141
  stance 172
Covid-19 50, 52, 144, 201, 227, 229
cowards 110–1, 113, 133
Creagh, Patrick 3, 15, 74–5, 102
creativity 2, 7, 22, 31, 97, 103, 145–8, 158, 170–2
Critique of Practical Reason 134, 157
cruelty 51, 74, 76–8, 81, 113, 121–2, 152, 155–6
Cullors, Patrisse 175
cure 16, 55, 84, 99–100, 111, 116, 122, 133
customs *see also* habits 60–2, 74, 81

D'Intino, Franco 22, 69
da Canal, Niccolò 22
damaged life 157
darkness 21, 51, 99, 111, 113, 147, 167, 174, 191
Darwin, Charles 58, 91, 104, 184
Dasgupta Review on the Economics of Biodiversity 148

death 10, 22, 26, 33, 39, 43, 50, 52–4, 57–8, 60–2, 65, 72–4, 76–7, 83, 96, 104, 108, 114, 116, 117, 124–5, 128, 131, 133, 137–41, 160, 166, 186, 191, 199
de Buffon, Comte 58, 104, 137–141
de Fontenelle, Bernard le Bovier 29, 137–8, 157–8, 160, 186
de Lorenzo, Giuseppe 132
decline 9, 23, 48
defeat 12, 34, 48, 114, 131
degeneracy of life 57–8, 67
Del Puppo, Dario 117, 129
denial 7, 133, 143, 197, 222
Descartes, René 35, 88
despair 11, 12, 21, 54, 83–5, 97, 101, 119, 122, 124, 132, 137, 142, 143, 146, 172–4, 176, 197
destruction 1, 6, 10, 48, 52–3, 55–6, 61, 70, 78, 80, 123, 125, 129, 147–8, 151, 168, 170, 175, 181
Di Rosa, Rossella 68–71, 73, 91, 205
Dialogue Concerning the Two Chief World Systems 29, 89
dialogues 22, 24–9, 34, 37–8, 46–7, 54–67, 69–73, 79–80, 85, 90–93, 95–6, 100, 107–8, 122–3, 126, 133–4, 138, 140–1, 178, 180–1, 183, 190
dichotomy 20, 30, 145
dignity 105, 107, 123, 131, 135
disasters 22, 5–1, 53, 77–8, 84, 197
disenchantment 60, 63, 124, 192
'The Dominant Idea' 110–1
dominion 42–3, 63
dreams 4, 55, 108, 170–1, 174–5, 181
dualism 45–6, 152

'The Earth and the Moon' 66–7, 134, 180, 183
Earth's resources 5, 43–5, 78, 93–4, 150, 154–5, 160, 164, 168, 179
earthly things 9
earthquakes 6, 76–7, 83, 196

ecological limits 146, 149, 150
ecosystems 2, 6, 10, 84, 92, 145, 148, 186
eighteenth century 5, 15, 21, 29, 74, 77, 110, 120, 153, 184, 213
enemy 31, 69, 74, 77, 145, 150-1, 155, 175, 218
Enlightenment 2, 11, 21, 25, 33-4, 48-9, 55, 57, 62, 64, 78, 82, 102, 129, 153, 155, 177-8, 184, 187
Ensler, Eve 167
enthusiasm 2, 13, 28, 31, 101, 123-6, 128, 181, 189, 194
environmental crisis 2, 4, 6, 7, 9, 11-12, 17, 21, 34, 45, 84, 92, 94, 96, 103, 131, 143-4, 164, 176, 186, 190-2, 194, 218
environmental defenders 150
environmental limits 146-7, 150
Epictetus 4, 127-8, 130, 192
epigraph 51, 129
Esposito, Roberto 18, 48-9, 62-4, 67, 118
ethics 3, 5, 8, 10-2, 14-6, 19, 35, 59, 73, 100-1, 104, 132, 141, 145, 151, 154-8, 179, 187, 194
evil 33, 38, 48, 57, 71-2, 74, 78, 83, 101, 109, 127, 155, 193
exceptionalism 90, 167
existence 68-70, 81, 109, 112, 130, 140, 153, 171
   as a spot 38, 110, 134
   multitude of 80, 158
expense 7, 93-4, 165, 168
exploitation 1, 7, 92, 175
   of escapism 174
   of nature 5, 43
   process of 168
extinction 1, 54, 65, 139, 159, 164, 181
extraction 1, 5, 7, 39, 42-5, 57, 150, 186

fables 25-6, 28-9, 106, 108, 120-1, 213
Fanon, Frantz 180

farmers 7, 146
'Fashion and Death' 10, 57, 60, 61
Fattorini, Teresa 73
fear 78, 102
   almost 39
   calming 133, 137
   confronting 181
   of death 104, 138-40
   and despair 172-3
   and hope 176-7, 194
   examining 133
   fearfulness 113
   framework 54
   fueled by 131
   inclined towards 96, 145
   kindling 175
   of nature 123
   overcoming 13, 103
   responding to 116
   weaponised 192
feelings *see also* enthusiasm 30, 39, 101, 126, 172, 180, 186
   of death 139-41
   deep 119-20, 123
   force of 103
   of nothingness 125
   transcending 11
   as weapons 28, 123
female form 68, 167
Figueres, Christiana 95, 173
finitude 113, 118, 136, 164, 174
flourishing 2, 85, 167-8, 173, 187, 216
folly 12, 55, 65, 67, 71-2, 96, 104, 129
food 1, 117-8, 146, 149, 212, 216-7
fortitude 11, 154
fossil fuels 94, 143, 163-5, 167, 191, 195
fragility 37, 56-7, 59, 73, 113-4, 122, 179
frailty 59, 63, 112, 130, 141
Frankfurt School 177

Index

'Frederick Ruysch and his Mummies' 138–141
freedom 7, 48, 95, 114–5, 132, 158, 172, 181
French Revolution 29, 48, 62
Freud, Sigmund 21, 50–4, 73, 76–7, 91, 96, 145, 147, 191
Friedrich Schreiber, Johann 138
Fubini, Mario 25, 79, 127
future 94–5, 115, 125, 143, 190
   better 174, 181
   different 103
   generations 6, 162–3, 171, 176
   imagining 179
   invention of 169
   machinic 160
   profits 167
   reinterpreting 8, 194
   question of 8
   thinking about 170
   visions of 55, 145

Galassi, Jonathan 23
Galileo, Galilei 29, 88–9, 91, 199, 207
Genealogy of Morals 172
Genetically Modified Organisms, see GMO 146, 217
Gentile, Giovanni 25
Geologic time 56
de Staël, Germaine 10, 29–30, 118, 213
Gilroy, Paul 10–1, 19, 33, 41, 88, 146, 156, 177–81
Giordani, Pietro 24, 27
'La ginestra' 10, 13, 16, 24, 28, 66, 74, 77, 80, 82, 85, 91, 96–7, 99, 101–3, 107–8, 110–3, 121–4, 126, 128, 130–1, 134, 136–7, 141, 143, 147, 152, 158–60, 168, 173, 176, 186, 189, 191, 194, 211
Glanvill, Joseph 43
Global Climate Coalition 165
global warming 166

Global Witness 150
globalisation 1, 146, 149
globe 6, 59, 86, 88, 90, 158, 179–80
GMO, see Genetically Modified Organisms 146, 217
Goethe, Johann Wolfgang 3, 9, 18, 105, 210
goodness 131
Gospel of John 51, 111, 191
Gozzi, Gasparo 29
grace 111, 116, 172, 181, 189
Gramsci, Antonio 10–1, 103, 173, 191
Gray, John 18, 48–9
Greeks 8, 49, 57, 141, 184
Green New Deal 6, 43, 195
Green Revolution 43, 146
grief 142
   in art 211–12
   and hope 175
   Freud's philosophy of 50, 52–3, 96, 191
   personal 101, 133

Habermas, Jürgen 177
habits see also customs 4–5, 67, 69, 72
Hadot, Pierre 136, 215
Hall, Stuart 8, 10–1, 18, 40–2, 53, 120, 152, 157, 173, 194
Hamilton, Paul 135
Handbook 127, 130
Hạnh, Thích Nhất 172
Hansen, James 6, 162–6
Haraway, Donna 12
harm 5, 47, 61, 71, 75–6, 130, 142, 148, 150, 167
harmony 108–9, 133, 150, 168
Harrison, Peter 43
Harrison, Thomas 153–4
health 2, 3, 5, 62–3, 144, 169, 172, 181–3, 185, 194, 196, 209, 220–1
Hegel, Georg 24
helplessness 51, 74, 76

'Hercules and Atlas' 26, 57–9, 180, 194
hierarchy 90, 139, 153, 179
historical amnesia 41–2, 96
history 1, 3, 6, 14–6, 18, 22–4, 28, 30, 34, 36, 41, 44, 46, 52–3, 58, 64, 78–9, 82, 86–7, 89, 97, 101, 106–7, 118, 120, 130, 138–9, 148, 155–6, 159, 163, 170, 174, 178, 182–3, 185, 190
History of Astronomy 3, 86
hope 19, 24, 33, 71, 73, 75–6, 83, 96, 103, 110, 123, 127, 129, 145–6, 169–71, 173–7, 180–1, 189, 193–5
hopelessness 113
hostility 68, 70, 74, 129, 152–3, 155
Hulme, Peter 152
human entitlement 91, 130, 153
humanism 42, 64, 111, 156, 177, 179–81, 223
humanity 1, 6, 7, 20, 39, 42, 49, 55, 68, 71–3, 75, 84–6, 89, 92, 96, 99, 100–1, 106, 121, 135, 139, 142, 149, 155, 157, 167, 181
humility 116, 172
humour 2, 25, 27, 55, 61, 96, 100, 118–9, 122–3, 192

'Icaromenippus, An Aerial Expedition' 66
identity politics 41, 151, 178–9
illusions 7, 11, 19, 47, 49, 74, 76, 129–30, 132, 135, 142, 159, 195
imagination 2, 12, 28–32, 34, 74–5, 89, 103, 117, 119, 123, 140, 145, 153–4, 174, 185
'An Imp and a Gnome' 57, 65, 70, 88, 107, 183
inaction 6, 128, 176
indifference 53, 76, 124–5, 192
inequality 7, 84, 149, 168
infanticide 68–9

infinity 37–9, 64, 101, 109, 117
'Infinity' 77, 106
innocence 73–4, 77, 101, 153
interconnectedness 151, 181
Intergovernmental Science-Policy Platform on Biodiversity and Ecosystem Services, *see* IPBES 1, 148
IPBES, see Intergovernmental Science-Policy Platform on Biodiversity and Ecosystem Services 1, 148

Jefferson, Thomas 58
Job 14
Jones, Esther 169–70
Jones, Tom 37
Judeo-Christian Tradition 43, 85
justice 5–8, 14–5, 19, 94–5, 102, 134, 144, 151, 162–4, 168, 170–2, 208, 222

Kant, Immanuel 25, 35, 108, 134–6, 157
King, Martin Luther 171–4
Klein, Naomi 43, 55, 164
Kolbert, Elizabeth 1, 164

lamps 93, 155, 161
Latour, Bruno 142
Le Monnier, Felice 26, 105
legacy 56, 65
Leibniz, Gottfried Wilhelm 21, 35–8, 57, 74, 77, 81–4, 108–9, 143, 190
Leopardi, Paolina 199
Leopardi, Pietrino 126
liberation 16, 19, 117, 132
lions 59, 126
Lisbon Earthquake 15, 37, 39, 51, 73, 77–9, 81–3, 122, 128–9, 189
literature 3, 14, 17–8, 23, 30, 32, 45, 78, 128, 170, 173, 184, 209
Looney, Dennis 91, 95, 116
Lord Byron 9

Index

love 2, 21–2, 47, 50–1, 60, 62, 99, 103, 105, 110–1, 113, 117, 123, 125, 141, 147, 172, 176–7, 191, 211–12, 216, 222
Lucian of Samosata 9, 27, 28, 29, 66
Luporini, Cesare 16, 25

Mahatma, Gandhi 168, 174
Malm, Andrea 143, 192
Marche 2
marginalisation 7, 64, 168, 170, 184
Marie-Monique, Robin 146
Marxism 9, 21, 104
materialism 25, 33, 48, 82, 112, 117
Medea 68
Meditations 69, 136–7
Merchant, Carolyn 43–5, 55
merchants 78, 122
misanthropy 51, 71, 99–100, 117
misery 14, 27, 40, 55, 60, 74, 83–4, 92
misogyny 68, 168–9
modernity 8, 10, 16, 21, 23, 33–4, 39, 47, 55, 96, 100, 132, 142, 156, 158–9, 177–8
Monsanto 146, 217
Moore, Henrietta 147–8, 150
moral framework 130, 179
morality 6, 74, 77, 103–4, 113
Moro, Aldo 14
mortality 10, 54, 105, 107, 114, 125, 131, 133, 136, 138, 141, 189
mother 44, 68, 74, 119, 126, 133, 148, 161–2, 174, 218
Mount Vesuvius 13, 18, 26, 80, 123, 128–9, 158–60, 189
multinational corporations *see also* corporate interests 217, 143, 163–6, 195
multiplicity 151–2
multitudes 23, 76, 80, 122, 134–5, 157–8, 167–8, 171, 186
Murdoch, Iris 212
mystery 43, 88, 96

Nakate, Vanessa 6
nature 43, 68, 70, 86
   as benign 52, 70, 78, 80, 123
   damaged relationship with 19, 145, 150
   as destructive 72–3, 75–6, 100, 157
   destruction of 1, 6, 10, 144, 147–8, 168
   as guilty 74, 162
   as a machine 153
   as mother 44, 68, 148, 161, 218
   as stepmother 68, 74, 162
   life according to 6, 72, 168
   processes of 2, 52, 75, 137
   severance from 167
   two faces of 68
   violence of 73, 93, 96
   working with 144
'Nature and an Icelander' 57, 66, 69, 70–3, 75–6, 79–80, 99–100, 145
Negri, Antonio 9, 13–6, 23–6, 33–4, 57, 65, 102, 117, 132, 141, 158–9, 169, 192, 204
neighbours 71, 78, 100, 113, 122, 151, 173, 186
Net Zero 163, 165
Nietzsche, Friedrich 9, 11, 16, 18, 22, 24, 26, 29, 34–5, 46–7, 64, 89, 102–7, 110–1, 172, 191
nihilism 46, 104, 142–3
Nobel Peace Prize 172
nobility 114, 119, 131, 172, 177, 181, 187, 189
   examples in Leopardi's work 110–11, 125–6
   the Broom 103, 113
   in *Corinne* 10
   Nietzsche's morality of 104
   farmer 102, 113, 121, 123, 173, 194
non-humans 2, 70, 151, 190
nothingness 47, 124–5, 177, 186, 192
Nussbaum, Martha 134–5

Olberding, Amy 133
Operette Morali 3, 9, 15, 20–2, 24–9, 37, 42, 46, 51, 54–7, 66–7, 70, 74–5, 85, 87, 89, 91, 96, 99, 102, 104–7, 127, 131, 138, 141, 183, 194
On Truth and Lies in the Nonmoral Sense 106
One Health 182–3, 185
oppression 76, 114–6, 151, 169, 179
optimism 5, 27, 33, 103, 109–11, 130, 173–4
   in Gramsci's thought 11, 103
   metaphysical 21, 27, 35–9, 77–82, 84, 107–8, 133–4, 143
optimistic will 8, 11, 173, 191

pain 39, 72, 80, 83–4, 119, 140
   emotional 13
   enduring 60
   and death 76–7, 125, 139–40
   in our destiny 114
   and intellectual powers 136–7
   as normal 172
   preventing 84
   shared nature of 130
   and solitude 24, 169
   taking measure of 52–4
   universal 101
Pale Rider 52, 96
paradigms 36, 91, 95, 135, 145, 150, 181
'Parini, or Concerning Fame' 127
patents 146
patriarchal thinking 44, 68, 168
Collins, Patricia Hill 151, 154, 157, 190
peace 1, 126, 135, 144–6
persecution 69, 78–9, 129
perseverance 11, 173, 191
perspective 16, 26, 32, 37, 55, 87, 92, 104, 109, 136–8, 143, 148, 154, 168, 179
pessimism 3, 9, 13, 16, 38–9, 42, 57, 66–7, 73–4, 99, 109, 112, 114–5, 117, 135, 137, 162, 173, 178, 190, 197

philology 3, 24, 36
philosophy 2, 5, 9–11, 14–6, 18, 21, 23, 25, 27–32, 35–6, 41, 48, 50–2, 55, 64, 69–70, 73, 77–8, 81, 85–6, 88, 96, 99, 100, 103–5, 107, 110–11, 116, 122, 126–8, 132, 136, 141–2, 145, 151, 156–7, 164, 169, 176, 180, 182–4, 186, 190–2, 194
   ancient 35
   modern 35, 88
Pignotti, Lorenzo 28–9, 117, 120–1
pinprick 38, 134
Piperno, Martina 18, 79
pity 59, 116, 123
planetary humanism 156, 177, 179–81, 189, 223
plurality 87, 138, 157–8, 160, 186, 224
plurality of worlds 138, 157–8, 186, 224
poet-thinker 9, 42, 62, 105, 154
poetry 16, 18, 20, 23–6, 28–33, 64, 75, 78–9, 96, 132, 181, 183, 187, 190
pollution 1, 94, 144, 148, 165
poor century 28, 121, 123
Pope Paul III 85, 185
Pope, Alexander 27, 36–9, 57, 73–4, 77, 81–5, 109, 122, 143, 190
Postcolonial Melancholia 41, 88
posthumanism 89
presumptuousness 65–6, 88, 107
pride 12, 110, 113, 131, 136, 189
profits 6, 61, 143, 148, 163–4, 167
progress 4, 7, 9, 23–5, 39, 41, 48, 55, 75, 77, 83, 92–3, 107–8, 110, 123, 145, 147, 148, 150, 156, 161, 182
prosperity 147–8, 150
psychoanalysis 8, 53

racial slavery 42, 45, 156, 178
Ranieri, Antonio 26, 105, 199
rationalism 29, 37, 48–9, 60, 62–3, 69, 72

reason 6, 8, 14–5, 23, 27–31, 33, 48,
    54, 63, 70, 74, 80, 83, 86, 90–1,
    95, 100, 108, 111, 114, 119,
    154, 156–7, 162, 166, 176, 212
Recanati 2, 32, 39
reconstruction 2, 8, 11, 16, 132, 145,
    159, 194
recovery 108, 117, 144, 148
renewables 94
renewal 9, 10, 94, 120, 142
resignifying 8, 120, 194
resistance 8, 25, 53, 102, 141, 154,
    158, 175, 181, 192
responsibility 7, 145–6, 165–6
revival 8–10, 33–4, 57, 96, 107–8,
    124, 129, 186, 192, 204
Rich, Nathaniel 6–7, 164, 166
Rivett-Carnac, Tom 95, 173
Romans 8, 49, 57, 141, 184
Rome 13, 126, 128–9, 134, 173
Rose, Gillian 141
Rose, Jacqueline 21, 50, 96
Rousseau, Jean-Jacques 35, 66, 77,
    82–5, 97, 122, 128, 143, 207
Royal Academy of Sciences 138
Royal Society 43
Ruysch, Frederick 137–41

Schiller, Friedrich 60
Schopenhauer, Arthur 9, 11, 17, 105,
    115
science 18, 23, 35, 42–5, 49, 60, 92,
    95, 138, 142, 144, 165–6, 182,
    184
seeds 146, 154, 180, 184, 191, 217
Seneca, Lucius Annaeus 4, 9, 26,
    104, 110, 126, 133–6, 140, 184,
    190
senses 2, 136, 167
separation 117, 139–40, 150, 155,
    224
seventeenth century 29, 43–4, 204
Severino, Emanuele 46–7, 103, 125, 154
Shiva, Vandana 1, 5, 7, 96, 145–150,
    164, 168, 180–1, 185, 190, 195

Simplicius of Cilicia 128
singularity 132, 159
sister 60, 199, 212
slavery 39–42, 45, 155–6, 177–8, 217
Sofri, Adriano 161, 164
solidarity 2, 5, 8, 10, 12, 20, 34, 55, 73–
    5, 77, 100–1, 103, 115, 128–31,
    145–6, 150–1, 164, 172, 173,
    179–81, 187–90, 191, 194
stanza 77, 128–131
solitude 24, 72, 99, 169
Solmi, Sergio 68, 70
Solnit, Rebecca 19–20, 75, 96, 171,
    175–6, 194–5
Sontag, Susan 11, 34
soul 18, 48–9, 62, 64, 117, 119, 123–6,
    139–40, 193, 212
Spanish flu 52, 54, 96
speck in metaphysics 38, 109–10
speck in the universe 38, 109, 132,
    134, 137
speculative fiction 66, 169–70
speculative poetry 25
Spinney, Laura 52, 96
Spinoza, Baruch 14, 16, 117
spiritual exercise 136
Sprat, Thomas 43
statues 119, 126, 173
Stoicism 4, 9, 26, 38, 72, 105, 108,
    114–7, 127, 132, 134–7, 142,
    186
strength 8, 10, 20–1, 53, 63, 85, 97,
    102, 118, 124–6, 131, 164, 167,
    172, 177, 181–2, 184, 187, 189,
    191–2, 197, 203, 212, 222
style 25, 66, 80, 89, 101, 106, 133
sugar 10, 39–41, 81–2
sunflowers 50–1, 147, 191, 193
survival 8, 10, 117, 148, 169, 170,
    194

Terán, Manuel 'Tortuguita' 150
Thacker, Eugene 11, 99
Thunberg, Greta 6
'Timander and Eleander' 75, 122–3

Timpanaro, Sebastiano 10, 47–9, 73, 76–7, 82, 103, 105, 107, 112, 114, 115–7, 122, 124–5, 131, 133, 142–3, 153, 161–2, 164, 192
'To Silvia' 73
tragedy 27, 50, 52, 65
trifles 19, 27, 86, 88–9, 107
Triple planetary crisis 94, 144
'Trips to the Moon' 168

ultra-fast fashion 61
unhappiness 23, 39, 40, 75–6, 80, 116, 124

Vallance, Patrick 1, 148
vices 19, 25, 27, 28, 67, 96, 120, 205
Vico, Giambattista 18, 35, 62, 64
view from above 134, 136
Villa delle Ginestre 26, 189
violence 7, 68, 73, 93, 96, 135, 140, 145–6, 150, 151, 167–8, 172, 177, 180
vision 5, 8, 19, 35, 43, 55, 62, 74, 138, 145, 147, 162, 169, 170–1, 175, 181, 189, 191, 193, 221
vitality 4, 12, 33–4, 49, 58, 61–2, 64, 96, 103, 108, 118, 164, 167, 194
volcano 76, 79
Volkswagen Scandal 166
Voltaire 51, 73, 97, 128, 143, 145, 190
  and nature 77–9, 81, 121–2
  dialogues of 29, 80–5
  rejection of optimism 108
  solidarity among men 129
  and slavery 155–6
  work of 37–9, 80, 126
von Bülow, Freiherr Hans Guido 105
von Bunsen, Karl 129

war
  against nature 5, 70, 143, 146, 149, 150, 186
  against people *see also* against inhabitants 6, 7, 65, 76, 85, 150–1
  warnings 4–6, 23, 49, 92–4, 143, 145, 148, 167, 170, 189, 192
Washington DC 164, 171, 195
weakness 76, 117, 151, 159, 161, 177, 186
  of character 131
  human 115
  of mind 51
  political 179
  sense of 92
wealth 7, 16, 19, 149, 164, 194
weapons of ridicule 121, 123
web of life 92, 145
Weber, Max 150
Weelaunee forest 150
Western philosophy 9, 46–7, 145, 154, 183–4
Western tradition 46–7, 154
White, Lynn Junior 45, 55, 152
Will to Power 22
Williams, Pamela 110, 127–32, 179, 189, 192
womb 44, 123
works of genius *see also* ancients 124–5

Zetkin Collective 143
Zibaldone 4–5, 8, 17–8, 20–4, 26–9, 34–6, 39, 46, 48, 62–3, 68–9, 73, 87–9, 93, 96, 99, 102, 107–8, 114, 118, 124, 126, 128, 131, 133–4, 136, 139, 141, 157

www.ingramcontent.com/pod-product-compliance
Lightning Source LLC
Chambersburg PA
CBHW071825300426
44116CB00009B/1442